A History of Violence

A History of Violence

Living and Dying in Central America

Óscar Martínez

Translated by
John B. Washington
and
Daniela Ugaz

Foreword by
Jon Lee Anderson

VERSO
London • New York

First published by Verso 2016
Translation © John B. Washington and Daniela Ugaz 2016
Foreword © Jon Lee Anderson 2016

This book is based on a series of articles Óscar Martínez wrote for
the Latin American news website elfaro.net and published under the
rubric "Sala Negra."

1 3 5 7 9 10 8 6 4 2

Verso
UK: 6 Meard Street, London W1F 0EG
US: 20 Jay Street, Suite 1010, Brooklyn, NY 11201
versobooks.com

Verso is the imprint of New Left Books

ISBN-13: 978-1-78478-168-2
ISBN-13: 978-1-78478-443-0 (EXPORT)
eISBN-13: 978-1-78478-169-9 (US)
eISBN-13: 978-1-78478-170-5 (UK)

British Library Cataloguing in Publication Data
A catalogue record for this book is available from the British Library

Library of Congress Cataloging-in-Publication Data
A catalog record for this book is available from the Library of Congress

Typeset in Sabon by MJ & N Gavan, Truro, Cornwall
Printed in the US by Maple Press

For Marcela and Maria—for caring for me,
for loving me, for their calming presence,
for staying by my side in this part of the world

"Violence will keep changing in name, but violence will always remain as long as there's no change at the root, from where all these horrible things are sprouting."

— Archbishop Óscar Arnulfo Romero, 1977

"They've offered me no other way."

— Kid Hollywood, a little over a year before his assassination in 2014

Contents

Foreword by Jon Lee Anderson   xi
Preface   xvii

PART 1. EMPTINESS

1. The State Against Chepe Furia   3
2. The Lords of the Border   27
3. Guatemala Is Spelled with a Z   43
4. A Nobody in the Land of Narcos   61
5. Narco: Made in Central America   81

PART 2. MADNESS

6. Our Bottomless Well   95
7. The Most Miserable of Traitors   109
8. El Niño Hollywood's Death Foretold   129
9. The Massacre of Salcajá   143
10. Men Who Pull Out Nails   169

PART 3. FLEEING

11. The Tamed Coyotes   191
12. Men Who Sell Women   211
13. The Prayers of El Salvador's Anti-Gang Police Unit   237
14. The Unfortunate History of an Undocumented
    Man Who Was Sold, Extorted and Deported   247

Foreword
by Jon Lee Anderson

In *A History of Violence*, Óscar Martínez befriends a contract killer living in a small Salvadoran town. The killer, the Hollywood Kid, has ratted out numerous former accomplices to police, but, sensing that the government doesn't care enough to protect him, he fretfully awaits his execution at their hands. The Hollywood Kid has a shotgun to defend himself, but when the moment finally comes, he is defenseless, on his way home from his baby daughter's baptism. At the burial, Óscar is accosted by his dead friend's enemies, who appear in the cemetery to gloat and swagger.

One night, a swashbuckling Honduran police official nicknamed El Tigre—The Tiger—with a fearsome notoriety as the leader of a death squad that executes criminal suspects, and who tells Óscar, "Everyone knows not to fuck with me," concedes defeat as the two drive along a lonely rural stretch of the border where the narcos are more powerful than any law he could hope to impose.

Another evening, as a group of terrified families pack up their homes in a slum in the Salvadoran capital to flee a threatened massacre at the hands of a drug gang, Óscar is on the scene. A police official arrives and pleads with the families to stay. But, instead of offering security guarantees, he asks them to put their faith in God, and invites them to join him in a prayer ceremony. One of the men, powerless to alter his family's circumstances, weeps quietly and tells Óscar of the humiliation he feels.

As he prowls the back roads, bars and police precincts of Central America in a stubborn search for truth, Óscar Martínez exhibits the instincts of a detective and the soul of a poet. His sources are window washers, prostitutes, would-be migrants, killers—*sicarios*—good and bad cops, judges and prosecutors. Óscar is a Marlowe in a world that is long on injustice and short on much of anything else.

Óscar's previous book, *The Beast*, was a gritty firsthand chronicle of the dramatic journeys undertaken by Central American migrants on their journey northwards through Mexico to the United States.

This book, a collection of fourteen investigative pieces written by Óscar over the past several years from Central America itself, is intended to explain to Americans why it is that Central Americans flee—they don't migrate—from their homelands, due to the violence generated there, year after year, with a great deal of American participation.

Óscar is himself a Salvadoran, and what he sees when he looks at his country, and its immediate neighbors, is a war zone. It has been that way for most of his life. Martínez was born in 1983, three years into a brutal twelve-year civil war, which by the time it ended in an impunity-for-all 1992 peace deal had killed 75,000 people and wrecked the lives of many more. But, in a sense, the conflict, in which the US played a preponderant role, never really ended. Along with former guerrillas and ex-soldiers, the offspring of returned war refugees soon formed a crazy quilt of gangs—*Maras*—inspired by the ones in Los Angeles, where many of them had been raised. Today criminal violence has replaced the political violence with levels of bloodshed that comes, at times, chillingly close to those of wartime. Outside of the contemporary killing grounds of Syria and Iraq, in fact, few regions are as consistently murderous as is "peacetime" Central America.

One of the main reasons for the violence is the drug trade. Just as Central America's geography once made it a strategic battleground of the Cold War, that same geography today has determined that the region is the ultimate corridor for narcotics shipments from Colombia to the US consumer market. That fact, together with Central America's chronic poverty and its widespread lawlessness, has turned an astonishing number of people into gangsters. Policemen, judges, and politicians are as likely to be corrupt as to be honest. There are as many as 50,000 Salvadorans directly involved in gangs and up to half a million more, out of a population of 6 million, who are economically dependent on them.

Neighboring Honduras, too, has become the stomping ground for hyper-violent drug gangs and corrupt police—and, accordingly, for the past several years, the country has had the highest murder rates of any country in the world. With El Salvador, Guatemala and Belize close behind.

To give an idea of what this means, consider the fact that the United States, usually regarded as a violent country, has a current average of 4.5 murders per 100,000 inhabitants. Honduras has 90. In 2015, El Salvador's murder rate began to skyrocket, and, by the end of summer, with an average of one murder taking place every hour, and a tally of around 4,000 dead already for the year, it looked ready to edge Honduras out of first place. According to an August 2015 article in the *Guardian*, the latest murder statistics suggest that El Salvador is "twenty times more violent than the United States, ninety times more violent than Great Britain."

Indignation over this state of affairs is partly what motivates Óscar, who runs Sala Negra, a crime investigations unit for *El Faro*, the groundbreaking investigative Central American online magazine based in El Salvador. A slow-burning outrage about the incapacity of the Central American states to provide protection and justice for its citizens pervades Óscar's pieces assembled in this book.

Reporting on the flight of civilian families from the gang-threatened San Salvador slum, for instance, Óscar writes:

Breaking news this Tuesday, January 20, 2015. There is a live audience, watching as if it were a soccer game: people peeking out from their kitchen windows as they eat lunch. Live and direct: more than a dozen families fleeing their San Valentín condos in the city of Mejicanos. There are also film crews, cops directing traffic, and other idling spectators. The police are offering protection for families who have been threatened by the Barrio 18 gang. Gang members threatened to kill by tonight. The residents of San Valentín, taking the threat seriously, are now fleeing on live national television.

Óscar similarly laments the execution of the Hollywood Kid, but not because he thought he was a nice guy. He wasn't. As he told Óscar, he'd personally killed fifty-four people, including several women. Óscar's lamentation was over the inadequacy of the Salvadoran state, which had failed in its promise to protect its witness, who, despite his criminal past had helped bring numerous other killers to justice. "Without his help, thirty killers would be running loose in El Salvador," writes Óscar.

In an article published in July 2015, Óscar and two of his Sala Negra colleagues, Daniel Valencia Caravantes and Roberto Valencia, reported the explosive results of their inquiry into a supposed March shootout between gangsters and police, in which eight Maras, including a young woman, were killed. They revealed that what the police had alleged was untrue, and that the Maras, as well as a couple of innocent bystanders, were murdered in cold blood. It had been a massacre, and there had been a cover-up. Even before this story broke, the Sala Negra team had received death threats, and on the day before publication, Óscar and his two coauthors left San Salvador, to be on the safe side.

On their return, the death threats continued. Óscar carried on with his reporting, but his daily routine now involved a host of new security precautions. In an email message he sent me on

September 18, he promised, "I've taken the decision to leave the country for a period, to give my family a break from this, and some peace of mind. For me, it will be a pause in the combat." The pause was shortlived, and it was not long before Óscar was back reporting on what for him, clearly, has become a kind of war of his own.

One senses that, in the end, what Óscar Martínez is fighting for is a reality where families like his, and those of the people he reports on, can finally live in peace, without fear of being murdered, a Central America where its citizens do not have to leave in order to survive.

Preface

Since October 2013 I've traveled to many cities presenting *The Beast*, the book I wrote about the migrant trail from Central America to the United States. In these talks and presentations I've come to understand—or at least I believe I have—that those of you outside of Latin America are very rational when it comes to reacting to these types of stories. In Latin America, the questions I most heard were along the lines of "Was I scared to be riding the train?" Or "Did anything bad ever happen to me?" Or "Which story affected me most?" Outside of the region, the most common question was "What's your solution?"

It made me realize how infrequently journalists ask themselves this. What can I propose to bring an end to these terrifying stories? It's a deceptive question, because there is no real answer. There's nothing I can suggest that will prevent women being raped on the Mexican migrant trails tomorrow; nor is there anything I can do so that the young Salvadoran boy fleeing his country for yours turns around. I can't make him go back. I definitely can't bring safety or dignity to the place he has abandoned. Journalism only has one method of boring into reality, and it is the same method that the sea uses against the coast: the constant lapping of the waves, whether they are gentle or turbulent.

So, what is my reply to this insistent question? My response is that you should realize what is happening, that you should know more, that you should understand what these people are living through. I want you to be transported by your reading to a barrio ruled by Central American gangs. You need to listen to an indigenous man from the Petén jungle and confront the mother of a boy murdered by Los Zetas. My suggestion is that you realize what happened to a woman who was sold into sex slavery as she tried to reach your borders— or, depending on how you want to see it, as she tried to flee from my country. My proposal is that you know what is going on. Because I believe that knowing is different from not knowing. I believe that knowing, especially with people like yours, who know how to wield politics, is the beginning of a solution. I believe, sticking with the metaphor of the sea and the rock, that knowing is what moves the waves. You can be one of the waves.

Having got that straight, I want to respond to a question I expect to hear when I present this new book somewhere near you: Why should people read this? Here is my reply.

First, I think you should read it because it is about people who surround you. This book isn't about Martians. It doesn't chronicle the tragic life stories of distant, faraway people living in the wilderness, without the Internet, eating nothing but millet. It doesn't discuss people you will never see up close or see only on television. This book is about the lives of people who serve you coffee every morning. It tells the stories of people who cut your lawn and fix your plumbing. These lives are very similar to the lives of about 6 million people living in your midst. It tells the story of the more than 1,000 human beings who every day leave the three northern Central American countries to try to enter, without permission, the United States and other countries of the North.

Second, you should read this book because the broken puppet that we are as a region was mostly armed by American politicians. This is a book about the most murderous corner of the world. In Guatemala, Honduras and El Salvador we have suffered an epidemic of violence for years. It has been established that if a country suffers from a disease that affects ten out of every 100,000 inhabitants, this country is experiencing an epidemic. By that standard, Central America is gravely sick. In the last five years not one of these three countries has averaged fewer than thirty-two murders for every 100,000 inhabitants. In El Salvador, the ratio is more than eighty. This month, the epidemic has been particularly bad, raging in a country of only 13,000 square miles, home to 6.2 million people, and yet averaging twenty-three murders a day. By comparison, during the sixteen-year Civil War, which ended in 1992, the average murder rate was sixteen. Today's violence makes nonsense of the words "war" and "peace."

Our society is a cauldron of oppressive military governance, the result of a failed peace process. We're living with government corruption and incompetent politicians. We are living with violence, with death always close at hand: in a traffic accident, a soccer brawl, or in defense of our families. We are ignorant of peace. We haven't had the chance to get to know it. We are a corridor for the transit of drugs. We are also their consumers. We are a poor society, and poorly educated, with public schools that flood and hospitals that induce nausea. We are a society with a minimum monthly wage you could earn working a single day as a day laborer in Los Angeles. We are unequal: There are families in Central America, though very few, that could live with the rich and famous of Miami; and there are families, tens of thousands of them, that can't always put food on the table. There are families, you can count them on one hand, who have their own private jets; and there are families, tens of thousands of them, that don't have electricity or running water. We are all of this. And we are also something more.

We are also the product of certain American politicians who tried to settle the Cold War in this small part of the world. I don't need to elaborate—the evidence abounds. But whoever doesn't believe me should type into Google the words "School of the Americas." Or "Iran-Contra Affair." Or "Miami Six."

Or "Ronald Reagan Central American Millions Military Aid."
There's a lot you can type in to get the same result. We didn't
just live through our own war here. We lived through your
war. Or at least your politicians' war.

We are also the product of your politics of deportation and
national security. In May 2015, El Salvador was hemorrhag-
ing, straight from the aorta: that month was the deadliest
of this century, and this June is on track to outdo the 635
murders recorded in May. The response of the authorities is
that this is the result of the recrudescence of the war between
rival gangs, or between the gangs and the state. For most of
us, these gangs are part of our everyday life. That's why we
don't ask anymore how this started, why they are growing so
quickly. We only ask how to survive. And it's understood that
survival takes precedence over anything else.

But these gangs—La Mara Salvatrucha, Barrio 18, Mirada
Lokotes 13—weren't born in Guatemala or Honduras or
El Salvador. They came from the United States, Southern
California to be precise. They began with migrants fleeing a
US-sponsored war. And, in fleeing, some of these young men
found themselves living in an ecosystem of gangs already
established in California. And so they came together to defend
themselves, and they established a name, and now this name
is what we call our fear: Mara Salvatrucha, Barrio 18. By the
end of the 1980s and the beginning of the '90s, a few experts,
a member of Congress, and a president came up with a stu-
pendous idea about how to get rid of these problematic gangs.
With the logic of an ape, they decided the problem could
simply be booted to the other side of the border. They acted
like a scared child who closes his eyes in the hope that what
frightens him will simply disappear. It was in these years that
about 4,000 gang members, all with criminal records, were
deported. They were sent to countries at war. Those 4,000 are
now 60,000, just in El Salvador. The experts, the congressman, that president didn't have a clue what circular migration

was. They spat straight up into the sky. Today these gangs are thriving both in Central America and in the United States.

Everything that is happening to us is tangled up with the United States. We can't untie ourselves. Some of the stories in this book show just how knottily we're tied together.

This book is divided into three parts: Emptiness (or the absence or disinterest of the state); Madness (what is festering in the emptiness); and Fleeing (the only option for many desperate people). Within these three sections are the fourteen chronicles that, working as a journalist for elfaro.net, I researched and wrote from 2011 to 2015, all set in the northern triangle of Central America, this terrifying little corner of the world.

Last, I believe you should read this book for one simple reason: for the sake of humanity. I want you to understand what thousands of Central Americans are forced to live through. Then you can understand why they keep coming, and will continue to come, despite having to leave their families behind, despite having to cross Mexico, despite the wall and the Border Patrol, despite the crazy hunters of men who stalk the borderlands, and despite the difficult life waiting for them as undocumented people.

There are probably other hooks I could use to get a reader's attention. I could, for example, tell you to read this book because every one of the fourteen chapters mentions, multiple times, the United States. I could explain that a few of the stories discuss California and Texas. But I prefer to simply say that my response to the question "What is the solution?" is the following: It's up to you. The solution is up to you. The crisis will be solved when people understand, and worsens when they don't. It's that simple. And it's that complicated.

Óscar Martínez
September 2015

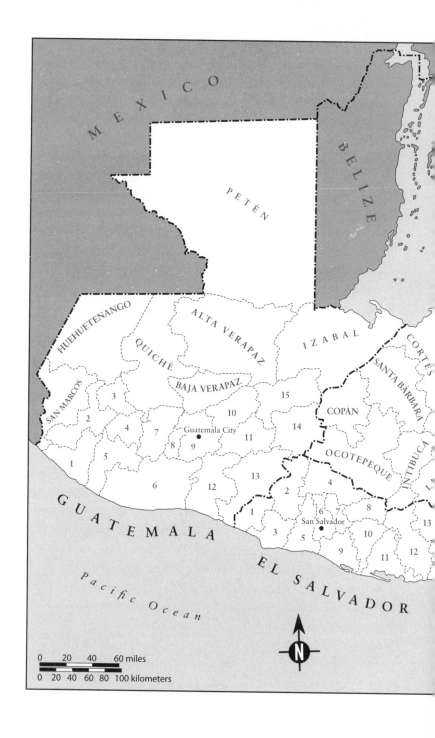

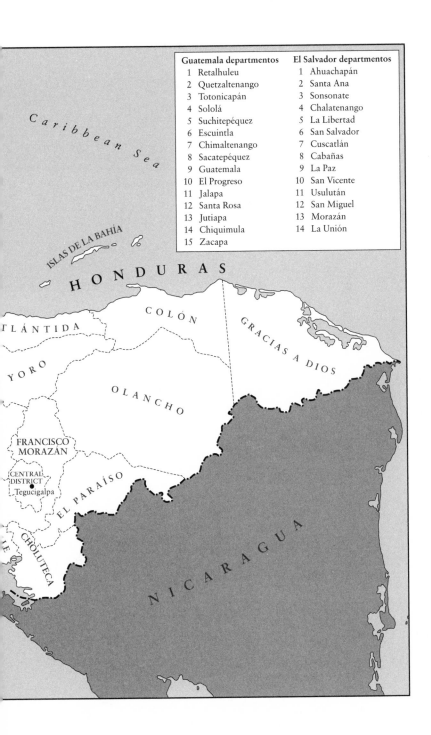

Guatemala departmentos	El Salvador departmentos
1 Retalhuleu	1 Ahuachapán
2 Quetzaltenango	2 Santa Ana
3 Totonicapán	3 Sonsonate
4 Sololá	4 Chalatenango
5 Suchitepéquez	5 La Libertad
6 Escuintla	6 San Salvador
7 Chimaltenango	7 Cuscatlán
8 Sacatepéquez	8 Cabañas
9 Guatemala	9 La Paz
10 El Progreso	10 San Vicente
11 Jalapa	11 Usulután
12 Santa Rosa	12 San Miguel
13 Jutiapa	13 Morazán
14 Chiquimula	14 La Unión
15 Zacapa	

Caribbean Sea

ISLAS DE LA BAHÍA

H O N D U R A S

ATLÁNTIDA

COLÓN

GRACIAS A DIOS

YORO

OLANCHO

FRANCISCO MORAZÁN

CENTRAL DISTRICT
Tegucigalpa

EL PARAÍSO

CHOLUTECA

N I C A R A G U A

Part 1. Emptiness

Here live the nobodies. When the authorities leave or don't do their jobs, the nobodies remain, living alone and according to laws set up by those filling the power vacuum, the laws of the blade and the bullet.

1

The State Against Chepe Furia

March 2013

This is the story of a veteran Mara Salvatrucha gangster who raised his own private army. A man, blacklisted by the United States Treasury Department, whom the Salvadoran authorities refused to call a marero, insisting instead on calling him the Mafioso, the Brain, the Intellectual, or, simply, Don José. These are the traces left behind of a criminal who penetrated deep into a state that was often his principal accomplice. To win the fight against Chepe Furia, the state had to take up arms against itself.

The Chief Inspector of the police investigation branch of El Refugio received a judicial order at the beginning of March 2011: You need to capture José Antonio Terán, better known as Chepe Furia. The Inspector, furious, thought to himself, "You got to be fucking kidding me."

Just a year previously the Inspector first arrived in Ahuachapán, a Salvadoran state that runs along the border of Guatemala. He's an old-school cop, with nearly twenty years of experience as an agent for the Centers for Police and Penitentiary Intelligence where he developed a strong network of street informants. The Inspector became a sort of expert in the Mara Salvatrucha gang (MS). Perhaps his interest was seeded in the two years he spent researching the hierarchy of the jailed gang members, surveilling their conversations and flipping informants. He discovered that the MS was far more organized and had a far more complex leadership system than its rival gang, Barrio 18.

The Inspector is obsessed with organizing his subjects: taking multiple photographs of each gang member, scanning them, arranging them, shifting the head shots around on his old desktop computer according to rank, clique, founder and *ranflero* (a gang-specific term meaning something like lieutenant). He pins even more photographs onto maps on his walls. He can't stand it when his intricate puzzles are missing a piece, missing a head shot.

It was because of his obsession with the complicated structure of gangs that he knew exactly who he'd been asked to capture. José Antonio Terán, aka Chepe Furia, a forty-six-year-old man described as looking like an "Apache," was one of the most frequent faces to turn up in the Inspector's puzzles. Chepe, from the Hollywood Locos Salvatrucha clique, was part of the Mara Salvatrucha gang, and the Inspector had placed Chepe Furia's face at the top of his maps, next to the words "leader" and "veteran."

The Hollywood clique has a fierce reputation within the Mara Salvatrucha. Formed in Los Angeles, near MacArthur Park, in the early 1980s, it's the clique that gave birth to the national leader of the MS, Borromeo Henríquez, El Diablito de Hollywood.

The Inspector knows he isn't researching just any ordinary gangbanger. Chepe Furia wasn't a triggerman, a soldier, or any of the other ranks listed under most of the faces in his catalogs: beardless young men with just a murder or two to their names. In fact, the entire reason the Inspector had moved to El Refugio was because of Chepe Furia. He thought that by escaping to a more rural town he'd be outside of Chepe's sphere of influence, far from any of the gangster's collaborators in the Atiquizaya police force.

He didn't understand how the same judge, Tomás Salinas, a short and mannerly man who seemed to speak only in juridical terms, could release Chepe Furia from prison for the second time.

How could this judge, who knew so much about organized crime, have believed that Chepe Furia, the king of spades in the card deck of Salvadoran gangsters, would not run upon being released on a $25,000 bail? He had killed a protected witness, he had infiltrated the police department, he had somehow finagled a letter of good conduct from the mayor of Atiquizaya, and he'd been singled out by the ex-minister of security and justice, Manuel Melgar, as having transcended the ranking of "gangster" and secured the title of "mobster."

"You got to be fucking kidding," the Inspector thought to himself.

In early 2010, in a poor neighborhood on the outskirts of Atiquizaya, a twenty-seven-year-old leans against the door of his tiny shack and smokes his fifth crack rock of the day. The door secures with a metal hasp lock, but he doesn't have it in place. As he takes a big hit into his lungs, he hears the creaking of the door opening behind him. He holds the smoke in and hears the cocking of a pistol. Reaching both hands for his belt, he pulls out a .40-caliber with his right hand and a .357 with his left.

"Hey, cool it. I know you're armed."

El Niño recognizes the calm voice of Detective Pozo, from the office at El Refugio.

"I've been smoking," El Niño says.

"I just want to talk."

"I'm pretty blazed."

"Son of a bitch. So you don't think we can talk?"

Detective Pozo decides to try his luck. He doesn't fire when El Niño, still holding a pistol in each hand, stands up. Locking eyes with the detective, El Niño walks past him and outside the shack. Without putting down a weapon he gets in the back of the pickup and says, "Let's roll."

The detective holsters his pistol and, his heart in his hands, drives the empty streets back toward his office, an armed assassin from the Hollywood Locos Salvatrucha seated behind him. Detective Pozo has finally found a high-ranking member of the clique founded by Chepe Furia who will at least consider becoming a protected witness.

Meet El Niño from the Hollywood Locos Salvatrucha, the Hollywood Kid.

El Niño was a successful assassin for the MS, rising to third in the ranks of the local Atiquizaya clique. Some people might think that revealing his nickname is a risk for him. Whoever thinks that doesn't understand how deeply the MS, especially Chepe Furia, has infiltrated the state, or how poorly the state can protect its witnesses. El Niño had already received calls from gang leaders inside the Ciudad Barrios prison, where only MS members are detained, telling him that sooner or later he would be killed. "You'll be leaving here smelling like pine," they told him.

"They don't make coffins out of pine around here," he responded. "They make them out of mango and conacaste trees."

It wasn't the first time that investigators from El Refugio (who've asked to remain anonymous) had tried to get El Niño to collaborate. The Inspector is an expert in both sowing friction and harvesting protected witnesses. He's threatened several gang members with dropping them off in enemy territory after they claimed they didn't belong to any gang. He's used his cell phone to film them denying they are part of the MS and then later, after their interrogation, sobbing. In just a year of intelligence gathering he was able to complete the puzzle of the clique's leadership. Since then, in late 2009, he's dedicated himself to flipping one witness after another, getting them to reveal names. It wasn't until he figured out that El Niño was connected to the murder of a fifteen-year-old girl that he started getting close to Chepe Furia. The Inspector told Detective Pozo to do whatever he had to do to make sure El

Niño talked. Pozo made El Niño a simple offer: You talk or you pay for your murders.

Now that he's become a plea-bargain witness (a *testigo criteriado* in El Salvador is a witness who was involved in a crime and agrees to testify in exchange for a reduced sentence) in a court case against forty-two members of Chepe Furia's gang, El Niño lives in a small shack close to the police station. After more than twenty hours of conversation and at least fifteen visits with El Niño, I've come to understand that he's so much more than a witness. He is a living testimony as to how a clique is born, as to how kids as young as thirteen, who once sought out trouble by roughhousing with each other, become members of one of the most dangerous and powerful gangs in the country. He is living testimony as to how a man deported from Los Angeles, California, changed the life of these scrappy young boys. That man was Chepe Furia.

"It's 'cause we were such idiots, man. Then he showed up talking all different and flashing his goods, his truck, living like a king. And we, the gang here, we were his business."

El Niño speaks in broken sentences, sucking in and expelling clouds of smoke, then quick-sucking the smoke back in, holding his breath, moving his lips like a fish. He's getting high while his girlfriend, eighteen years old, coos over their newborn daughter and his police guard dozes in the next shack over. The only place you can catch a glimpse of the movie-like glamour of living as a protected witness in El Salvador is in the movies.

The story of El Niño begins in 1994, when he was already a young gangster. The names of the gangs he talks about, however, sound like play groups. He was part of a gang called Mara Gauchos Locos 13 (the Crazy Cowboy 13 Gang), who fought against other neighborhood gangs: Los Valerios, Los Meli 33 (the Twins 33), Los Chancletas (the Sandals) and Los Uvas (the Grapes). Most of their adventure consisted in going to the town's parties en masse and roughing up a few other kids. If, by chance, somebody had a bat, or one of them pulled a knife, he was hailed as the hero of the moment, and then it was over.

The playground of the young gangsters in Atiquizaya extended to the parties of El Refugio and Turín, but never to the neighboring city of Chalchuapa. The kids knew that only the big boys played there, a group of teenagers who called themselves Barrio 18 and were run by a twenty-year-old who had—a rarity in the first years after the war—an actual gun. The leader's name was Moncho Garrapata.

For most people living in that region, the word "criminal" meant a member of a group that robbed trucks, stole cattle or maybe kidnapped people. From those circles of criminals, El Niño explained to me, the names of a few—the most dangerous —stuck out: Nando Vulva, the brothers Víctor and Pedro Maraca, and Henry Méndez. Also, a twenty-six-year-old who had served with the National Guard during the war and had recently returned to Atiquizaya from California: Chepe Furia.

According to police records, Chepe Furia was deported from the United States on October 15, 2003. From 1994 to 2003 he lived and moved between the two countries. It was in Southern California that he became a founder of one of the most powerful MS cliques in the country: the Fulton Locos Salvatrucha. I confirmed this with two other sources, one of whom was kicked out of the gang by Chepe himself and wished to remain anonymous; the other was Ernesto Deras, better known by his nickname, Satan. He was also an ex-Salvadoran soldier who migrated to the United States and was a *palabrero* (leader) for the Fulton Locos in Los Angeles, where he still lives. Satan told me that José Antonio Terán was "known as El Veneno [the Poison] and had people's respect," but then "disappeared" from LA around 1995.

Recently returned to El Salvador, Chepe approached the scrappy gangs of boys and started preaching to them about a much bigger gang, the big family, the Mara Salvatrucha. Little by little, winning over the youngsters, his groups began to meet regularly in the San Antonio neighborhood of Atiquizaya.

El Niño remembers Chepe in the old days: "He converted us [literally 'ganged' us]. Cruising around in his double cabin ride, all armored up and rolling in cash."

Chepe Furia brought the kids together like a wise old man imparting wisdom to the youth of the tribe. He explained the meaning of words and told them stories of battles against the great enemy, Barrio 18. One night, El Niño told me, Chepe told the tale of the murder of Brenda Paz, one of the MS's most celebrated murders, carried out in the United States. Brenda Paz was a young Honduran woman, four months pregnant, who testified to the FBI and was later stabbed to death on the banks of Virginia's Shenandoah River. "Traitors smell worse than shit," Chepe Furia would tell his disciples.

For nights on end groups of ten or fifteen young men would gather in abandoned houses in the San Antonio neighborhood, forced to beat the hell out of each other. After the fights were over, Chepe would say to them, "Welcome to the Mara." He preached loyalty and courage above all else. He was sculpting his boys.

When he had about twenty-five of them under his command, Chepe Furia showed them his arsenal, which at the time consisted of two .22 pistols and one 9 millimeter. Around that time, in the late '90s, the leader of Barrio 18, Moncho Garrapata, was in prison, and Chepe Furia decided to wage an offensive against the rival gang. He named the offensive "Mission Hollywood." The once-young neighborhood rebels premiered as a deadly group of assassins.

El Niño told me he'd tried to impress Chepe Furia by killing Paletín, a baker and member of Barrio 18 who had just returned from Mexico after a failed attempt to cross into the United States. He took one of the clique's .22s and, together with Chepe, he walked to the outskirts of the village of El Zapote, where Chepe left him on his own. When Paletín showed up on his bicycle El Niño tried to shoot him, but the gun jammed. By the time he finally pulled a shot off, Paletín had started running toward him to take the gun away. El Niño pulled the trigger again and the bullet tore through Paletín's chest.

"Then I grabbed his head," El Niño remembered, "and finished him off with a knife so, since they said he was a witch, he wouldn't come back. And then I got out of there and went to El Naranjo, where I was living then."

As a reward, Chepe Furia sent him an ounce of marijuana, which El Niño accompanied with shots of Four Aces rum. He was fifteen years old. Chepe's boys were starting to pick fights with their rivals, or with pretty much anybody they came across.

Meanwhile, Chepe Furia worked his gang politics, bringing two more cliques into his fold: the Parvis de Turín and Los Ángeles de Ahuachapán, neither of which had a single firearm at that point. (The word *Parvis* comes from Parkview, the street in MacArthur Park in Los Angeles where some of the early members of the MS lived. The Salvadoran accent turns the word Parkview into *Parvis*). By this time the entire San Antonio neighborhood belonged to Chepe Furia, including the first house at the neighborhood's entrance, which a member known as El Cuto used as a lookout to make sure the police weren't snooping around. A block from the soccer field, which Chepe had paid to re-sod, was his two-story house with a two-car driveway. It was where assassins came to party, smoke pot and drink. Some of the assassins would show up at the house still wearing their school uniforms. As the boys were molting into killers, Chepe continued to recruit them into his own private army.

As evening settled into the sky above his small hut, El Niño explained to me that a lot of his boss's operations didn't have anything to do with the war against Barrio 18; nobody but Chepe knew the reasons behind the violence.

"He'd get in epic fights with important people I didn't know, political people, people from some drug cartel. He'd get paid to do a hit on somebody, but he'd get one of us to do it for him. So you'd do the hit and he'd get the money. You got cred from the boys, but he kept the bills. We were idiots, man. He'd be going to Guatemala, to San Miguel [on the western fringe of El Salvador], working these big shakedowns, making money. He was already the Boss around here."

The congressman shuffles hurriedly into his office. Inside, his seven staff members are all nearly suffocating in the heat. As soon as they see their boss, the staffers pretend to be hard at work. One of them frowns at a sheet on the desk in front of him. It's a blank piece of paper. The congressman tells everybody to leave, that he wants to be alone. In less than three minutes the office is empty. He closes the metal door that leads out to the street and throws the lock. Then he opens the metal blinds so his bodyguard can hear his order: "Stand by the door until I come out," he yells.

He sits down at his desk, looks at me and says, "Alright, so what do you want to know about Chepe Furia?"

It was early 2012 in Ahuachapán, the biggest city of the state with the same name. The congressman, who spoke to me on the condition of anonymity, talked to me of Chepe Furia's power, of his friendships with lawyers and prosecutors, police and criminals, customs agents and truck drivers. He spoke about his reputation as a benefactor of communities, of fixing potholes, repairing soccer fields, building fences. And yet what was most revealing that afternoon had nothing to do with anything the congressman said. It was that even in the emptied room, with the metal door locked and an armed officer standing guard outside, a national politician was convinced that in order to mention the name of Chepe Furia it was necessary to hide his own name.

"We're not talking about just any gangster," the congressman says to me. "He's a mafioso with tentacles in every part of the state. And one day I won't be in Congress anymore." He means that he won't be protected. In 2009 Chepe Furia was already the head of a powerful clique. The times of sloppy murders were over. He had led his boys into a long war with Barrio 18, fighting gun battles in the enemy territory of Chalchuapita. El Niño remembers that in the past nine years Chepe Furia left the region at least three times, for periods lasting at least a year. He'd leave when the fighting got close enough to home and wouldn't return until things calmed down. Whenever he came back he had weapons to hand out to his soldiers like souvenirs: .357 pistols, SAF submachine guns, a G3 rifle and, once, a "9 millimeter Beretta that he supposedly stole from a cop," El Niño told me.

Through various arrests of members of the Atiquizaya clique, including one arrest resulting from an attack on a police car, officers decommissioned three police-issued weapons. Two of the weapons, including a machine gun, were reportedly stolen from an officer, Subinspector Delgado Juárez, who was working on the other side of the country in San Miguel. Delgado, who had already reported his 9 millimeter pistol as stolen, said that he'd left the machine gun in the trunk of his car, parked in front of his house, when it was stolen.

In those years, Chepe could count on a hierarchically organized gang. He had become the veteran, founder and absolute leader of the clique of the Hollywood Locos Salvatrucha of Atiquizaya. He delegated the second-in-command position to a thirty-year-old gangster named José Guillermo Solito Escobar, known as El Extraño (the Stranger) who had just left prison after serving a two-year term for aggravated assault. Under the Stranger, serving as subchief was another thirty-year-old, Jorge Alberto González Navarrete, who had just been deported from the United States, also after being convicted for aggravated assault. González had numerous skull tattoos and was known in Maryland, where he had lived in the United States, as Baby Yorker, and in El Salvador as Liro Joker (*Liro* being the phonetic Spanish spelling of *Little*). "A real heavy son of a bitch, a killer," is how El Niño described Liro Joker to me. The treasurer of the Hollywood Locos was a skinny, pale, fine-featured thirty-eight-year-old man with a friendly face named Fredy Crespín Morán, known by fellow gangsters as El Maniático (the Maniac). El Maniático was a licensed electrician and an integral part of Chepe Furia's organization. Until he was captured in 2010 by a team led by the Chief Inspector, he was also a hired spokesman for the mayor of Atiquizaya, who belonged to the right-wing Arena Party. El Maniático would tour various communities throughout the region with a group of young assassins from the Hollywood Locos, official city business the perfect alibi for committing crimes.

Chepe Furia had established a system of trading assassins with the Normandie clique (another reference to a Los Angeles street name: Normandie Avenue, where the gang was born, thousands of miles away from these warm Central American border towns), which hustled out of the coastal state of Sonsonate. Los Normandies were headed by a member of the MS whom the ex-minister of security referred to in a 2011 interview as a narcotrafficking gangster. His name was Moris Bercián Manchón, though he was known as Barney. He was once arrested with a stash of cocaine valued at $160 million, and yet he managed to avoid prison time. He slipped sentencing in another case as well, where he was linked to fifty different homicides, some of which involved dismembered bodies left in plastic bags in the streets.

Thanks to collaboration with Manchón, as well as other treaties, the Hollywood Locos had recruited one of the best assassins in the country: an ex-cop from Sonsonate known as Loco Trece (Crazy 13) who, back when he was still wearing blue, was named Edgardo Geovanni Morán. A loud and spirited man, he was short but intimidating. In late 2012 Loco

Trece was the last gangster of the Chepe Furia generation to be captured. Earlier, he was nearly caught by two policemen in Atiquizaya, but he struggled out of their grasp, leaving them with nothing but his T-shirt.

The clique alliance caused the Inspector numerous headaches. He struggled with finding where the newly arrived assassins from Sonsonate—men who had no history in Atiquizaya but had long records on the coast—fit into his puzzle. With a growing infrastructure underneath him, Chepe Furia started turning himself into a businessman. By now his relation with the mayor's office had been formalized: He bought a dump truck that he loaned out for city trash collection. His first white Isuzu truck made him $2,500 a month.

In the middle of 2012 when I asked Atiquizaya Mayor Ana Luisa Rodríguez de González how it was possible that she had such a high-profile gangster in her administration, she told me that she had never heard of Chepe Furia, that she only knew "Mr. José Terán, president of the San Antonio Neighborhood Association." She also told me she'd already been through these questions when a few detectives from the Central Division of Police Investigation came to talk to her. And her responses hadn't changed: She didn't know anyone named Chepe Furia; Mr. José Terán had signed a standard garbage collection contract; he was the friendly head of a neighborhood association; he actively participated in cleaning up his neighborhood; she'd never heard of El Maniático; she knew Mr. Fredy, who came recommended by the ex-councilman Doctor Avilés; she honestly didn't know what they were into; and she really missed them when they were captured and accused of "all those horrible things."

Months later, when I asked Mario Martínez Jacobo, the chief prosecutor of all of Ahuachapán state, if he thought it was believable that someone in Atiquizaya didn't know who Chepe Furia was, he told me: "No, I don't think it's believable." The money Chepe was making on his trash collection was a pittance compared to what he was making from his illicit businesses.

El Niño told me about a time, in 2010, when Chepe Furia ordered him and two other members to burn a Toyota SUV. It didn't make sense to El Niño. The gang didn't usually burn such fancy cars. He explained his confusion: "'If the owner owes so much to Chepe, why doesn't he just send me to kill him?' was how I was thinking in my hit man's mind." He later pieced it together: Torching the SUV had to do with an extortion Chepe was running with a businessman known as El Viejo Oso (the Old Bear) who hadn't paid Chepe his half of the $80,000 they had made together, "but was forking it over bit by bit, seven grand and then another seven grand." Chepe Furia wasn't pleased. El Niño was there when El Viejo Oso came to the store in San Antonio where Chepe was passing the day in various meetings and told him: "Look, Chepito, someone burned my ride." Chepe consoled El Viejo Oso, telling him that if he paid what he owed, he himself would lend him money to buy another car. Chepe, it turned out, knew more tricks than just how to pull the trigger.

Despite the fact that working with the mayor was not his main source of income, he knew he needed to be on good terms with the city government, that the relationship would serve him well. At the beginning of 2012 a cop working under the Inspector introduced me to one of the mayor's staff members. If I was surprised about the congressman taking so many precautions in meeting with me, I found the staff member's dance to border on the ridiculous. The first time we met was on a corner, five blocks from Atiquizaya's Central Park. He saw me, shook my hand, slipped me a phone number and then split. I called him afterward and he arranged to have our interview on the outskirts of Atiquizaya, on an almost empty plot of land next to an industrial motor that was running loudly enough that nobody else could have heard a word we said to each other. It seemed that he had years of practice having conversations like this. He started talking to me in a deep, gravelly voice that sounded like it was coming from somewhere beyond the grave. I asked him what had happened to him and he told me that he was distorting his voice on purpose. After I assured him that nobody would hear the recording, he conceded to use his normal voice. What he told me was scattered, like teenager's gossip, and I had to piece it back together afterward. "He [Chepe Furia] has a tight relationship with City Council. He has special privileges, he meets with managers and bosses in City Hall, arranges to work with transport and that kind of thing because it helps him with his other businesses." The man looked over his shoulder, then leaned in closer to my ear. "He's got them all working for him, but they only work in MS zones, and they all work with official licenses ... El Maniático is the promoter and works on recruiting new people into the gang."

Huddled with me next to that industrial motor, he ranted on for an hour. A lot of what he said clarified some of the other info I'd been getting. The man explained, for example, how Chepe Furia established a relationship, through a third-party ex-prosecutor who also ran a car dealership, with Public Administrator José Mario Mirasol. According to public records, Chepe Furia had been detained more than once while driving his double-cab pickup truck. There were even photographs of Chepe posing in front of the tinted windows of his ride, the license plates of which were registered to Álex Iván Retana. Retana, better known as El Diablo, was a lawyer from Chalchuapa who served as public prosecutor in the vehicle theft division. According to a police report, El Diablo was also the owner of the dealership Auto Repuestos Iván in Santa Ana, of which "Chepe Furia was a partner who would bring in trucks of suspicious origins with Guatemalan plates to dismantle and sell off in parts." Chepe seemed to have various friends in the world of stripping or junking cars. In 2010

Chepe crossed into Guatemala at Anguiatú in a car whose plates, according to the police registry, belonged to Dilmark Giovanni Ascencio, the son of the ex-congressman Antonio Ascencio, of the National Conciliation Party, who together with his father owned an auto parts store in Santa Ana.

The informant said that Chepe Furia met with the mayor as often as he wanted, without even having to set up an appointment. Another city employee, speaking to me on similar conditions of anonymity, had told me the same. It was Chepe who paid for the entire bar tab at the mayor's 2011 New Year celebration at the El Jícaro restaurant, when he and the mayor chatted away most of the night. Once, the second informant told me, Chepe came to pacify a city employee strike. "He showed up [to the strike] with this arrogant attitude, but since all his men were armed, he was able to persuade the strikers. He told them, 'Let's go back to work, so the people aren't left without services.' And, just like that, the strike was over."

According to both sources, every September 15, Election Day in El Salvador, Chepe would loan his vehicles to the mayor's office to help transport voters. An official police report was even more specific: "For the 2004 presidential elections [Chepe Furia] coordinated the transportation of persons to voting polls for the Arena Party."

Don Chepito came and went out of the mayor's office when he pleased, maintaining and building a powerful and diverse network of contacts. El Niño told me about a judge Chepe would sometimes talk to. He remembers hearing him once tell the judge: "I heard that a couple crazy kids got picked up for racketeering. Do you think you could let them out for me by Monday morning, please?" When the boys were released that Monday morning, Chepe told them to stay off the streets for a while. His machinery was running smoothly, and at a low cost. His many hit men kept him out of danger. El Niño explains: "He paid us three pistols to kill some guy, when he got paid $25,000."

The corporate-like infrastructure of the Hollywood Locos Salvatrucha was made up of a tremendous network of legal businesses, quasi-legal businesses and outright criminal businesses, and was far larger than the network of the greater Mara Salvatrucha gang. Chepe kept the monthly dues of $7 per gang member going to the national gang, but besides that pittance, everything else went into his own pocket. The Inspector explained that it was clear that the near total control Chepe had established in San Antonio allowed him the luxury of dismantling cars and storing shipments of drugs right in his own neighborhood.

By the end of 2011, even before Chepe Furia was captured, El Niño figured his boss had it coming to him: "He's making money with the gang's name, and he's not dishing out any [to the greater national gang, the MS]. That's going to come back and haunt him."

Subdirector of Police in Atiquizaya Mauricio Ramírez Landaverde told me that by early 2012 the Hollywood Locos Salvatrucha clique was an "example of a gang that had reached the status of organized crime group. They are organized to deal in contraband, drugs, assassinations and the trafficking of persons." He explained that to become so well organized it's key that a clique have an ambitious leader who understands how to deal with bloodthirsty youth. This guarantees that any other ambitious criminals in the area have to come to terms with them.

Chepe was making alliances in every direction, including at a national level. At the Santa Ana festivals in July 2011, police officers started following Roberto "El Burro" Herrera, who is currently detained at a maximum-security prison and has been identified as the leader of the Texis Cartel. Their chase led them to the Drive Inn restaurant, where Herrera was seated in a private room with El Maniático and Chepe Furia.

What Chepe didn't know at that point was that the Inspector had finished piecing together his puzzle, that El Niño had told all his secrets, that Chepe's fight with the state was about to begin, and that there were in fact two different states he was going to have to deal with: a friendly state and an enemy state.

More than 500 policemen were deployed to the cavalry regiment of San Juan Opico, about an hour away from Atiquizaya. It was October 2010. The cops had received orders to conduct seventy different raids on houses belonging to members of Chepe Furia's Hollywood Locos clique. In caravans of buses, they arrived in Atiquizaya's Central Park, regrouped and then were sent off on their missions. Atiquizaya has a population of a little more than 30,000 people, with many of its streets still stone or dirt. The Inspector led a team of fifty agents directly toward the San Antonio neighborhood. There were seven different targets in the area, but the Inspector was only interested in one: taking down his king of spades, Chepe Furia himself.

It's well known that the network of influence Chepe Furia has spun extends from police to garbage collectors to contacts far outside of the city. One of the detectives participating in the raid was Sergeant José Wilfredo Tejada, a man who would later be accused of turning over an informant for Chepe Furia to torture and kill. What was odd about the raid was that it seemed that the police expected to find Chepe at home, asleep and completely unaware of the heavy troop movement around him.

When the brigade first crossed into San Antonio, the gangs cut the electricity of the whole neighborhood. Perhaps as a joke, the only gang member found in the neighborhood was El Cuto, son of the tortilla man who kept an eye on the neighborhood entrance. The chief prosecutor for western El Salvador, Mario Martínez Jacobo, later traveled to San Antonio to interview some of the residents who told him that Chepe had been whisked away to safety in a car about ten minutes before the police arrived. In the following days, however, the police did round up twenty-five other gangsters, who would later be tried for eleven known murders. Another thirty members, including Chepe Furia, were charged in absentia, for racketeering.

Chepe didn't show his face in Atiquizaya for another two months. Finally, on December 24, 2010, soldiers identified and arrested Chepe in one of his stores. The kingpin had been relaxing alongside his dad, greeting visitors. As soon as the Inspector heard that Chepe was back in town he convinced a deputy judge to sign another arrest warrant so he himself could go to San Antonio and snag his prey. Circuit Judge Tomás Salinas, however, who was on vacation at the time, supposedly didn't buy the story against Chepe and refused to issue a new arrest warrant after the last failed raid. This was despite the fact that a month previously, the Special Prosecuting Office Against Organized Crime had assured Judge Salinas that there was indeed sufficient evidence against Chepe for leading an organized crime group and had recommended he issue the warrant.

The Inspector knew that Chepe Furia's own lawyer was "pulling out his hair in fear." Why, he asked himself, would a deputy judge be willing to sign the arrest order, while a circuit judge refused? Chepe Furia, meanwhile, calmly watched the scene unfolding before him.

Chepe, who refused to self-identify as a gang member, was soon transferred to the Apanteos prison in Santa Ana. Chepe seemed to realize what El Niño had said about him long before, that he "had it coming" for not paying his dues to the national leaders of the MS. The prison warden says that on Chepe's first day of being in the "civilian" prison wing, where non–gang-affiliated inmates are placed, three different inmates asked for a visit with him. All three of them asked the warden, "Don't you know who you've put in the civilian wing?" One of them referred to Chepe as "Don Chepe, the mafia mayor of the West." In the end, the warden decided to move Chepe to "the Island," an isolated cell block for problem inmates. Chepe didn't seem to make any friends there either.

After a couple of nights living with two leaders of La Raza, a prison gang, and another gangster from La Mirada Loca (the Crazy Look), Chepe admitted that he was a member of the MS, signing a paper that identified his rank and clique. He was then transferred to the MS wing, where he did his best to keep a low profile.

But he didn't stay in jail for long. Circuit Court Judge Salinas came back from vacation and immediately approved Chepe's lawyer's petition, granting an appeal of the case just thirty-eight days after his initial arrest. The judge would go on to determine that, "just because a policeman and a plea-bargain witness" say so, it doesn't mean a man is a gang leader. The judge explained that Chepe Furia wasn't being charged with murder, but with "fulfilling the role of [gang] leader, [which requires proof] that the person was the author of various murders." He reiterated that he was "not going to penalize someone on account of what the media or a prosecutor claims." Plus, the judge continued, "this person has a contractual position with the municipal mayor's office of Atiquizaya," so it would be unlikely that he would attempt to escape. Nonetheless, he set a $25,000 bail, which Chepe financed through two mortgages. He was asked for his passport and was told to present himself every Friday at a police office in Atiquizaya. And then he walked free. For the second time in two years the same judge ordered the door to his prison cell opened.

The following Friday Chepe didn't show at the police station. He didn't show up the next Friday either, nor a single Friday for the rest of the year. Thanks to the leniency of Circuit Court Judge Salinas, Chepe had disappeared.

Prosecutors scrambled to ask the court to reconsider the judge's "poor decision," since it was based on the same arguments he had used once before to undermine Chepe's arrest, and which the court had ultimately ordered the judge to reverse. The court ruled, again, that the judge's decision was "incomplete and invalid ... and completely erroneous." It determined that evidence, including a letter from the mayor explaining Chepe's contract in collecting the city's trash, the birth certificate of his child, a testimony of a doctor claiming to know Chepe, four house titles, along with water and power bills made out to another person's name were not sufficient to conclude that the gangster wouldn't skip town. The only thing the documents did prove, the court went on to explain, was that the accused had "a considerable amount of property," one of which was two stories and larger than any other house in San Antonio. Taking away his passport to try to keep him in the country was another absurd notion, given that "he can [cross] with another form of ID or at nonofficial points of entry."

The court ruled that Judge Salinas had committed a "summarily grave" error. Salinas had not applied for a "suspended effect," as he and other judges typically did, which would have given prosecutors the opportunity to appeal before the accused was released on bail. It's a common procedure, taken to avoid exactly what happened: that the accused slips out of the state's grasp.

I asked the chief prosecutor of western El Salvador if he thought the judge tried his best to let Chepe Furia out.

"That's exactly what he did," he responded.

For two months I called and left messages for Judge Salinas. He never responded. But then, at the beginning of 2012, we met face to face. He was obviously frustrated when I asked him about the Chepe Furia case and his extraordinary decision to free a man who had failed to fulfill his parole requirements once before. The judge assured me that he had his reasons and insisted we talk about something else. I was never able to get him to comment on his Chepe decision.

Nonetheless, the court had by then ordered Chepe recaptured. The story started all over again.

~

In March of 2011, the Inspector received a judicial order for the arrest of José Antonio Terán, better known as Chepe Furia. The first thing he thought was, "You got to be fucking kidding me."

It took a year of grueling work just to get close to the "King of Atiquizaya," and now the new arrest orders were demanding that the Inspector capture him (once again) in just seven days. And it wasn't as if Chepe was working alone; he had a network of minions that were doing all they could to protect him. The Inspector's men picked up on his scent a number of times when their informants told them that Chepe was moving back and forth across the Guatemalan border, pushing drugs. One of the informants asked for $300 in exchange for a license plate number and a signal whenever Chepe came back to Santa Ana. The police decided not to take the offer.

On March 10, 2012, police officers noticed a man acting suspiciously in Bella Santa Ana, an upper-middle-class neighborhood. When the man saw the officers, he ran inside a house. The officers followed, detaining the suspect who they were surprised to find out was none other than Chepe Furia. After searching the house they discovered a .30-30 carbine with seventeen cartridges, two 12-gauge shotguns and ammo for a .25-caliber pistol.

When he heard of the detention, the western regional police chief, Douglas Omar García Funes, better known as Carabinero (Carabineer), went to the prison just to see the catch with his own eyes.

"It's incredible how sharp he is," García Funes told me later. "When you hear him talk he almost convinces you that he's just a businessman. He is always polite, steering the conversation where he wants. He told me that we were colleagues, that he had once been a National Policeman."

Everything seemed to be going down the same trodden path. Chepe Furia would be marched in front of the same judge and charged with the same crime, "racketeering," which, as a gang leader, could send him to prison for six to nine years. But this time the Inspector had a trick up his sleeve. Thanks to gaining the confidence of El Niño, he had more than just formal confessions; he had corroborating evidence linking him to murder. El Niño had told him about an afternoon in November 2009 when Chepe and some others left Atiquizaya to go to the state of Usulután for the funeral of a murdered gang member. Chepe drove there in his pickup along with El Extraño and Liro Joker. On the way, they stopped to grab a couple of ropes (one blue and one white), which Chepe had ordered a young twenty-three-year-old gangster to buy for him. Chepe paid a dollar for each rope and the young man got in the pickup. That same day, on the western edge of El Salvador in the city of Berlín, Usulután, the body of a young man was found on the side of the highway. The victim was identified as Samuel Menjívar Trejo, a twenty-three-year-old vegetable seller in the Ahuachapán market and an extortion collector for Chepe. He was a known MS gang member who went by the nickname Rambito. He was also an informant for the Atiquizaya police, who attempted to sell out his boss. Rambito's body, showing signs of having been tortured, was found tied with the same blue and white ropes that El Niño had seen him hand over to Chepe. His face was destroyed by various shots from a 9 millimeter pistol.

Police Sergeants José Wilfredo Tejada and Walter Misael Hernández, both from the Atiquizaya force, were seen in their vehicles earlier that day, along with Rambito, just before he sold the ropes to Chepe. That same morning Tejada had radioed his fellow officers to find Rambito. El Niño would later point out both police officers in photographs and claim to have seen them, on more than one occasion, conversing with Chepe Furia. Both sergeants, however, remain free.

During the conversation with El Niño in his shack in 2012, he told me, without making a big deal out of it, that Tejada had once come to him and asked him to accuse other gang members of having killed Rambito. Tejada said he would tell El Niño whom to point his finger at. None of the men Tejada wanted him to name were Chepe Furia.

Chief Prosecutor Rodolfo Delgado of the Special Prosecuting Office Against Organized Crime explained to me that due to the involvement of state investigators and the complexity of the case, as well as in consideration of their own safety, they had decided to move the trial to the national appeals court. Delgado told me that the entire situation was bizarre: Two sergeants (instead of detectives) had detained the informant-turned-victim. The sergeants took Rambito to a station, from where he left accompanied by Tejada and Hernández, and the next time he was seen, he was getting into Chepe's pickup truck.

In December 2012, after Chepe had been found guilty of Rambito's murder, Judge Salinas tried for the third time to clear him of his charges. On August 20, 2012, almost four months after his recapture, Salinas decided that there wasn't sufficient proof against Chepe and granted him a "provisional dismissal." This time, however, the extra charge of murder kept him in jail. The circuit court reminded Judge Salinas that, according to a witness, Chepe "facilitated [the trafficking of] weapons that were used in murder; he was 'the brains' behind a gang; has connections with the police; and frequently leaves the country for Guatemala to make drug and weapons sales." The circuit court also reminded Judge Salinas that "he has been part of this group [Hollywood Locos Salvatrucha] and it has acted" on his behalf.

For the murder of Rambito, Chepe was sentenced to twenty years. He is currently serving the time in Gotera prison, which is far from fellow members of the Mara Salvatrucha.

El Niño would continue living in his shack, testifying against other former gang members of the Hollywood Locos Salvatrucha. About Chepe Furia, he had already told all he knew, and yet he was convinced that the story wasn't over.

"Traitors are worse than shit," he remembers Chepe telling him.

Before Chepe had received his sentence, a policeman El Niño didn't know came to his shack and offered him $1,000 to go and kill someone on the outskirts of Atiquizaya. "I'll give you a ride," the cop said to him. El Niño asked for the gun to do the deed. "I'll give it to you when we get there," the cop responded.

El Niño told me later: "I'm no fucking idiot."

2

The Lords of the Border

August 2011

A tough police chief, boasting about not being scared of narcos, arrests a high-flying border mayor. The fallout follows fast, revealing the intricate web of power in Honduran and Guatemalan narco politics. The Lords of the Border, the criminal power players, have contacts at the highest echelons of national politics. This is a brief tour of the state of Copán, the passageway that connects Guatemala to Honduras, the so-called Corridor of Death.

On the side of the highway to La Entrada (a border town whose name literally means "the Entrance"), a chubby cowboy is taking a leak behind his car. Night is falling on the northern border of Honduras, and Police Commissioner Juan Carlos "El Tigre" ("the Tiger") Bonilla orders his subordinate, Rivera Tomas, to check out the drunkard. El Tigre is leading a convoy of twenty-five policemen on a scouting mission. Accompanying the fat cowboy, who is still pissing, is a bodyguard and a woman, both waiting inside the car. Unsurprisingly, Tomas discovers that there are two guns stashed in the car. The bodyguard hands over the permits for both guns. The cowboy shouts something to Tomas, and, on the other side of the highway, a van climbs the slope, *norteña* music blasting at full volume. Perhaps struck by the scene, the driver of the van squeals to a halt and six armed men jump out. Without a second thought, about twenty police officers from El Tigre's convoy surround them and take aim.

"I'm the mayor of La Jigua, you idiots!" shouts the fattest of the new arrivals as he pushes away the agent trying to inspect him.

El Tigre can't contain himself when he sees his police officers being pushed around. "What the fuck is going on here?" he intervenes.

The mayor of La Jigua, Germán Guerra, takes one look at El Tigre and hands over not only one, but all three of the guns he has on him. Two of them, it turns out, lack permits. This scene, typical along this stretch of the border, took place just a few miles from El Paraíso (the Paradise).

El Paraíso is a disaster: empty and, depending on the season, either dusty or muddy. Currently, it's all mud. It's not at all like what I've heard. People told me it was a shocking place. A place you may never get out of alive if you dare show up unannounced.

But, really there's just little to see. City Hall, though, is a palace, a monumental palace. It stands tall in the center of El Paraíso, with five long pillars framing its exterior and, as if a lot of folks in El Paraíso ride around in helicopters, it has a heliport on its rooftop.

I'd been told I couldn't simply swing in like a disoriented tourist. That, with some luck, I'd merely be expelled from El Paraíso. That's why I had to come in as I did, in a convoy. It's obvious that anyone guarding El Paraíso spotted us as soon as we descended from the cliffs and down the muddy and turbulent path that leads to the Honduran city bordering Izabal, Guatemala—the city known as the golden gate for cocaine being ferried to the United States.

In Honduras, everyone is quick to warn you against entering organized-crime territory.

You can't just go.

They see everything.

If ... God knows how ... you manage to enter, you'll never come back.

For me this started at the beginning of my journey, at the capital of Tegucigalpa, an eight-hour car ride from El Paraíso.

It was a Saturday afternoon and I was sitting at a table with two expert reporters from Honduras. Both had experience covering organized crime. A little later, one of their trusted sources joined us, a prosecutor who had worked on several cases against families involved in organized crime, which, in Honduras, usually dedicates itself to the trafficking of drugs, people or wood.

To talk more intimately, we left the breezy terrace and, as one of them suggested, locked ourselves into one of their apartments to whisper away the rest of our conversation. "We talk on the streets and we're dead," one of the reporters told me.

The lawyer laid down his limits: "We can find you some contacts in Copán. I have someone I trust in Santa Rosa, but that's as far as my reach goes. From that point to the border with Guate is drug-lord territory. Everything's up for grabs over there."

That's the first time I heard talk of El Paraíso. And they made it seem like something far away, without name: a place, thanks to its palatial City Hall, of myths.

As one of the journalists put it: "There's a small town in the middle of that border zone that is really fucked. They say that they have a helicopter landing pad on the roof of the mayor's office and that the mayor boasts of never lacking anything, that they don't need to cooperate because they have more than enough money."

And, as the prosecutor put it: "The state hasn't even assigned prosecutors to that region, they have few policemen, but nobody to investigate crimes, no special units. The government has decided to hand the area over to the drug lords."

~

El Tigre isn't satisfied. It's past ten at night when we leave for El Paraíso. The twenty-five policemen that make up the showy caravan are tired. The impetus they showed at the beginning of their journey, when they energetically searched each vehicle that stumbled down these roads, has dissipated. They tremble with cold. Their uniforms are soaking. They miserably pile into the backs of the pickups. But El Tigre Bonilla wants more.

The police commissioner Juan Carlos Bonilla, El Tigre, is forty-five years old. He's spent twenty-five years serving as an officer and currently oversees three Honduran states on the border with Guatemala and El Salvador. He's in charge of Copán on the border with Izabal and Zacapa, two states under the control of the Mendoza and the Lorenzana families who, according to the Guatemalan police, are two of the most powerful families of the Guatemalan narco world. He also oversees Nueva Ocotepeque on the border of Chiquimula, Guatemala and Chalatenango, El Salvador. This Honduran state is known to be run by the Texis Cartel, a Salvadoran gang made up of mayors, politicians, policemen, gangsters and businessmen, and has been recognized as a gang by the United Nations. El Tigre is also chief of police in Lempira, on the border with Chalatenango and Cabañas in El Salvador. Because El Tigre rules over Copán, he essentially rules over the stretch of border known as the Corridor of Death, where cocaine is shipped from the Honduran state of Gracias a Dios (Thanks to God), on the border of Nicaragua, and is routed alongside the coast of four other Honduran states before reaching the border of Guatemala. Among those states is Atlántida, the most violent state in Central America.

Over six feet tall, El Tigre is a massive man with a face (as if sculpted out of rock) reminiscent of the Mexican Olmec heads. He's famous among his colleagues for being rough-and-tumble, a characterization he likes to cultivate.

"Everyone knows not to fuck with me," he often says.

In 2002, the Police Unit of Internal Affairs accused El Tigre of participating in a delinquent death squad in San Pedro Sula, one of the most violent cities of Central America, with a homicide rate of 119 for every 100,000 inhabitants. A witness even came forward in court, testifying that he had seen one such execution by the police-led death squad, known to bombastically call themselves "the Magnificents." El Tigre paid a bond of 100,000 lempiras (about $5,000), and in a series of events that many saw as rigged, with the lead prosecutor fired mid-trial, he was ultimately exonerated.

"Have you killed outside the rule of law?" I asked him as we left behind El Paraíso.

He answered evasively: "There are certain things you take to the grave. The only thing I can say is that I love my country and I'm ready to defend it by any means, and that I've done things to defend it. That's all I can say."

Investigator María Luisa Borja told the Honduran media that during his interrogation El Tigre had said something that struck her. "If they want to send me to court like a scapegoat then this police force is going to implode, because I can tell the Ministry of Security to its face that the only thing I did was follow its own orders." El Tigre had also said to Borja that the national deputy minister of security, Óscar Álvarez, would go down with him as the number one go-to in his office.

El Tigre is trying to prove me wrong. I told him that officials, mayors, reporters, human rights defenders, priests, men and women who wish to remain anonymous, all have told me that certain areas of the border of Copán, of his border, are completely controlled by narcotraffickers. By the lords, as they say. By the Lords of the Border.

One afternoon, El Tigre told me to choose where we would go that day, so that I could see with my own eyes that he can go wherever he pleases.

"El Paraíso," I said. "I want to go to El Paraíso."

"That's fine … I can go wherever … Look, girl," he says

to his secretary. "Leave those reports and round up a good entourage, call up the guards, but don't tell them where we're going, let it be a surprise."

El Tigre doesn't trust his police. He says there's only one person he trusts: himself.

The Honduran intelligence agent was the most nervous government agent I had spoken with from anywhere in Central America. One agent from Nicaragua even drank a few beers with me on the Caribbean beach. This Honduran, though, wouldn't even get out of his car. We did loops through Tegucigalpa for the whole hour we talked, loops whose only pattern was not going down the same street twice.

I wanted to know a little bit about Copán, find a way in, but throughout most of the ride he was the one asking the questions. When he finally answered some of mine, he talked of a region of ranches and cowboys.

"Santa Rosa de Copán is a retreat for those men, a place to get away. They go to make deals, get together, bring their families, relax. They have political meetings, make deals with the police, mayors, other officials."

The agent described the difference between Copán and other Honduran states, especially Olancho and Gracias a Dios, other entryways for cocaine coming from Colombia on its way to the United States. In those states the noise of gunfights is like background music. Yesterday there was a two-hour shootout in Catacamas, the second biggest city in Olancho. It was a fight between the local narcos and the family that runs the state capital in Juticalpa. In Copán, however, there is always intermittent peace. When a fight ends, one person gets to call himself king. For a while, the others let him reign. For a while.

"In Copán everybody knows who's in charge now. It's people connected with the Sinaloa Cartel, though it's not all theirs. They work as sort of freelancers for whoever pays, but right now they have a tight relationship with the Sinaloans.

We're on constant alert because we know that El Chapo Guzmán [once the head of the Sinaloa Cartel] comes to this area. And this year we've detected the presence of Los Zetas. Their interest in the region will change the whole landscape."

We kept driving in circles through Tegucigalpa. We'd pull into a residential zone and then, a few minutes later, turn out onto a main street just to turn back off again. He went on, describing Copán as the state with the most organized, most experienced narcos. He explained that the border was largely controlled by the Valle family, who are based in El Espíritu, a town with just about 4,000 inhabitants an hour away from the Guatemalan border. The border there is pure mountain: no customs officials or border gates.

The agent defended the theory that Guatemala is the center of US-bound cocaine trafficking, full of men trusted by both the Mexicans and Colombians. And yet the Honduran cartels in the western part of the country, like in Copán, have a lot of experience and wield important leverage. Mexican cartel emissaries often go to cities like Santa Rosa de Copán to negotiate without the intermediary Guatemalans.

"That's enough," the agent tells me. "Today was for us to get to know each other and I've already started talking." He had pulled the car over to the sidewalk in a remote neighborhood I hardly knew. Every time he stopped the car he'd put a hand over the holster of his Beretta. With a slight nod, he invited me to get out. I did, and he pulled away.

Here a man without a gun isn't considered a man. That's not an exaggeration; it's life in Copán. Since we began the tour at noon until we left El Paraíso, with El Tigre searching the drivers of every car we stopped (fourteen in total), only two of the men sported no gun. Only one of them, a poor farmer in an old beat-up car, didn't have a license for his revolver. El Tigre's men cuffed him and stuck him in the bed of the pickup truck that was driving behind us as security.

Pistols and rifles are common on these dirt roads, but you also find them further up the path, once the mud gives way to pavement. We turn down a paved road that leads back toward El Paraíso and the nearby town of La Entrada, about an hour from the Guatemalan border. You can't get to Paradise without walking through the Entrance, which leads to El Espíritu (the Spirit), which leads to the border where the lords move at will, expanding their control, pushing cocaine and stolen goods across the border. La Entrada marks the line between civilized Copán and pistol-wielding Copán.

El Tigre orders his men to search a chubby cowboy taking a leak, when the mayor of La Jigua rolls up in a pickup full of armed men. Suddenly, twenty policemen are all pointing their guns at the mayor. He guffaws loudly, insulting the policemen.

"Hey, what the fuck is going on here?" El Tigre intervenes.

Germán Guerra, the mayor of La Jigua, notices El Tigre for the first time and then turns over his guns, all three pistols. Two of them aren't licensed.

"Hi, Tiger. Nice to see you again. You can go ahead and take these little guns from me, but I need to hurry up and get to a wake," he pleads.

"Talk it over with Rivera Tomas," El Tigre responds with disdain. He approaches Rivera Tomas, takes his arm and says, "Book him. He's already starting to shake. Book the scaredy-pants. Just like you did with the little Indian with the revolver, take him away."

Rivera Tomas gives orders to handcuff the men, including the mayor, load them into the pickup and take them to the station at La Entrada. He seems nervous. It's clear that the mayor of La Jigua changed his attitude once he saw El Tigre. And it's also clear that he was used to ordering around his police like servants.

"See," El Tigre boasts. "They don't fuck around with me."

~

"If I thought using my name would change something, I'd tell you my name," the ex-mayor explained to me why he wanted to remain anonymous. "But it doesn't matter, because these lords who rule the border aren't alone. Behind them are the men in suits that govern the country."

We met for breakfast in a restaurant on the outskirts of Santa Rosa de Copán. Before agreeing to meet, the ex-mayor made me go through the typical security protocol: One of his confidants told him that he trusted me, that I wouldn't publish his name, wouldn't mention the name or location of our meeting place and wouldn't take any photos. After that, he agreed to meet.

"Look, you might think it's all lies, invention, exaggeration, but it's not. They do what they want because they have all the political support they need. Even El Chapo Guzmán has been around here; everybody knows it. He was on a ranch in El Espíritu, protected by the Valle family, the biggest money launderers in the region, with hotels in Santa Rosa, plus a ton of other businesses. He [El Chapo] even went to El Paraíso."

For the first time I asked direct questions about El Paraíso, about its wealth, its heliport and the new mayor who's known to run the place like a fiefdom.

"Look, all the mayors in the region know how the mayor of El Paraíso operates. He doesn't always offer you money directly, but when you have a festival in your town he gives you what you want: bullfights and famous Mexican *norteño* bands to draw big crowds and make you a lot of money. And then he asks you a favor. It's happened to most of us. And then you wonder, if my city is just as poor and rural as his, how does he pay for famous Mexican musicians who charge thousands of dollars for a show?"

What the ex-mayor told me over breakfast I had heard from another mayor who had also received offers and booty from the mayor of El Paraíso, Alexander Ardón. Ardón travels in an armored pickup truck with a convoy of two more trucks and twenty armed men whose job it is to guard him day and night.

The media's interest in El Paraíso spiked in 2008 when Honduras's ex-minister of security, Jorge Gamero, called the city "the black stain of Copán," a state already famous for being a hub of cocaine trafficking.

In an interview published in *La Prensa* newspaper in August 2008 (the only interview the mayor of El Paraíso, Ardón, would give) he boasted about having only gone to school through the fifth grade, having been raised poor and coming to have millions of lempiras in the bank. He explained that his city is rich, and that he was now a millionaire thanks to milk and cattle.

Ardón described himself as a humble man, and yet he also claimed to be "King of the Pueblo." He denied any connection to narcotrafficking, and yet accepted that along the border many ranchers, himself included, have benefited from some transborder cattle trafficking. That was the only interview he ever gave.

The bishop of Copán, Luis Santos, however, has been more open to the press. His interviews have been rife with phrases that could stand as banner headlines if they weren't just typical descriptions of his state: "All we have left in El Paraíso is the church; the rest has been bought up by the narcos." "In El Paraíso young women won't date a boy unless he has a brand-new pickup truck, like the narcos have." This is his description of an isolated town in an isolated tract of the Honduran-Guatemalan border, a town only accessible by mud roads.

"There are things we all know," the ex-mayor told me over breakfast. "Like in the 2009 elections in El Paraíso the ballot boxes closed at eleven in the morning and were guarded by armed men who'd been paid 3,000 lempiras by the Liberal Party. At eleven at night, they took away the ballot boxes and filled the ballots up on their own."

Two other sources confirmed the story of the 2009 elections. One of them was a member of the National Party, the same party Ardón belongs to. The statistics themselves also pointed to irregularities. Of a population of 12,536, there were 9,583 votes counted, by far the highest voting turnout in all of Copán. Of the 9,583 votes, only 670 were for the Liberal Party. All the 8,151 other votes were for the National Party. The difference was so great that the National Party was only 1,000 votes shy of gaining another state deputy. In the other twenty-two municipalities of Copán, no party won by more than 600 votes, while in El Paraíso, Ardón's party won by 7,481 votes.

If anyone comes to Copán asking about narcos, the names of El Paraíso and its mayor inevitably come up. This was the case with Steven Dudley, a researcher from the Woodrow Wilson Center and the University of San Diego, who came to Copán in 2010 and found, from studying police intelligence reports, that Ardón was working directly with the Sinaloa Cartel. The reports detailed parties with guests that included Central American and Mexican drug lords. In February 2010, the acting minister of security, Óscar Álvarez, said in an interview with the Mexican Radio Fórmula that El Chapo was known to vacation in El Paraíso. He also mentioned that the internationally popular band Los Tigres del Norte came to play at parties organized by Ardón. And yet, despite all the folklore about the town, few people point out what my informant, the ex-mayor, told me over breakfast.

He summed up the situation: "With all of his notoriety, Ardón is a mayor of a lost little town, and yet he's capable of bringing people together, including some of the most important businessmen in the country, like he did for the inauguration of his City Hall with the heliport on the roof. That's why he didn't let anybody take photographs at the event. But how did we get here? The most efficient way to safeguard yourself as a border lord is to finance political campaigns, whether municipal or national. That way, any future problem you have you can fix it with a quick call to a political friend."

According to the mayors and ex-mayors I spoke with, that luxurious city hall inauguration in El Paraíso was a red-carpet event full of politicians, businessmen and nationally known figures.

El Tigre second-guesses the orders he gave to Rivera Tomas. He's stressing. Paperwork isn't his strong suit. Instead of following up with the consequences of his arrest order, he leaves the office and drives full speed to find a stolen truck and tractor. A semitrailer had been stolen earlier in the day and then found pulled over on the road to La Entrada. When we arrive, however, the tractor that had been hooked to the truck's trailer bed had disappeared again, which meant that it had been stolen sometime between five in the morning—when El Tigre got a call alerting him that the stolen truck had been found— and eleven o'clock at night when we finally arrive at the scene.

"They're not simple highway robbers," El Tigre explains to me. "This is the border. These guys are criminal lords."

El Tigre orders the two policemen standing outside, pointing their M16s toward the dark hills, to get a move on. "Alright, it's good, let's roll! That tractor is probably already crossing into El Salvador somewhere around Ocotepeque."

A half hour later we're back at the station so El Tigre can check on the mayor of La Jigua. He rushes to sign the arrest papers. In the office are ten more men who act as El Tigre's bodyguards. They pat me down when I walk in, film me with their cell phone cameras and speak loudly into their phones: "We're taking [the mayor] away. These idiots don't know who they're messing with. We're going to call the boss. We're taking him away now."

But then El Tigre changes his mind. Rivera Tomas stands in the corner, blushing, begging him to be careful, to let the mayor of La Jigua go back home for the night. But before a decision is made, we're out the door again. I follow El Tigre into his pickup. It's just the two of us in the cabin. In the bed are three of his guards. We drive in silence for a while, and then he gets a call.

"What the?" El Tigre shouts into his phone. "He called Barralaga? I don't give a fuck! Keep him in there!"

Jorge Barralaga is the police chief of the state of Copán. El Tigre is his regional chief, and they don't get along at all. El Tigre wanted Barralaga investigated for having loaned out sixty cops as security for the inauguration of the luxurious City Hall of El Paraíso. "Where do you get off leaving an entire state unprotected just to take care of a single crazy mayor?" El Tigre asks. And yet it wasn't just sixty policemen. According to an internal police report I saw in Tegucigalpa, there were twenty other police dispatched, on top of the sixty mentioned by El Tigre, and even some soldiers: an entire army guarding an event at a city of some 18,000 people. Meanwhile, in other parts of the state, the only security for some cities is a single traffic cop. The eighty police guards were lined up after the event and each given 1,000 lempiras (about $50) in thanks. That's nearly $5,000 in total. In his letter of protest, El Tigre complained that the payments represented "a violation and a smearing of the image" of the mayor's office as it showed that "our police are in the service of individuals who dedicate themselves to el narco." El Tigre's letter only drew attention to the bad relationships he has with border-town mayors.

We ride down the highway in silence for about five minutes, and then another call comes in.

"Yeah, what is it? What the? He called the minister of security asking why a mayor had been detained? Well, as long as he doesn't tell us to let him go, keep him locked up."

He hangs up.

"These damn people," he tells me. "They never stop trying to pull their strings."

We continue on in silence for another three minutes. And then another call comes in.

"Yeah, yeah. What? ... Yeah, I arrested him. Publish it ... Yeah, so it's not information you want? You want me to release the mayor?"

He covers his phone and whispers to me that it's a big-time local journalist. Then he puts the phone on speaker.

A woman's voice sounds out: "Look, the Deputy Marcio Vega Pinto [a state legislator] called me and told me to do something. He knows I know you."

"But you know that I can't help you here," El Tigre responds.

"All the other mayors will get you back. They're all friends."

"Yeah, I already know the brutes will never forget me."

"Just be careful. They're saying that this guy partners with Los Valles, from El Espíritu."

"And what, bullets don't hit the Valle people?"

He turns off the speaker and says good-bye to the journalist. "My phone's not going to stop ringing," El Tigre tells me. "Not until I let the mayor go."

The domain of these border lords isn't restricted by muddy roads. When they pick up the phone, people listen, even if they're far from the border. We ride in silence. El Tigre is starting to look uncomfortable.

"Yeah fine," he says, half talking to himself. "If you're asking me whether the lords control the border and know every time I step foot into El Paraíso or El Espíritu, fine, I tell you the answer is yes. And I ask myself how they know, and I have to answer that my people have been infiltrated."

We ride in an uncomfortable silence with El Tigre continually turning to me, as if waiting for me to speak.

"He's worried," I tell him, meaning the mayor.

"Yeah, but it's fine. If you ask me if the drug lords freely traffic along this border, I'll tell you that it's true, because I've never decommissioned even a speck of cocaine here."

According to the minister of security an annual average of

300 tons of cocaine cross the borders of Honduras. Copán is considered the principal drug trafficking route leading to Guatemala.

I ask, "You haven't decommissioned any coke in all three border states all year?"

"Not a speck. And I ask myself why. Because nobody gets me by the balls! Am I right or am I right?"

"It's true," I admit. "The mayor didn't get the best of you. But what did that get you?"

We ride in silence until Santa Rosa de Copán.

3

Guatemala Is Spelled with a Z

June 2011

There was a time when Guatemalan drug traffickers lived under a pact of mutual respect. A time when you could still count on one hand the number of black sheep who would break that pact. One of these black sheep proposed that a drug family contract a hit man from a Mexican cartel expanding control throughout the country.

Intelligence officers, soldiers, workers inside the world of narcotrafficking, as well as a controversial declaration of a state of emergency, all point to the single factor that shattered criminal stability in Guatemala: Los Zetas.

The last time he cooked was three years ago. It was six years into his sentence when a group of cons came to his cell looking for the foreigner who knew about chemicals.

"What do you want?" he asked them.

On his cot they unpacked a plastic wrap of cocaine paste and asked him what else he would need to cook. Bicarbonate, he told them. By the next day they'd gotten it for him, and the men were able to smoke their crack. That was the last time the Colombian cooked. Before, in an earlier life, he would cook every day. It was how he made his living.

The Colombian didn't seem to mind the asphyxiating prison heat. He was used to it. When he first came to Guatemala in 1997, he settled in Mazatenango, the capital of Suchitepéquez state. Two hundred kilometers from the border with El Salvador and 150 kilometers from the Mexican border, Mazatenango suffers from an oceanfront heat that boils over onto the isolated strip of coastline. Devoid of important ports or touristy hotels, the state is peppered with unincorporated fishing villages like El Chupadero or Bisabaj.

Some of the inmates I saw as I walked through the prison the day I talked with the Colombian were playing soccer, chatting in the corners, eating in the dining halls or being transferred between buildings in handcuffs. In this prison inmates are divided between common or civilian inmates—also known as *paisas*, or country folk—and gang members, almost all of whom belong to either the Mara Salvatrucha or Barrio 18, two of the biggest gangs in the Americas.

The loud thirty-five-year-old man known as the Colombian and I snuck away to a solitary commissary stall so we could talk without having to whisper. The Colombian was cleanly shaven and was wearing a pair of new white Nikes. He was a firsthand witness to the decade-long evolving relationship between the various drug traffickers in Guatemala. He knew that the good days had passed, that outside there was a new law, and that this new law had been laid out by some men from Mexico. He also knew that he didn't want anything to do with it.

Until he was imprisoned, the Colombian was what is known in the drug world as a free agent. He didn't work exclusively for one cartel: He was never the chemist for the Cali or the Norte del Valle cartels in Colombia; he didn't come to Guatemala contracted by a Chiapan drug family, nor was he contracted by any other Mexican group. He simply stumbled into Guatemala while on route to the United States. He was a free agent, a man who, like his father, knew how to mix acetone, bicarbonate, amphetamines and ammonium.

He was arrested, along with his father and a Guatemalan soldier who was helping them, in a house in Mazatenango. He's convinced it was a setup. The door was knocked down at the exact moment the Colombian put his hands into twenty-two kilos of coke.

"It's like this, see," he told me. "This was the game. If they had money, I put together a kilo in twenty minutes, started the mixing and was all ready to cook."

The Colombian mostly worked with clients who were desperate because a batch of theirs had gone bad, a package had gotten wet during transport or, simply, because they had all the necessary ingredients but lacked the knowledge to turn them into white powder.

When he first arrived in Guatemala, the Colombian would work with anybody who made an offer. He soon got in with traditional drug families, the Mendozas and the Lorenzanas, who had contacts throughout Central America. But he also worked with lesser-known groups on the western border, in the volatile city of Tecún Umán just across the river from Mexico, groups whose bread and butter were migrants and contraband. He worked with whoever paid. Though it may seem odd in a world of narcos, working with competing families never incited suspicion among his clients.

"It's like this. Here there was no cartel that ruled everybody or messed with any other cartel. They didn't kill you for working with somebody else. You delivered your goods, and that was enough. You go where you need to go and do what you need to do, because I'm paid up and I'm happy."

Those were, according to the Colombian, happy times. Guatemala was a good place to be a free agent. But ten years have passed since then, and a lot has changed on the outside.

"When you get out," I asked him, "would you start working again?"

"I don't think so, my friend. It's a mess out there. Everything changed with Los Zetas. Those brutes don't understand pacts. They don't negotiate. They get into every kind of crime, and so they squeeze you, and they heat you up."

"How do you know that?"

"Look, friend. Look where I am. All sorts of people come in here. Here you get to know what's going on better than if you're on the outside."

If you believe the tidy formula that, in terms of drug trafficking, Mexico is the backyard of the United States, then you should be able to extrapolate and say that Central America is the backyard of Mexico, albeit a neglected and overgrown backyard, connected to Mexico by a single gate: the Guatemalan border.

But with a coastline on the Atlantic and the Pacific and close to 600 miles of shared border with Mexico, it's actually more of a gaping cavity than a backyard gate. Drug traffickers have known about this for decades. In contrast to El Salvador, where the past decade has seen a renaissance of narcotrafficking, in Guatemala old families have been working the trade since the '70s, when war drums were beating all across Central America.

In order to understand the effect Los Zetas have had on Guatemala, it's important to journey back to the '70s, and Edgar Gutiérrez, an economist and mathematician, is the perfect guide. Fifty years old, Gutiérrez has founded various organizations dedicated to easing the return of Guatemalan refugees, as well as fighting impunity and preserving historical memory. He's also worked for the government: From 2000 to 2002 he was secretary of strategic analysis—that's to say he was the chief of Guatemalan intelligence services—and from 2002 to 2004 he was the minister of foreign relations. Currently, he works as a security analyst for governments and organizations throughout Latin American and Europe.

Easy to talk to and organized in his thinking, Gutiérrez lays out the evolution of drug-trafficking in Guatemala, explaining how it became one of the pillars of the country's power structure. His chronology checks out, verified by ground soldiers up to military intelligence officers.

"Drug trafficking was never what it is today, in terms of the volume of cocaine passing through and the size of the overall market. I'm talking about the '60s to the mid-'70s. Around that time, Cubans were migrating en masse to Miami, and then from Miami to Guatemala, attracted by tax policies. Those Cubans served as a bridge to the Colombians and hid their drug operations within other businesses, mostly shrimp exportation. They would export shrimp to Miami with drugs hidden inside the containers. But something happened in the '70s and those same people abandoned trafficking for legal businesses."

Finding evidence from this period of drug trafficking can be complicated. Gutiérrez is basing his claims on people he knows who were directly involved.

The second period of trafficking in Guatemala, however, attracted lots of international attention and is rife with documents from US intelligence agencies.

"You remember the Iran-Contra scandal, which ended with the prohibition of US funding to the Contras. In that period, the early '80s, the United States was making its first efforts to put a stop to the Colombian narcos, and the CIA decided that the cocaine and heroine passing through Central America would be trafficked by various military forces instead. They involved the Salvadorans, Guatemalans and Hondurans, who used their illicit earnings to finance the Contras. There are testimonies from the US Senate and Congress where Argentine financial advisors, working alongside the CIA, lay it out in numbers: as much as $2 million a week.

"Between 1985 and 1986 the Iran-Contra affair hit the headlines, with the discovery that the United States had illegally sold more than $40 million worth of arms to Iran during its war against Iraq. But the story didn't end there: President Reagan admitted in a press conference that around $12 million in arms-sales profit went to the Contras. After the scandal broke, the money stopped flowing. That's when the second phase began, one that has never been completely understood, even with the passing of time. In 1996, the *San Jose Mercury News* published a report that tied cocaine and crack trafficking in LA in the late '80s to the financing of the Contras, all with the CIA's approval. The scandal reached the US Senate, which opened an investigation. According to the report, Central American military acted as traffickers for the drugs passing north. But it went beyond the military: A few heads of the largest trafficking families smelled profit and walked right through the door that had been opened by the CIA.

"The United States' permissive attitude led to the arrival of the Colombians in Central America in the '90s, landing mostly in Guatemala. The first real godfathers in the country were the Colombians who brought over their entire administrative and financial teams. When they found a slice of the market and found they needed to make connections with Mexico to ship north, they contacted the Guatemalan officials, the Army. They hired ex-customs officials, military officers and Army specialists."

"Why them?"

"Because they're the ones on the ground and they know the border. They might have already left their active employment with the state, but they still had their contacts. The bosses would use their drug profits to buy more land, open lines of transport, gas stations and businesses to wash money, but they were also establishing themselves [legally]. That's when the Mendoza family came, whose market is in Izabal. And then the Lorenzana family in Zacapa. Waldemar Lorenzana was first a customs official and then a cattle rustler. Very successful in his business."

These are the times that the Colombian was harking back to, when there was relative peace in Narcolandia, when Guatemala became the gaping cavity of Central America. What came next were a few unwanted guests.

~

A small and angry indigenous Q'eqchi' man asks me what sounds like a threatening question: "Would you let your kids play in a park where there are a bunch of drunks sitting around with rifles?"

He stares at me, eagerly awaiting my response.

"No," I say.

He looks happy, almost relieved, nodding his head and repeating, "That's the difference. That's the difference."

The man is an informant for the Guatemalan Army. I met up with him after a contact introduced us in Cobán, the chilly capital of the northern state of Alta Verapaz. Thanks to his testimony, the state discovered a safe house used by Los Zetas to store weapons. He was one of the many people who, despite the fear, offered intel to soldiers who arrived with the state of emergency in Cobán. Getting angry at the new cartel members, however, didn't seem to be a productive outlet for his fear. As courageous as he was, he set up our meeting on a busy corner of the market outside of a bus terminal. The crowd, he was hoping, would act as our shield.

He is about to ask another rhetorical question. I can see it coming. He explained that it's not drug trafficking that so infuriates him, but how trafficking affects people's lives. He used to take his kids out to the San Marcos park, close to the center of town, but toward the end of last year until the day the military arrived, those men would sit there, keeping guard, their guns flashing in the open, drinking beer and catcalling the women. The men were Los Zetas.

His question finally comes: "Who would you rather help: those who do their work but don't bother you, or those who put your life in danger?"

It's obvious he's already asked himself this same question. Before Los Zetas had taken over the park, a few employees for the Overdick family, the local narcos who used to be in charge, worked in the park as lookouts. The man tells me that they would say hello to you. And if they were packing, a pistol perhaps, they kept it tucked away, and instead of getting drunk they just permanently milled outside of the church entrance. One time, the man tells me, he even let the lookouts know when he saw a military checkpoint while on a bus returning from the capital. The only communication he has with the drunks with the rifles is when he grimaces at them.

On December 19, 2010, Guatemalan President Álvaro Colom declared a state of emergency in Alta Verapaz. A state of emergency, as established in the Law of Public Order, is one step shy of declaring war: limiting the open transit of citizens and permitting warrantless searches. According to a number of my sources, including an ex-minister of defense, an ex-head of military intelligence, a colonel, a general and an ex-chancellor, most people seem to think the state of emergency was a publicity ploy that had little actual effect in the streets. In Cobán, instead of a state of emergency, a state of prevention was declared, which resulted in more police, more soldiers and more prosecutors, as well as a network of open checkpoints, all leading to more cases and decommissions for the justice system to handle. And yet, as all my sources say, the Army never had control of the streets of Cobán; it was always the Public Ministry (a municipal office). Two of my sources referred to the use of the military as "a show."

By the end of 2008 Los Zetas chose Alta Verapaz as their base of operations in Guatemala and, according to some, for their Central American headquarters. It seemed an obvious choice. Alta Verapaz is the bottleneck on the way to Petén, a Guatemalan state twice the size of El Salvador, which is the state that shares the most border with Mexico. Alta Verapaz has also traditionally been the main trafficking hub for both weapons and drugs. It's almost impossible to reach Petén without passing through Alta Verapaz, which is also only a three-hour drive from Guatemala City.

When the situation got bad enough, soldiers from the Army, agents of the Public Ministry, and police officers were all eventually replaced in Cobán. News from the foggy city had started sounding like it was coming from some narco-controlled town on the US-Mexican border: gangsters raping indigenous women in once-peaceful streets, capos placing perimeter security around a McDonald's so they could eat a combo meal, and drunk men in the park joking around and openly carrying AK-47s.

"No! Don Overdick didn't work like that," the Q'eqchi' man tells me. "I don't know what they were involved in, but they were respectful toward the people who lived here. They even helped us."

That is the response the indigenous man gives me when I ask my own rhetorical question: "Are Los Zetas the same as the Overdick family?"

And yet, I think, certainly some blame should be attributed to whoever let the fox into the henhouse: the Overdick soldier who first hired Los Zetas to execute a hit.

"Of course. They were trying to fool themselves, but now they have no choice but to confront the situation head on."

I'm speaking with a military official who was in Cobán in December when they instituted the dubious state of emergency. He sketches out a scene of the family patriarchs watching passively as their own guests ransacked their homes. Juan Ortiz Chamalé on the Mexican border with contraband and immigrants; Waldemar Lorenzana on the border between El Salvador and Honduras; Walter Overdick in Alta Verapaz; and the Mendozas in Petén, the uncut jungle border of Mexico. All of them wanted by the United States. All of them left stunned by their terrible guests.

We're sitting in the restaurant of the tiny hotel I've been staying at in Guatemala City. I have two objectives with this chatty and blunt military official: to find out whether the military intelligence assumes as fact that Los Zetas used the murder of narco Juancho León as their ticket into the country;

and to get a sense of just how much an operation like the one in Alta Verapaz is for show.

On the first point, our conversation is brief. The answer is an unequivocal yes.

In March 2008, a half-hour-long violent clash between two groups of at least fifteen men resulted in a sheet of bodies laid over the hotel and waterpark, La Laguna, in the state of Zacapa, bordering Honduras. One of those bodies belonged to Juan José "Juancho" León, an infamous forty-two-year-old Guatemalan narcotrafficker who was the leader of the León family and ran their operations out of Izabal, a state wedged between Petén, Belize, the Caribbean Sea, Honduras and Zacapa. The murder of Juancho León is often referred to as the breaking point in the pact of coexistence among the various Guatemalan "families."

Edgar Gutiérrez, former chief of intelligence, told me that Juancho León, who was once a deputy and son-in-law of the leader of the Lorenzana family, began to amass too much power, diversify his businesses and, what was worse, become known as a loudmouth.

"He was a threat because he was bragger," Gutiérrez told me during one of our first interviews. "I got this president [of the country] elected, I got that other one elected ... And the other groups started to say, 'This guy's a monopolizer. He's breaking our equilibrium, he's picking up contacts north and south.'"

When I share this theory with the military intelligence official, he nods, smiling, and raises a finger toward the skyline of the pleasant courtyard in the colonial hotel of downtown Guatemala City. "That's true," he says, "but one thing is missing from that equation: Juancho was the guy that made petty thieving fashionable. A great part of his economic power came from all the drugs he stole."

The famous purse snatchings, drug robberies among narcotraffickers. It goes to show that the pact between the families was only glued together with spit—even before Los Zetas came around.

Juancho León, like other narcotraffickers and even police chiefs, was involved in complicated intelligence operations to find out where, when and how many drugs were going to be transported by, say, the Lorenzana family. The shipments would come through some isolated and well-hidden spot lost on the Honduran border, and León's men would wait for it a little further along, near Alta Verapaz, to steal the drugs and sell them to another family who would later traffic them through another point along the border. It would be naïve to think that the victims of robbery had no idea who had stolen their cargo.

According to the military official, now sipping a cappuccino in the hotel patio, the straw that broke the camel's back was one such purse snatching that Juancho León orchestrated against the Lorenzana family in early 2008. The shipment in question was a cargo of cocaine destined for the Sinaloa Cartel, at the time the most powerful cartel on the continent. That, alongside his well-known loud-mouthing and his increased control of turf, led to a new pact between the Mendozas and the Lorenzanas: the promise to kill Juancho León, though the man had an army at his beck and call, had always been heavily guarded and, as of 2003 after the murder of his brother, Mario León, had amped up his personal security even further. And so, for help, the two families turned to the experts who had already been invited to Guatemala several times before: called to protect particularly special cargo, or to train hit men, or to recruit Kaibiles, the Guatemalan foot soldiers trained in the thick of jungle with the mantra "move, kill and destroy." It was exactly then that the two largest families opened their doors for the last and final time to the terrible Mexican guest.

That very month, March 2008, Los Zetas called Juancho León for a meeting at the Hotel La Laguna with the pretext of negotiating a cocaine shipment that was to cross into his territory. They attacked him with AK-47s and a Russian-made RPG-7 rocket grenade launcher. Three people were detained after the battle, all of them Mexicans from the northern state of Tamaulipas, the headquarters of Los Zetas.

The families achieved their goal, but it seems they had failed to appreciate the murderous muscle of Los Zetas. They hadn't reflected on the fact that the group, led by elite ex-military officials, had recently split from their parent, the Gulf Cartel, and were newly orphaned and, to make up for their lack of contacts in South America, were in search of new territory. The families didn't look beyond their guests' capacity to kill and intimidate, a mistake the families still haven't lived down.

Guatemala imposed a state of emergency in Cobán as an attempt to impose rules on the troublesome guest. They put up a sign, reminding the guest that he was in someone else's house. They wagged their fingers. Nothing more. Los Zetas guessed that the state's show of anger would soon dissipate, and so they decided to ignore it.

She jokes that her husband may have lied about going to load drug vans for Los Zetas, and instead went to meet another woman in Cobán. We're in El Gallito, a neighborhood in Guatemala City known for being the hub of narco operations. Most of the smaller streets here are blocked off by metal highway dividers, used to restrict access, especially to cops, and funnel any visitors onto specific streets. The woman has agreed to meet me at the house of my contact. We share a beer as we wait for her husband, who left for Cobán a week ago and still hasn't turned up. She grumbles discontentedly. Finally, late into the night, her husband comes home. He's short, dark skinned, with straight hair and a mustache—a prototypical-looking Guatemalan man, except that tonight he looks like a rag doll, so exhausted that his wife masks her anger and greets him with a halfhearted reproach.

"Just look at how those savages left you!"

He takes a sip of beer and responds dryly, "Yeah, I thought it time to come back. Those loads were fucking hell. We filled trucks and trucks, from six in the morning until midnight, and we were never done. I told them, 'You better pay me now because I'm done.'"

"What were you carrying?" I ask.

"Bags and boxes … of stuff."

I let them talk, knowing that more is revealed among neighbors and family. That's when I pick up on the details. He left a week ago, a week after the state of emergency was instated. An old man known to be a Zeta offered fifteen laborers the job to fill and empty trucks in the suburbs of Cobán. They were the worker bees of Los Zetas, in charge of getting most of the merchandise out of the "danger zone." This bone-tired man was one of the fifteen.

Two days have passed since my conversation with the stevedore in El Gallito, and now I'm in Cobán in the Sixth Infantry Brigade that houses the 300 military officials ordered to deal with the state of emergency. I'm greeted by the second in command, Colonel Díaz Santos. Outside, a platoon of his men file out for the first patrol-round of the afternoon. This has been going on for a month and a half, and now they only get drunk drivers or, at most, some petty thief armed with a knife.

"Since we came in," the colonel says, "they got the message. [Los Zetas] became more respectful. They're no longer running around the street like mad men with rifles."

They got the message and decided to avoid confrontation. Better to bring in the load carriers than bring out the hit men. It's a strange thing that Los Zetas decided to put on the brakes this time, something they hardly do, even in Mexico.

I tell the colonel that I've heard that Los Zetas recently shipped so much merchandise out of Cobán that they had to work in twenty-four-hour shifts. I'm expecting he'll contradict me, but instead he adds to my story.

"Sure. If they were warned about our raids, and they still had a large part of their cargo in the area ... We were only able to get what was left behind."

Every day, a certain version of events gains more credibility: Two informants living in Cobán told me that on Saturday, December 18, the day before the state of emergency was instated, some Zetas members played a game of soccer with a group of police, prosecutors and local government clerks. When they finished their game, they butchered a cow and roasted it and then, as the narcotraffickers had loads to carry before daybreak, they called it a night.

A few days earlier, in Guatemala City, I met with General Vásquez Sánchez, who oversees Colonel Díaz Santos. He spoke to me of the Army's achievements in Cobán. They had seized forty-five vehicles, most of them luxury SUVs; thirty-nine assault rifles; twenty-three MG 34, 7.62-caliber machine guns ("The same model our soldiers use in the area," the general added); and thirty-five guns, including a Five-seven, known in Mexico as the "kill-a-cop" for its ability to pierce through bulletproof vests.

Both the general and the colonel noted that they had informants to thank for their success. The military, far from boasting of a complicated intelligence operation, attribute their relative success to sheer hate: the people's hate of Los Zetas. Everyday citizens pointed out their hidden workshops and safe houses: That's where they outfit their cars to hide the cargo. Everyday citizens showed them their ranches: They hide their weapons over there, in Otoniel Turcios's ranch. Everyday citizens revealed their infrastructure: Just go right over there, a little over a mile from downtown Cobán, and you'll see the runway, you'll see the pilots who, like black-market taxi drivers, fly without permits, taking cargo for who-knows-who to who-knows-where.

Alta Verapaz had been so abandoned that even the state-owned runway was left to Los Zetas. There was no air traffic controller, no scheduled flights and no record of who would pilot which plane at what time. Sometimes Los Zetas even used the runway for their monster car shows, their horse races and parties. For all practical purposes, the runway was theirs to use as they pleased.

"It's strange," the general said, "that no one has come to reclaim the five unregistered planes we seized. Would you forget about your plane just like that?"

The general seemed to think that Los Zetas had learned their lesson, that they understood the reprimand and wouldn't fight to regain what had been seized. We'll have to see just how long the slap on the wrist will curb their bad behavior.

"Unlike the good narcos," the general told me, "who keep their turf in peace and make gentlemen agreements with the other families, these guys have a history of going around raping and shooting."

Los Zetas have never fought under the flag of subtlety. What's surprising in the case of Cobán is their decision not to counterattack. Other than that, they have been following the usual handbook and behaving as they do on their home turf, in Mexico. To every question I asked, the general responded with a yes, even adding a detail or two. Did they buy out children and women, taxi drivers and street vendors to be their lookouts? And the general responded that yes, only here they call them flaggers. Do they have businesses other than drug trafficking? And the general nodded and listed kidnappings, money laundering, coffee and cardamom plantations, extortions. Do they work with police, mayors and prosecutors? And the general admitted the facts: Due to a sweeping lack of trust, the government had to relocate 350 state policemen. The general added another affirmative when I ask him if they took over the local gangs, only he went even further: "Los Zetas have come to undermine the local gangs. They've started using a nickname for the local narcos: *narquitos*. They want them to stop operating independently. They took control of, if not all of Guatemala, then a large part of it. And the traditional local narcos have diminished their control. They're operating in the shadow of Los Zetas, and those who haven't joined them are subject to death threats."

They're following their handbook. I think of something the police officer I spoke with in Guatemala City said to me a few days ago, and I think of what many people told me in Mexico when I was reporting on Los Zetas over the course of a year. The police officer followed strict protocol when talking about Los Zetas: Before speaking he took me to a corner of the building, looked behind him and in every direction, and then, still worried that someone might overhear, spoke to me in a whisper. He told me that as soon as you reach the outer limits of Cobán, Los Zetas stop soldiers, give them $500 and say they'll call if they ever need anything. Then they'll take out a cell phone and ask them to comb their hair nicely so that they can take their picture.

The colonel stops me before I leave his office. He knows that everything we've spoken about, and everything I've spoken about with the general, would lead me to think that even after the state of emergency, the fact is that the military will soon leave and Los Zetas will return (all their lessons learned) to take over the old Guatemalan families, the "good narcos."

"I know they're waiting for us to leave, but we're here to stay," the colonel says in parting.

On March 1, I find myself at a dinner surrounded by police chiefs, military men and security gurus. We're making predictions about the future of Guatemala, about how Los Zetas are going to react. Amid the crowd I pick out one of my informants from Cobán. I say hello and then gesture that we skip out of the hotel restaurant. He tells me to wait a second and to meet him in the patio.

A few minutes later he greets me with a question: "So, did you publish the article?"

"Not yet. I'm about to finish it."

"You saw that the state of emergency is over?"

"Yeah, on Friday, February 18. What's happened since?"

"Well, Los Zetas are back. They're back in the streets, armed, but a little more cautious. They stick out with their huge trucks."

At daybreak on February 25, one week after President Álvaro Colom traveled to Cobán to pronounce an end to the state of emergency, an armed convoy drove into a used car lot, lit three cars on fire and then shot up a number of other cars with his AK-47. My informant told me that it was Los Zetas, who, little by little, were starting to claim their vengeance. This time it was cars, but soon it will be people. Now that the state of emergency is over, now that Cobán has returned to normal, my informant asks his own rhetorical question.

"What's next?"

4

A Nobody in the Land of Narcos

November 2011

Petén—the vast, mostly jungle state in Guatemala—is a gaping aperture where drugs passing through Central America cross the border into Mexico. All the major organized crime families have a presence in Petén. The state is also a stark example of how everything relating to organized crime is a tangle in which the word "narco" is often tied up with the word "politician." The government here has decided not to get in the ring with the biggest players; instead, they hunt the weakest prey in the jungle.

"So this is where all you narcotraffickers live?"

"Yep, right here," Venustiano says. "Follow me. I'll introduce you to everyone."

He opens the gate and out peek two men, one tiny and wrinkled, the other leathery and gray. The latter is bathing himself with a bucket of water in the middle of the patio. The wrinkled man yells in the indigenous language of Q'eqchi'. A few older women, as well as about twenty children, appear from several shacks.

This is Petén, the northern state of Guatemala, on the outskirts of a town called La Libertad, or Freedom. In order to get here we've left behind the ruckus of the market, we've retreated from all the tuk-tuks (motorized bicycle-taxis with tarpaulin roofs) and we've wound our way down a dusty, cracked path. The hamlet is the size of half of a soccer field and consists of seven scattered shacks, all made of plastic, cardboard and sticks. In the middle of the hamlet is an oily puddle littered with bobbing food scraps. It smells like a dead animal. In one of the shacks, women are cooking lunch over an enormous *comal*. The meal: tortillas with tortillas.

Everyone gathers around Venustiano. They're all dirty. The children are rail thin, with round, protruding bellies. They don't say anything to me because very few of them speak Spanish. They just look at me and wait.

I say: "You guys are the narcotraffickers from Centro Uno?"

"Yep. That's us," says Venustiano, stepping forward as the leader of these moribund people. "What do you think?"

"I don't know what to tell you, Venustiano."

The Mexican authorities call the northern state of Sonora the Golden Gate to the United States. That's where the old smuggling routes are, and that's where people who are "in the business" live and prosper. Under that same logic, Petén could be called the Central American Golden Gate to Mexico.

Petén is the biggest state in Guatemala. It spans more than 20,000 square miles and shares close to 400 miles of jungle and river with Mexico. The Guatemalan military is well aware that this is the country's most problematic stretch of border. The formula they use is this: the closer to the Pacific Ocean, the more migrants, criminal organizations, human trafficking, prostitution, machetes, guns and contraband of all kinds. Then, heading inland, the more transnational cartels, assault weapons and political ties.

Petén and Sonora are not only similar in that they serve as the headquarters for the big leagues of organized crime; they also share similar demographic characteristics. Much of the land in both states is only accessible by air or off-road vehicles and is thus largely uninhabited. While Guatemala has an average of 337 inhabitants per square mile, that number in Petén barely reaches forty.

Here, land is measured by a unit called *caballería,* which is equivalent to about 110 acres.

The region south of Petén is increasingly privatized, with multinational corporations buying caballería upon caballería to grow African palm. The small species of palm is used to extract vegetable oil, a commodity hardly touched in Central America, though in the rest of the world it is one of the most widely used cooking oils. Right in the middle of the state is a long urban stretch that runs north to south, petering out at its tips into a green and indomitable jungle forest only inhabited by the rare family, many of whom are accused of being involved in organized crime. Even Álvaro Colom, the president of Guatemala, has wagged his finger at them. In the northern ridge of Guatemala is a strip of land narrower than the farms of African palm but wider than the urban belt that is blanketed by forest reserves where no one can cut down a tree without a permit. Or so the law says. Petén remains unpopulated because most of it is either privately owned or reserved for agriculture and construction.

This well-preserved, privatized look of Petén has to do, according to a widely publicized report (more on the report soon), not only with the protected forest, but also with the many caballerías amassed by the big African palm companies and criminal organizations.

The complex dynamic between state nature reserve and privately owned corporate farm has tacked the label of "narco" on Venustiano and his people. Meanwhile, they live in a circle of shacks huddled around a puddle that smells like dead animals.

Those familiar with the inner workings of this jungle know that there are eyes and ears everywhere. Before setting foot in Petén, I spent a week securing trustworthy sources willing to put me up for a night. In Guatemala City I spoke with five people who had lived or were currently living in Petén.

I even got a number for a religious group who told me that under no circumstances could I ever come visit them in Petén, though one of their members did agree to speak with me anonymously.

We're set to meet in Santa Elena, the biggest city in the urban belt of Petén, in an office where a powerful standing fan saves us from the heavy heat and whining mosquitoes. I find myself talking to a respected activist who works with dozens of community organizations.

These days, the national media always finds one reason or another to showcase Petén in their front-page headlines. In the Sierra del Lacandón National Park, on the border with Mexico, the eviction of an entire community of peasants gained national media attention. The minister of interior, Carlos Menocal, accused the peasants of drug trafficking, and TV media seemed to be celebrating the displacement of 300 families who were supposedly working for infamous narcos.

"They've kicked out the narcos again!" says the activist, and bursts into laughter.

I ask him what's so funny.

"With all that's brewing here, to have the indecency to say that they are ... Well, what can you do? Now all the journalists report something about narcos, and they hardly mention that this was a group of peasants. People who have lost their land, who have been kicked off their land and are now wondering where in the fucking world they're going to plant their corn, their beans, their seeds. And when they find a place in the middle of nowhere they'll be accused of being narcos again, they'll be kicked out and left to beg."

"But they've invaded protected forest land," I say, playing devil's advocate.

"We'd do the same. Didn't I tell you they have nowhere to grow their food? And that's all they know how to do. If you didn't have anything, and you knew that someone would soon take your land away, and some guy told you he'd pay you 1,500 quetzales (some $190) to load and unload a small plane, would you do it?"

I don't have to answer.

"They have a lot of mouths to feed. Campesinos have a lot of kids." Again the activist erupts into laughter.

I tell him I want to speak with them, with the campesinos, the peasants, the supposed narcotraffickers. He laughs again. This time it's weary laughter, as if he's tired of having to explain things to me. He says I'd have to go deep into a land crawling with organized crime.

"And anyway," he says, "I don't know if they even would talk to you. They're sick of journalists looking for the same answer to the same question: You guys work with narcos?"

He said it would be better to speak with communities who have already been kicked off their land.

In 1959 the Guatemalan government, in order to exploit the region's agricultural potential, created a plan to populate Petén and integrate it with the rest of the country. The government handed over huge swaths of property to big corporations, but also to the campesinos who knew how to work the land.

"That's true," the activist says, "and for a while the campesinos grew their crops and ate them and lived off of them. They came from all over the country, but we're talking fifty years ago. There were no good roads, and no one was really interested in hoarding big chunks of land. There were a lot of businessmen who had large properties but they were never on them."

"What changed?"

"Well, now there are two highways linking Petén to the rest of the country, and ever since 2000, the African palm has been all the rage, as well as timber trees like teak and melina, and suddenly everyone has their eyes set on the campesinos' little parcels of land. And, of course, many narcotraffickers and smugglers and all kinds of dealers want to accumulate land on the border with Mexico. The easy access through Petén sparked their interest."

"So you're telling me that the campesinos sold their land?"

"There are many ways to sell. Let me explain: If the lawyer of a company visits you time and again and talks to you about five-figure numbers, and you're a Q'eqchi' campesino, your eyes start glowing and then you sell without knowing a thing. If you're a campesino, indigenous or otherwise, and the narcos want your land, then you're even more fucked, because they'll simply tell you that you need to sell your land for such and such a price, and that's it."

"And if you refuse?"

"There used to be a famous saying about a decade ago: If you don't sell now, your widow's gonna sell herself for cheap later."

This activist knows what he's talking about. Every month he meets with dozens of campesinos who have been pressured to sell their land and, if they haven't been paid, or if they don't understand their contract because they didn't read the fine print, or if they simply don't know how to read, he advises them.

This is what it breaks down to: The government uses two different sticks for punishment. One stick is stiff, and they use it to punish the weak; the other stick is soft, and they use it to make it seem that they are cracking down on their rivals, though they are ultimately leaving them unpunished.

"International organizations have pumped Guatemala with money intended to protect forested areas and archeological sites. How does the state show the donors they're tough? By targeting the weakest, and accusing them of being narcotraffickers, which makes the state look even stronger."

The activist tends to laugh loudly and sarcastically.

"Look, when we go to that area, when we talk to the campesinos, there's no question that the infamous narco families, like the Mendozas, the Leóns and the Lorenzanas, have their hands in protected forest land like the national parks Sierra del Lacandón and Laguna del Tigre."

He isn't the only one making the point that the narcos are treading on protected land. Even government informants have confirmed that, to quote the famous Salvadoran archbishop Óscar Romero, the laws of Petén are like snakes—they only bite those who walk barefoot.

Nestled in Zone 18 of Guatemala City, the wind blows heavily through the café, and napkins are flying off the nearby empty tables. From the terrace you can see the rooftops of various houses in this lower-middle-class neighborhood. Despite the cold, we opt for the seclusion of the outdoor terrace.

Colonel Díaz Santos orders a black tea. We first met at the beginning of 2011, soon after he was picked as the military's second in command in managing President Álvaro Colom's state of emergency, which was meant to weaken the influx of Los Zetas in Alta Verapaz, the state just south of Petén. The colonel is now in charge of the Northern Task Force of Petén, including Sayaxché, a town known for both its African palm and the drugs smuggled down the La Pasión River, which is flanked on all sides by land held by wealthy narco families. He also oversees southeast Petén, which includes part of La Libertad, where the stretch of civilization peters out as you near Mexico, finally disappearing into thick forest. That's where you'll find El Naranjo, a border town known, to lean on an outdated stereotype, as the Tijuana of Guatemala: a place rife with drug smuggling, human smuggling, human trafficking and undocumented immigration.

The first time the colonel and I met, we were at the military headquarters of Cobán, the capital of the state of Alta Verapaz. Santos was in uniform and spoke openly about Los Zetas and the local narco families. Now, in civilian clothing and on his day off, he's more measured when speaking about Petén. I have to tease out his double meanings.

The colonel is familiar with the area the 300 campes-inos were displaced from. He was actually involved in that operation. Again and again he reminds me that they were following the orders of the Public Ministry, that they had to evict people living on protected land, and that, yes, what they found were humble people: women, a lot of old women, and children. He said that he was never told anything about any narcotraffickers.

I remind him that the Ministry of the Interior as well as the official government press release stated that the operation targeted people linked to drug trafficking. It was straightforward: "Areas controlled by narcotraffickers" is how they defined the campesino settlement. The colonel bites his tongue. It doesn't make sense to keep pushing him. The government's position is absurd, continually contradicting itself. Evicting narcotraffickers because they're living on protected land is like arresting a murderer because he also stole his victim's cell phone.

The colonel is quiet. He sips his tea, then reiterates that his opinion is his own and that in no way is he speaking for Security Advisor Menocal. I interrupt him and ask if he ever had reason to believe that he was working with drug dealers.

"No," he says. "Though I don't think you can deny that more than one campesino is in the business. You just can't generalize. Many are simply forced to live on protected land. They sell their land to people growing African palm ... And where can they go? The only place left to grow food is protected land."

"You know the area, Colonel. People say that there are huge stretches of land belonging to the Mendoza family, or, by proxy, the Lorenzanas. What do you think? Do you think there are powerful people working out of protected areas?"

"I think so."

"Groups that smuggle drugs, wood and contraband?"

"I think so."

The report *Power Brokers in Petén: Territory, Politics and*

Business, published in July of 2011 and financed by the Open Society Foundations, reveals that some of these swaths of land are legally registered to known drug traffickers. Even high-up military personnel like General Eduardo Morales, who orchestrated the state of emergency in Petén, believe that the northern part of the state, made up of protected land like Laguna del Tigre, is teeming with drug lords who organize shipments by planes that are later burned in order to get rid of all traces. A few days ago, Morales told me that some forested areas were deteriorating due the building of runways and plane graveyards. He told me about a hotel that can accommodate a hundred people in Sierra del Lacandón, and a recent landing site in Laguna del Tigre where an official and two soldiers confronted forty armed men who ultimately ran them off. "It's sad to admit," Morales said, "but that's how it is."

I tell Colonel Díaz Santos that it seems very strange to me that the National Council of Protected Areas (CONAP) doesn't know about any of this, and yet knows about the illegal campesino settlements; or that the police who help with CONAP's surveillance operation are still in the dark. I ask him if he trusts these authorities.

"Oof! I'd rather not answer that."

"Well, Colonel. What do you think about the report that's been circulating all over Petén? Do you think it's credible?"

"I'll tell you what a friend once told me: 'The report is only good for reminding you what you need to talk about and who you need to talk to.'"

While the report garnered national attention in Guatemala, especially in Petén, not one local media source covered it. And yet there was not one person from Petén, be it an activist, an official or even a soldier with whom I spoke during my trip, who hadn't read the report. It circulated from hand to hand, from mouth to mouth, from email to email.

The authors—researchers of various nationalities and fields—wrote the report anonymously. None of them have spoken to the media. They fear for their lives and ask for no one to even guess at their nationality. After going through many intermediaries, I was able to get two of them to talk with me through Skype. The report was explicit, rich in official sources. All of its data on land ownership I found to be substantiated with publicly registered cadastres; the rest was based on other official data, international reports, already published testimonies, and interviews with key informants in Petén.

During our Skype conversations the authors told me that they published the report anonymously because they knew well that the powerful people they referenced had strings to pull even on an international level. They assured me that they were prudent in publishing their findings. "We only published what we could prove, even though there are many unregistered properties in protected land that belong to organized crime groups in a de facto way."

Petén is depicted as a land fertile for political corruption, drug trafficking and the concentration of power in very few hands. Petén, as described in the report, is not a place for humble people.

In the analysis of Petén's local political parties, the findings are shocking: One can only be mayor or a city council member by being directly a part of or having close ties with organized crime. The report lists the full names of people in all political parties, without exception, who benefit from such alliances.

The accusations reach the highest level of government. Presidential candidate of the Renewed Democratic Liberty Party, Manuel Baldizón (originally from Petén) came from a family who achieved its economic prowess thanks to, in large part, the smuggling of archeological artifacts. The report cites anonymous testimonies of those who participated in the group raids of Mayan ruins, stealing pieces to sell them to foreign collectors.

The report also explains how the powerful families of

organized crime, like the Mendozas, who are originally from the strategically located state of Izabal, which borders both Honduras and Belize, have appropriated huge plantations in Petén. The Mendozas own twenty-three plantations spread out over four municipalities. Many of the properties skirt the banks of the La Pasión River, and at least one of them boasts a mansion with a pool and a runway.

Not one authority figure has publicly exposed these landowners. The report explains that the greater part of this land, like the 250 caballerías registered to the Mendozas or their proxies, are largely part of the protected forest of Sierra del Lacandón, the very national park from which the state displaced 300 campesinos, many of whom, with nowhere else to go, set up camp in the jungle on the Mexican side of the border. The colonel and the general both explained that the problem isn't organized crime groups taking over land that isn't theirs, but the illicit businesses they set up on those lands. Even General Morales points out that Los Zetas have training camps and lodges in Laguna del Tigre.

The drug traffickers aren't very discreet. General Morales described finding an enormous stash house about three years ago. His men even found a boat in mid construction. "A big boat, one to ferry cars. A prosecutor likened it to Noah's Ark."

Narco land reaches all the way to the Mexican border, to the Usumacinta River. "Each property," reads the report, "is equipped with armed guards."

Petén has become a sort of condominium for the big families of organized crime. The Mendozas aren't the only ones in the limelight. The Leóns, originally from Zacapa, a state bordering Honduras, own 316 caballerías in Petén that are nestled, so the report explains, "in strategic places along the drug route." The Lorenzanas, also from Zacapa, own four ranches within the nationally protected park of Laguna del Tigre. One of these ranches—proof of the broken system— was openly registered under the name of the family patriarch,

Waldemar Lorenzana, who in 2011 was extradited to the United States for drug-trafficking charges.

The report concludes that the property linked to organized crime groups reaches a four-digit figure: 1,179 caballerías. That's equivalent to seven times the area of San Salvador, or about two and a half times the size of Boston. Meanwhile, the African palm plantations officially occupy 1,027 caballerías.

According to the National Council of Protected Areas, by 2007, close to 8,000 people had been displaced from 902 caballerías in and around the municipality of Sayaxché. Twenty-seven campesino communities ceded their land to African palm companies and other buyers. And yet officials refuse to acknowledge that the campesinos, who are often left with no other option but accepting the narcos' offers, are also having to protect themselves from encroaching transnational companies who know how to get what they want: more land.

It's six o'clock in the morning and there's a faint, comforting sunshine. I'm on a bus headed out of the town of El Subín, near Sayaxché, to the Petén town of Santa Elena. The bus is nearly empty: Only two other passengers are riding near the back. One of them, who I guess is a campesino, quietly speaks to the man next to him, who looks like a construction worker.

The campesino asks if it's easy to find construction work these days. The worker says yes, that there's a lot of construction in Santa Elena. The campesino says he should consider himself lucky, that there's no work on the land these days, that "if you have good land, they'll just take it from you." Now all that's left is all "dry, dead land." He says that further south, by Sayaxché, the only work is in the African palm industry, because "the *señores* ["Mister" or "Lord," a common way to refer to a high-level narco] who own the good land don't need anyone to farm it."

In Santa Elena, I'm greeted by Alfredo Che, a short and stout campesino, with the slow and clipped style of Spanish commonly spoken by the Q'eqchi'. He is a member of the Association of Indigenous Campesino Communities for the Integral Development of Petén, which is part of the National Coordination of Campesino Organizations. The organization's central demand is the relocation of displaced campesinos. With no place left to go, they ask that campesinos be allowed to return to the protected forest land they once inhabited, under the condition that they would limit expansion of their settlements, and that they would farm under rules that respect the ecosystem.

Che is angry—his face contorts when he speaks—though his voice never rises above a whisper. He complains that in Petén even the killing of campesinos is used as an argument against campesinos. In May of 2011, on a plantation called Los Cocos, in an unpopulated stretch of land across La Libertad, there was a massacre of twenty-seven people. According to official reports, the perpetrators were Los Zetas. Their target was the plantation owner, but apparently they couldn't find him and they took out their revenge on the campesinos instead. Some were decapitated with chainsaws. An investigator showed me a picture of the bodies still wearing their heavy work boots.

Even the Ministry of the Interior identified the victims as campesinos hired to work the plantation, but Che says that the Petén authorities use massacres like this one as an argument that the campesinos are collaborating with "narco plantations," and are thus caught red-handed in the cross fire.

"They never displace the plantation owners," argues Che. "It's always the campesinos, the communities who farm what they eat. They might tell you that the land here is green, but the truth is that if you walk through Sierra del Lacandón, the Maya Biosphere, you'll no longer see pristine mountains. CONAP has guards to protect themselves, but they can't really do anything if they only carry tiny .38-caliber pistols. And even with the Nature Protection Unit ... the fact is that two policemen plus three guards cannot confront a group armed with assault rifles. So they keep on attacking defenseless communities and leave all plantation owners alone."

The campesinos aren't the only ones denouncing unequal treatment. Francisco Dall'Anesse, the lead prosecutor for the International Commission Against Impunity in Guatemala (CICIG, in its Spanish acronym) that was founded by the UN in 2006, has also pointed out this disparity. At a journalism conference in Argentina, he said that "there are indigenous groups being kicked off their land and pushed onto the streets," while no one is doing anything about the real narcos. He told the story of a UN high commissioner going to Los Cocos Plantation to bear witness to the massacre of campesinos. Narcos, armed to the teeth, stopped him and interrogated him about his intentions, forcing him to identify himself before letting him pass.

Che says that with all the narco threats and corporate pressures, campesinos are only getting some 50,000 quetzales for a piece of land that is worth around 200,000 quetzales (around $25,500). I ask him why they don't sue. He says that they've already done so many times, but that, in the best of cases, lawsuits only result in stacks of bureaucratic papers that end up getting shelved in some office of the Public Ministry.

He says that African palm companies often employ "coyotes," typically other campesinos, sent to repeatedly pressure their neighbors until they finally cave in and sign a contract they don't understand. He tells me that if I want to know more about these practices, I should speak to another member of his organization, Domingo Choc, who works in the municipality of Sayaxché, known for being the area most coveted by African palm transnationals.

Choc shows up later that evening.

"Companies are smart," he says. "They know how to suffuse a community with fear."

Their strategy is to pressure and divide. He explains that "if a coyote isn't able to do the job, they'll send someone better, until they get what they want." They insist, again and again, until they're able to divide the community and are left with only a few campesinos who they threaten to squeeze out between plantations of African palm. Private guards bar any leftover campesinos from going through lands owned by African palm plantations; they don't let cars pass that are transporting sacks of corn and beans to the market. The corporations only let the campesinos grow enough to eat, nothing more. That's how they're able to pressure those most hesitant to sell and become plantation day laborers with no contract, meaning they're paid less than the $63.70 quetzales a day (about $8), which is the minimum salary. This goes on until the campesinos grow tired of sweating and fighting over a sliver a land that once belonged to them and they leave, just as Venustiano did, to carve out a new piece of land in a protected forest zone, hoping not to be displaced or accused of being narcos.

This happened to José Cacxoj, a campesino I met from Sayaxché. At sixty-three years old, he grew tired of the daily visit he got from a supposed engineer named Gustavo who continuously threatened that he'd end up landlocked between plantations of African palm if he didn't sell his parcel of land in the hamlet of Las Camelias. He finally sold his parcel, which was barely half a caballería, for 100,000 quetzales. He's spent the last two years looking for land in a state that holds no interest for either the narcos or the palm companies, and yet, even with the prices at least twice what he was paid for his own land, he hasn't been able to find anything. So Cacxoj is wasting away his money by renting land under the agreement that he give half of his crop yield to the landowner. If something goes wrong with one of his two annual harvests, as happened last year, due to lack of rain, Cacxoj is ruined. He's thinking of spending the rest of his years on protected land and turning himself into an "invader," as campesinos are called by the state, or maybe turning into "a narco," as Venustiano and his community were called.

I ask Choc how many people have been displaced. He says he doesn't know the figure in people, but in communities and families.

"In the El Progreso community in Sayaxché, twenty-three families were finished. In the El Cubil community, thirty-two families were finished; they no longer exist. In El Canaleño, forty-six families. La Torre, seventy-six families. Santa Rosa, eighty-six families. Arroyo Santa María, forty-three families ... And the community that everyone remembers as the first community, the community known as Centro Uno, 164 families were finished; they no longer exist."

A day has passed since I met with Che and Choc. They helped me contact campesinos in Centro Uno. I'm now riding a bus on a sweltering, humid day, heading toward La Libertad. The windows are open and waves of dust waft in and stick to my sweaty skin, seeming to attract the tiny clouds of mosquitoes circling my face.

At the center of the town is an outdoor market. It's a marvel that the many tuk-tuks zigzagging around pedestrians aren't also running them over. Seemingly every small shop has a set of speakers blaring *norteña* music or a megaphone shouting its sales. I walk into a chicken rotisserie, and from the back room where an employee is scrubbing dishes, I call Venustiano, who says he knows the place and asks me to wait, that he'll be there soon with Santos, another ex-resident of Centro Uno.

Venustiano, at fifty-six years old, looks the typical campesino: rope-muscled, with a mustache and wearing a white threadbare shirt, jeans and black work boots. His skin is cracked like dried mud. He shows up with Santos, a sturdy, hairless Q'eqchi' man.

They speak in a tone somewhere between shame and gratitude. It doesn't seem like they're used to telling their story.

When his community was kicked off Centro Uno in 2009, the media only reported the official version. Venustiano says that no one ever asked him anything. Venustiano speaks of an infertile land, a land of plastics, lumber and shacks, of a miserable economy, of eight-hour workdays spent tilling someone else's dirt far from his makeshift home, of earning only thirty quetzales a day. He says that when you're "farming someone else's land, seeds don't sprout the same." I interrupt him and ask that he start at the beginning and tell me what Centro Uno was like in Sierra del Lacandón.

"What was it like?" he asks. He puts down the roasted chicken he's eating, wipes the grease off his mustache and slowly bats away the cloud of mosquitoes hovering in front of his face. He pauses and looks into the middle distance.

"Where we lived we had water. A stream and land. The stream was clear, you could see your feet through it. There was a dairy farm where you'd get pretty muddy, but it was beautiful. There was corn, beans, and we were happy. There were coconut trees, avocado trees, all of them bore fruit. There were oranges, lime, mango, and they grew like this," he stretches his arms out to symbolize the abundance. "We knew our land. There was cane, yucca, bananas, cocoyam. We couldn't be happier."

At ten in the morning on June 16, 2009, a caravan of 600 military personnel, policemen, forest guards, Public Ministry agents and Ombudsmen for the Defense of Human Rights (PDH) began a massive eviction of campesinos in the Centro Uno community of Petén. One hundred and sixty-four families were removed from the land that, albeit without permission, they had started settling before the 1996 Peace Accords, which put an end to the country's thirty-six-year-old Civil War. Some had moved there even earlier, around 1992. Most of them, however, apart from those first pioneers, trickled in within the next five years. Almost all were originally from Ixcán, Izabal, Quiché and Cobán and had been looking for a place to farm far from what had been a particularly deadly war zone. In these interior tracts of mostly indigenous-held land, only the words "massacre" and "genocide" can describe what went on during a war in which it is estimated that 200,000 Guatemalans were killed.

Centro Uno had never been a secret. The campesinos built two schools where 180 kids took classes from five community teachers who had actually been hired by the government. They have copies of old letters dated from 1990, in which community members pleaded with national and state authorities to legalize the settlement of Centro Uno, just as other communities had been able to do after proving that they had settled there before the forest was established as a protected area. The Centro Uno community gathered official letters of support from five deputy mayors of farming villages who testified that the founders of Centro Uno had been living there long before the community even had a name, since at least 1988.

"In the end," Venustiano continues, "on that day in 2009, they only gave us a half hour to pack our things. I was only able to gather my four kids. I left behind a field of corn. I also left behind ten fields of squash ready to be harvested. Everyone lost everything."

Estuardo Puga, head of the PDH in Petén, confirmed that they only allotted them a half hour to leave their land. He said the PDH left at 1:30 in the afternoon, but that the military and personnel of CONAP stayed behind. He also said that there were reports of looting. Venustiano says they took everything from them, that he saw vans ahead of them, hauling away their cattle, their sacks of produce, their power generators.

"Because they called us narcos, they were able to kick us out so easily. I think it was just an excuse used by the authorities, a cover-up," says Venustiano.

I ask him if someone in the community participated in drug-related activities.

"Narcotraffickers live in mansions. Narcotraffickers don't

live in tiny palm-thatch houses like the ones we lived in, and even less so in tarp shacks like the ones we live in now ... Do you want to see how we, the narcotraffickers of Centro Uno, live?"

We take a tuk-tuk out of the clamor of the market. It leaves us at the beginning of a dirt path. We walk for fifteen minutes until we get to his parcel of land.

"So this is where all you narcotraffickers live?"

"Yep, right here," Venustiano says. "Follow me. Let me introduce you to everyone."

He pulls open the stick-and-wire entrance gate and lets it fall to the ground.

5

Narco: Made in Central America

February 2012

Over a morning chat with a hotshot Nicaraguan narco I learn what it takes to be a narco free agent in Central America. The two most important factors: Get in with the police and build a solid social network.

I've been stood up by the Narco. We had an agreement. Today at five in the afternoon I was to be in San Jorge, Rivas state, Nicaragua, close to the border with Costa Rica, to meet up with the Narco. But here I am at the place and time we'd agreed upon and there's no Narco. I soon learn that I didn't get the date or hour wrong, or misunderstand his cryptic messages. Nor is it that he had just gotten a fresh tip about a shipment of cocaine worth stealing. No, the reason he isn't showing is a lot more mundane: Last night he drank an entire bottle of whiskey and now he can barely piece together a single sentence.

When I finally get him on the phone I hear an incomprehensible murmur. Ten minutes later I get another call, from the Narco's wife. She says she's sorry, but that her husband can't speak to me right now. Later on, when he's up to it, he'll call and let me know.

These sorts of meetings rarely pan out. Why would a narco want to talk to a journalist in the first place? The answer, though maybe not obvious, is always the same. Their own interest: They want to accuse somebody. Criminals, I've learned, always have a lot of fingers to point.

It's eleven at night when the Narco from Rivas calls my cell phone. I'm sitting in a restaurant on the shore of Lake Nicaragua. The Narco excuses himself: You know how it is, he says to me. It's hot, no? And all this heat makes you want a drink.

He says he feels better, except that a couple good friends just stopped over and they brought a few more bottles of whiskey ... so, he can't meet me today, either, but tomorrow morning I should swing by at seven sharp, and we'll be eating breakfast together by 7:30.

I decide to show up at 9.

San Jorge, a city with a population of about 8,000, is cut through by a single street that runs into a pier lined with boats for rent that will take you to the tourist island of Ometepe, in the middle of Lake Nicaragua. This lake is not the sea, but San Jorge has a marine spirit: The restaurants are called the Navegante (Seafarer) or El Timón (the Helm) and the hotels have names like El Pelícano or Las Hamacas. The city is slow, hot, dusty, and its residents spend most of their time in sandals and shorts.

Rivas is also the only Nicaraguan state that shares a border with Costa Rica. Besides Peñas Blancas, the only official border crossing, there are more than eighty other unguarded crossing points. Rivas is known as the gateway to Central America for Colombian drugs. According to the National Police, the Mexican cartels of Sinaloa, Gulf, Juárez and the Michoacán Family use the Rivas border with Costa Rica to push their drugs north toward the United States. On the Atlantic side, however, the Colombians drop off their shipments further north, in Honduras or Guatemala, charging the Mexicans a steeper transport price.

The difference between Pacific and Atlantic drug shipments is that the latter uses 800-horsepower speedboats that rocket north, pausing only to refuel. On the Pacific side, passing through Rivas, most of the drugs are shipped by land first, then transferred to boats to cross the lake on their way to the cities of Granada or Managua.

It's nine in the morning and, according to his wife, the Narco from Rivas has locked himself in his room to sleep off his hangover. But, she assures me, he'll get over it soon.

He calls me at 10.

"Stop on over. We'll have a little coffee to ease into the day. Where are you? I'll send someone to pick you up."

A lot of the narcos I've talked to seem to be cut from the same mold: chubby and dark-skinned, sweaty and with big hands, very polite, usually jovial, often smiley; they speak in sharp country slang and address you in endearing terms like brother, my friend, teacher, *viejo* (old man) or even *viejito* (little old man).

In Rivas there are four main bosses. The Narco I spoke with is one of them. Cartel bosses in Central America are less secretive than their Mexican counterparts; they are also less ostentatious, less rich, more accessible, and usually get their start in one of two ways: making the best of a network of their own contacts—maybe they were money changers along the border, or part of a band of criminals that trafficked cheese, or robbed truck trailers, or perhaps they were employed by the city—or they were already part of one of the drug networks and somehow managed to usurp power from their previous boss. This narco was a thief: He got started as a trafficker by robbing from other traffickers.

When we finally meet, he looks surprisingly sharp. He doesn't have red eyes or slow speech or seem hungover at all. He is sweaty, sure, but he is also happy and loud. He welcomes me into the front room of his small house, outside of which are two young bodyguards. Happily, almost shouting, he asks to see my ID. He looks it over, turns it over, reads it carefully. Then he hands it back and writes my name in a notebook.

Central American narcos, with the exception of a few ex-politicians or those coming from established Guatemalan or Honduran patriarchies, are considered free agents. They aren't part of the Mexican Sinaloan Cartel, nor do they work exclusively with the Colombian Norte del Valle Cartel. They work, rather, with those who pay, with those who call. The Narco from Rivas is a free agent. And not the sort of free agent who works a corner, pushing grams; he traffics in the ton.

He started by telling me the same thing the other narcos I interviewed told me: that they've left the business. These claims are like scratch-off lotto tickets: Just a little scrape of your finger and you start to see what's underneath. The truth usually ends up that they are exactly what they say they are not. El Narco from Rivas says that he's quit robbing drug shipments.

"Supposedly," he says to me, "I'm a robber. A shipment comes in and we raid it. If anybody was around during the war [the Nicaraguan Revolution] … they know how it goes."

According to his logic, if fighting in a civil war educates the population, then Central America is full of well-educated people. Three wars have been fought in the northern triangle in the last forty years.

Nicaragua is the best place in Central America to steal drug shipments. On the Atlantic side, speedboats set off from tiny remote villages close to the Honduran border to intercept shipments and resell them further up the line. On the Pacific side, armed groups intercept trucks, or sometimes the police step in to scrape a little off the top.

Roberto Orozco, from the Institute for Strategic Studies and Public Policy (IEEPP) a respected Nicaraguan think tank, describes Rivas as one of the four states with alarming levels of police corruption. An IEEPP investigation described the criminal groups in Rivas as "embryonic cartels" with much more capacity than solitary delinquents.

High levels of corruption and organized criminal activity are not secrets in Nicaragua, even among the police. National Police Chief Commissioner Aminta Granera admits that Rivas is a challenge: "We need to cooperate with our logistical base in Rivas even more than in the Atlantic, where drugs don't come over land. We just turned five [Rivas] police officers over to the courts. We have a lot of internal work to do throughout the Pacific, where we are more vulnerable to the corruption of organized crime."

I guess it's true that whiskey doesn't give you a hangover. The Narco from Rivas, who hasn't even reached for his water glass yet, keeps talking and talking to me. I ask him what sort of network you need to have to run a drug-stealing operation.

"Well, if you've been doing it for your whole life, well, then you know a lot of people. Even cartel people. I lived in Mexico for five years. And then they [cartels] call you 'cause the Colombians never pay up. So now they want you instead of the Colombians and they keep calling you. Or whoever never got paid for the last job comes looking for you. It's miserable work. You're always fucked, running around from country to country, and still always tied to your home ... And they [the police] take their cut. The Colombians aren't gonna send you 472 kilos. They send you 500. Whole numbers, for sure. But whenever police report decommissions, it's like eighty-seven, eighty-three, 940 kilos."

The drug robber, I learn, is just one player in a long line of thieves. In April of 2011, in Bilwi, the capital of the North Atlantic Autonomous Region, I asked various sources, from police officers to cocaine traffickers, how drug robbers stay alive when the cartels know who is robbing them. Very few of these robbers have the ability to hide an entire boat or truck trailer loaded with coke. In the Caribbean, I was told, there simply aren't foreign bases set up to transport the drugs, just local transfer points where it's best not to start problems. The best solution for the cartels is simply to buy their drugs (or buy their drugs back) from the robbers. In Rivas, as the drugs are moving over land, keeping a low profile is what matters.

"It's strange," the Narco from Rivas tells me. "We've seen some bodies dropped around here for robbing twenty, ten kilos. It's a small town, everybody knows each other. If you see some dude you don't recognize, the locals know they can fuck with him, and so they call you, look, *loco*, a couple of fellas are poking around doing this and that."

"After you rob [a shipment] you call the people in Guatemala or Honduras. Say to them: Look, some people robbed this much of the goods. Then you sell it to them. The world is made for the bold. The robber knows he's yanking on the bull's balls. Say you rob 500 kilos. The owner of that shipment has competition. The competition buys your 500 and sells it further up the line. But one day you're gonna lose out."

In Central America, as opposed to Mexico, where a narco needs to show that he's got balls made out of gold, discretion still has its role, just like it did in Mexico in the '80s or '90s. It's better to negotiate than to call too much attention to yourself, at least when things are getting a little dangerous. As the Narco from Rivas says, if you act crazy you either go to jail or you end up fucked. That's why there are so many nuts in jail.

The first rule of protection for a local player is that one word: local.

"To kill somebody from Rivas, you need to hire somebody from Rivas," the Narco from Rivas says to me, laughing proudly. He feels safe in his niche, where he knows how to read the signs. If a truck sits on the corner by his house for more than an hour, it's the cops. If certain cars follow him, it's the cops. If certain men sit close to him in a restaurant, more cops: He knows their names, their habits, their nicknames. He knows the cabbies, the barber, the mayor and the ferryman. He is like many a narco in Central America: He has his zone of control where he's intimate with every crack in the pavement. The neighborhood, the hillside, the beach, the city, the highway, the county, the ranch. And from this stronghold he does business with whoever's willing to do business with him.

From her office on one of the top floors of the Central Police Station, Aminta Granera assures me that Mexican cartels do not have a permanent presence in Nicaragua. The police, however, still need to concern themselves with the "national corporate structure" of the cartels. To do so, Nicaragua's policing strategy has changed over the past four years. According to Commissioner Juan Ramón Gradiz, Granera's right-hand man, the new strategy consists of "requisitioning material and capturing drug traffickers, although," he admits, "the network will remain." The police have recently conducted a series of raids, attempting to arrest criminals in the act of trafficking and decommissioning anything they can get their hands on: houses, businesses, weapons, vehicles. "Taking away their cover," Gradiz explains.

One of these operations was called Domino One and was carried out in Rivas on December 4, 2011. The results were twenty fishermen, drivers and other poor-looking men charged with drug trafficking; another nineteen charged with money laundering. The police justified the success of their new strategy with a graph titled "Seized Cocaine and Cells Neutralized 2000–2011." Below the title were two lines on a graph, one blue and the other red, dipping and rising around each other. The blue line represented decommissioned cocaine, which rose in tonnage to 15.1 in 2008 and then dropped to 4.05 in 2011. The red represented "neutralized cells," which was at zero until 2005 and then jumped up to sixteen in 2010, just as the blue line took its big fall. For the police, the lesson was obvious: They were decommissioning a smaller quantity of drugs because they were dismantling the trafficking networks; hence, a smaller quantity of drugs were being trafficked.

To Detective Orozco, however, the explanation is overly simplistic and simply wrong. First, because the border in this region continues to be an "open door," with eighty-two unguarded crossing points that he himself counted in his investigations. Second, because international agencies continue to report a steady level of cocaine production in the Andes, about 850 tons a year from 2009 on. It is estimated that 90 percent of those 850 tons passes through Central America on its way north. Orozco adds it all up and concludes that if consumption indexes in the United States have remained stable, Andean production has been steady for years, and Mexican and Central American consumption has gone up yearly, then the police are simply wrong when they say a smaller quantity of drugs are passing through Nicaragua.

Back inside the Narco's house, he tries to think of all the free agents that operate in town. He names fifteen, replacing one agent whose name he can't remember with the name of his friend, currently out of the business and serving time in a nearby prison.

To the Narco from Rivas, even if he admits that Domino One did sweep up "a few real narcos," the police logic doesn't square. And yet as we continue to talk, he contradicts himself.

"Everything goes down here. The Michoacán Family, the Sinaloa Cartel, the Zacapa Cartel, the Guatemalans ... All your compatriots [Salvadorans], plus the *ticos* [Costa Ricans]."

They may not all be locals, but the foreigners need the locals to show them around. According to the Narco from Rivas, for any local, it's the best option on the table.

"It's become a method of survival. There's nothing here but this or going out to the lake and fishing," he says, spreading his hands and showing his open palms, as if the decision were obvious.

Perhaps that's another rule for the Central American narco. Working at this level, as a free agent who moves big shipments for high bidders, who is living a life in which anything at all is better than what he has: There are no other options.

Two Salvadoran narcos whom I spoke with, for example, explained to me that they both started out very young, working in the markets, hauling sacks, setting up vegetable pyramids and unloading trucks. José Adán Salazar, known as Chepe Diablo, spent years sunning himself along the El Salvador/ Guatemala border, changing border crossers' money from quetzales to colones (before El Salvador adopted the American dollar as its official currency), earning a few cents for each transaction. He is now assumed to be one of the top drug lords of the Texis Cartel and was one of three traffickers mentioned in a 2014 letter, part of the Foreign Narcotics Kingpin Designation Act, from President Obama to the US Congress and Senate. On the Nicaraguan Caribbean coast, many of the cell leaders who work with the Colombians, as well as the drug robbers, were lobstermen in the Miskito Keys. Being a lobsterman there doesn't mean owning a boat and hauling in traps. The men are free divers, holding their breath for up to three minutes at a time to pull up a single lobster, earning about three dollars a head selling them to restaurants. A lot of the divers suffer brain atrophy from lack of oxygen and, later in life, end up half-paralyzed and laid out in their huts.

After mentioning the booming business and the influx of new clients demanding the services of free agents from Rivas, the Narco from Rivas describes who the foreigners are and what they're like. The Guatemalans and Hondurans are "heavy-handed." The Salvadorans are the most ballsy, many of them gangsters from the Mara Salvatrucha, coming down looking to move a vehicle loaded with a few kilos of coke. Rivas, he explains, has only two types of visitors: backpackers looking for the San Juan del Sur beaches and narcos looking to move their product. Police have recently been arresting Hondurans and Mexicans with not only drugs, but weapons as well. Three of the Mexicans who were arrested in 2007, for example, were from the much-hailed state of Sinaloa, the hotbed of some of the biggest capos in the world.

To the Narco from Rivas, the police's graph claiming that a smaller quantity of drugs are passing through the country doesn't make any sense. He tries to put it in perspective for me.

"I think that there are more drugs here right now than there are in Pereira, Colombia."

"Hey, what was that chief's name, that guy who went around with Marcial?" the Narco from Rivas asks into his phone. He's decided to make a call to help answer my question. He pauses to listen, then says, "And is he still working? ... Look, I'm here with a friend who's asking if we ever paid off the cops ourselves."

He turns on speakerphone so I can hear his friend's response. It sounds like he's at a party.

"Of course, yes. Do you want us to call somebody now?"

"You yourself paid them off?"

"Ha-ha!" the man laughs.

Sinaloans, gangbangers or even other Central Americans can come to Rivas and learn the lay of the land, but they'll never be locals. Knowing a place is not the same as being from a place. And in the free agent market, that difference has value.

Rivas is a village. All of rural Central America is village. Central American countries are capital cities surrounded by villages, even if some of the villages are called cities. In villages everybody knows everybody. For example, if I want a taxi to come and get me right now, all I have to do is say the name of the Narco from Rivas, and they'll know exactly where to find me.

The Narco from Rivas confirmed something I heard stressed a number of times: As a free agent, if you haven't infiltrated the police, you're nothing. This is a point that the police commissioner, the investigators from the IEEP and the Narco from Rivas completely agree upon.

The Narco lays it out for me: "I'm not talking about the head commissioner, or the other big shots. I'm talking about the department heads, the second in commands, the chiefs of the auxiliary police."

Orozco still thinks that the police in this country are the best in the region, that they're way better than the Hondurans, that "there are states where everybody collaborates against organized crime." He thinks the *nica* [Nicaraguan] problem with police corruption is just a few bad apples in the states, but he also thinks that if he doesn't get rid of it then it'll get worse.

Information is power. It's undeniable in a place like Rivas. There are families, like the Ponce family, who turned from humble fishermen into major narcos for one single reason: They knew people and they knew what was going on. They started working side jobs in little hotels for upper-class vacationers passing through and they kept their ears open, they asked questions and pretty soon they were established lieutenants in the Cali Cartel.

To know what's going on you need to have a lot of ears and a lot of eyes. I ask the Narco from Rivas what's the best way to manage, and he lays out what you need to do.

"The police. Sure you can win over a single highway patrolman, turn him into your trusted little dog. But if you're lazy they're gonna drive you out of the state. You got to have boys working for you, people who really know this area. People who can drive ahead of your shipment in a car or on a scooter, and then you got to have lookouts with cell phones in La Coyota, in La Virgen, in Cárdenas. Cabbies, gas station attendants, people who know what to look out for. Because before they go out on a sting the police have to go fill up at the gas station."

And yet, of course, seeing so much, knowing so much, has its costs.

"It's a terrible system. Up on the border, for $10,000 you can cross a full truck trailer. It's the police that work the checkpoint. You need to be big to work the border. If you want to pass three trailers, that's thirty grand. A local who sells bags and buys a kilo from Costa Rica, where things are cheaper, they can't work that."

For the smaller fish, the eighty-two unguarded crossing points that Orozco added up are the best option. But the smaller fish still have to pay for protection, for their lookouts, for their, as they call them, "flags."

"If you want to push a big load, 200 or 300 kilos, then it's about five grand for the flag. That's a stiff drink to swallow!"

All of it follows the logic of gaining position, moving up the ladder. A narco's business in Central America is to push as large a quantity of drugs north as he can. Kilometers equal dollars. The Narco from Rivas knows it well: A kilo of cocaine in Rivas is worth $6,000; in El Salvador that same kilo is worth $11,000, in Guatemala it goes up to $12,000; and then in Chiapas (southern Mexico) it's at $15,000, and by the time it gets to Matamoros (on the US-Mexico border) it's already up to $20,000. On the streets in US cities it is higher still.

The Narco from Rivas tells me that my time is up, that he needs to go to Managua to settle a certain matter, and that he'll drop me off at a gas station along the highway. As we drive he points out a motel, a convenience store and then a restaurant. For each locale he tells me which narco is the owner.

His cell phone rings.

"Yeah, what? Yeah. OK, Saturday. Four o'clock. You're sure it's safe? 'Cause I was planning on getting out of the country."

He hangs up and smiles proudly, as if he had just proven something to me.

"A shipment's coming through Saturday. So no more drugs around here? So the trade is over? Ha!"

Part 2. Madness

Amid the emptiness, far from any formal authorities, those who remain live according to the laws of violence. Madness, born in the emptiness, is the ultimate uncertainty.

6

Our Bottomless Well

April 2013

There are bodies down there. Not prosecutors, not gang members, not journalists, not policemen, not even the government doubts that in this exact spot, deep below ground level, there are bodies. And now that everybody knows, the question remains: What do we do? This is the story of a well—and of the country that surrounds it.

At the bottom of the well there are bodies. Maybe ten, maybe twelve, maybe as many as twenty. Definitely there are at least four. Entering into the small city of Turín, in western El Salvador, if you continue on the dirt road, cross over the train tracks, pass by the mud house and keep going through the cornfield, you'll come to the well. At the bottom of the well there are bodies.

December 2010

A man straps himself into a harness. He anchors a rope to a tree, hangs an oxygen tank to his back and takes up his flashlight. Then he drops down into the well. Darkness envelops him. He descends. Ten meters. Twenty meters. Thirty. The well is deeper than he thought. He figured it would be about thirty meters deep, about the depth of another well in the area he dove into a few months back. Forty meters. Fifty. Fifty-five, and then the man touches water at the bottom. He turns on his light. He sees socks, clothes, junk, a collection of bones, feet, toes. He gives the signal to come back up. The well is too old and seems too fragile to do any straight down pick-and-shovel excavating. But it's clear now: There are bodies in the bottom of the well.

The man's name is Israel Ticas, and he's the only working forensic investigator in the entire country, as well as the only person to descend into the well. There is nobody else but him in the entire country working to dig up graves, uncover bodies and send the evidence to the courts.

In November 2010, testimonies from two gang members came together to tell a single story about the well. One of the members was from the Hollywood Locos Salvatrucha clique. The other was from the Parvis Locos Salvatrucha. They were both part of the Mara Salvatrucha in the state of Ahuachapán. Both of the men turned against their own gangs. Neither of them have ever been to the United States, which means that they didn't know where Hollywood Boulevard or Park View Street was (in Macarthur Park of Los Angeles), or even where Hollywood was, which gave the cliques their names. Both of the young men are from outside of Turín, from the hills, the countryside. Both of their testimonies coincided exactly: Turning off the highway into Turín, following the dirt road, crossing over the train tracks, passing by the mud shack and then turning left on the next dirt path you come to, which is just wide enough for a car, and driving on past the cornfield, there you will see a field open up before you, where there is a jocote tree, a rudimentary sink and a well. At the bottom of this well there are bodies.

In early December 2010 investigators came to Turín for the first time. That was when Ticas dropped down into the well to confirm the testimonies of the young men, knowing that at the bottom he would uncover what for him would become the biggest challenge he would face since, in 2008, he began his work of digging up mass graves.

January 3, 2011

Excavate at a forty-five degree angle. That's Ticas's Plan A. They'll have to dig for the bodies; they can't just pull them up. And instead of digging straight down, they'll have to open up a thirty-yard-wide hole a hundred yards from the well and then shoot at a forty-five-degree angle to the bottom, aiming straight for the bodies. Once the tunnel hits the wall of the well, they'll knock a hole through to access the cadavers and drag out everything they find.

The Ministry of Public Works (MOP) loans Ticas the necessary equipment, a backhoe and a couple of dump trucks. Today is the first day of digging.

January 27, 2011

Bad news. Two cold fronts in a row set off a series of disasters, mostly in the interior of the country. The MOP needs its machines back. Tica is left without help. In the first twenty-four days of digging he was able to descend ten of the fifty-five meters. He was happy. At that pace he would finish digging before the wet season, which is the worst time to dig up bodies in El Salvador. In the wet season when you dig, the rain fills back in. You empty, the rain floods. Even reinforcing the walls of your holes won't keep the rain out. Without a backhoe or a digger it's going to be impossible. The MOP said they only needed their machines for a few days, to do some damage control and reconstruction, and then they'd send them back to Turín.

February, March, April, May, June, July, August, September, October, November 2011

The MOP doesn't give the machines back. The ten meters of progress remain only ten meters. A single policeman keeps guard over a hole nobody is bothering with. For nine months the guard moves himself in and out of the shade, standing watch. Ticas goes to the prosecutor of Ahuachapán, who tries to convince the minister of defense to loan out some new equipment, but nothing happens. The wooden cap to the well is replaced by a cement seal. Ticas tries advertising on his Facebook account: Looking for a backhoe, a dump truck, anything to help him dig some dead bodies out of a well in Turín. He'd be grateful for the hand.

December 23, 2011

El Niño Hollywood, of the Hollywood Locos Salvatrucha clique, is one of the witnesses whose testimony led Ticas to the well. The thirty-year-old loves to talk. He even likes to talk with prosecutors, though when he does so he cuts down on his colorful adjectives and skips over the guts and the gore. He likes it when prosecutors bring him other ex-gang members and they sit down and talk about comrades who died in the war against Barrio 18. He tries to impress people with his memory, his ability to read people, interpret candle flames, his knowledge of witchcraft. He's been living in a shack, down the street from the police station in El Refugio, since 2009, and is the key witness in the case against Chepe Furia. Today is the first day a journalist visits his little shack, and El Niño settles into his role as storyteller.

We talk for three hours. El Niño tells me how he joined the MS in '94, how his boss, Chepe Furia, was something between a mafia boss and a gangster, and then he tells me how many murders he's committed, how many murders he's witnessed and how many he's known about. He talks about drugs, extortion, death threats, traitors, corrupt cops and friendly judges. He tells me how a traitor can destroy an entire clique. He tells me how his own gang killed his brother. Another clique within the MS thought his brother, known as El Cheje, was a traitor. So they killed him. And then the murderers tried to kill El Niño so they wouldn't leave an enraged hit man on the loose. They tried to *take him for a walk* (and this is the most important phrase, *taking someone for a walk*, in his story) but it ended up being El Niño who *took them for a walk* instead.

When a gang member *takes you for a walk*, they trick you into accompanying them to some place where they kill you. Let's go grab a drink. Let's go visit that place. Let's go kill what's-his-name. That's when they pull the gun on you. Let's go smoke a J by the well in Turín.

He starts telling me about clique exchanges. When a gang member is hunted by the police in the clique's territory, he gets shipped out to a clique in another territory to work there for a while. That's where he *chills*, El Niño explains.

He tells me that his clique worked exchanges with other cliques, and that he himself would get moved to San Salvador sometimes, to *chill*, but that members who would get sent over to Hollywood territory didn't necessarily need to chill. Rather, they came because that's where the wells were.

"They came 'cause they figured there were skeletons in these wells. They'd bring homeboys or *bichas* [rivals] that they were *taking for a walk*, or homeboys that couldn't handle their shit, and they'd bring them to our wells, cause we have wells here. The Turín well is the one I gave up. The one in Atiquizaya was already filled up. I didn't give that one up because that was from the old days, from homeboys that are already dead, so what's the point? In the one in Turín, shit … I myself know of four skeletons."

March 12, 2012

"I'm standing here with my hands folded. I wish it weren't so deep and I could just dig it myself with a shovel and a pick, but nope."

Ticas is frustrated. He doesn't have anything to do. For twenty minutes he paces around the well and then stops and says, "See? The same ten meters." He points his finger at the excavated hole descending diagonally down toward the bottom of the well. "Digging in the winter is too dangerous. I've seen it before. The dirt on top mixes with all this stuff below and turns into sludge. Then it buries everything under all that sedimentation."

He sits down next to the well, looking at his hole, the cadavers deep below him.

"I feel hopeless. Duped. As public prosecutors, we've tried everything we could to combat this impunity. There are more than fifteen people down there. I'm sure of it. That's what the detectives have been telling me."

For the past month Ticas has had a backhoe at his disposal. The Civil Engineers of the Armed Forces—the only agency that has paid any attention to the Ahuachapán public prosecutors—loaned him the backhoe. But it doesn't do a thing for him if he doesn't have a couple of dump trucks to go with it. A single backhoe, scooping up one scoop, climbing out of the hole, driving a hundred yards and then getting back in the hole, over and over again, isn't worth the time or the gas.

"I'll say it again," Ticas says, as if his request will bear some new weight now that he's been saying it for the whole year, "a backhoe and two trucks. A backhoe and two trucks. A backhoe and two trucks ..."

It's worth remembering one other detail. A year ago, in January of 2011, Ticas had everything he needed, and in just twenty-four days he was able to dig down ten yards. As the well is fifty-five meters deep, if he had been able to keep digging at that same pace, he would have dug down to the bodies ten months ago.

April 3, 2012

"You seen the sink that's close to that well?" El Niño asks me from his little backyard garden. He's inspecting the radishes he's growing.

I have seen it. Someone had installed a basic sink, probably to carry water from the well where they could wash clothes under the jocote tree. That sink is the setting for El Niño's story, the story of a murder, the story of how every murder story in this country has a backstory. This backstory, however, is difficult to describe: In the gang war, if you're not in the middle of it, a lot of it doesn't seem to make sense.

An example: Members of El Niño's clique once killed an aspiring member because instead of saying he was "*pedo*," or high, after smoking marijuana, he said that he was "*peda*," the feminine version of the same word. The clique took the mistake as a terrible offense because everything they do is masculine and everything the enemy does is feminine. So they killed him, stabbed him to death on the spot. It's hard to understand. Wells don't get filled up with bodies killed for strategic reasons; there isn't even criminal logic to many of the murders in this country. There are bones in the bottom of wells for one simple reason: animal violence. Can I kill? Yes. Can I hide the body? Yes. Will it be hard for authorities to find the body? Yes. Will I be looked upon by fellow gang members as courageous? Yes. Thus, I kill. And after a few kills I get used to killing. Killing becomes part of everyday life. Thus, little by little, wells get filled.

The story El Niño tells is a story of a young man named Ronal Landaverde, the brother of El Gringo, who was, so El Niño and his fellow clique members suspected, an infiltrator from Barrio 18. Ronal wanted to be a salvatrucho. He started smoking with some of the members. The salvatruchos let him smoke until, one day, they changed their minds. They led him to the well in Turín where, they realized, none of them had remembered to bring a pistol. They poked around the area until, next to the sink, they found a cord used to hang clothes; they strangled Ronal with the cord. "Not with a knife," El Niño explains. "Because we didn't want blood in the well."

Reason inside madness.

The body of Ronal is one of the four being looked for by state prosecutors thanks to the testimony of El Niño. For those four bodies, prosecutors brought charges against forty-three members of three different cliques who had been caught after a series of interrogations. All forty-three were arrested in October 2010, which means that by October 2012, if nobody pulls the bodies out of the well, all the detained men, having served the maximum amount of time in jail without being sentenced, will be released. But it's not just those four bodies. Prosecutors expect to turn up many more. They've received information that the well was used as a body-dump by various cliques: Los Ángeles, Parvis, Hollywood, Acajutlas, Priding Gangsters, and Fulton.

May 25, 2012

Ticas is in a good mood. He's been up and down, but now he feels good. At the beginning of April he convinced the MOP to give him back the backhoe, the two trucks and the dump truck. At the end of April, however, they took back all the trucks. All he had left was the backhoe—useless on its own. But then, just a week ago, a surprise: Rumbling past the cornfield one day are three trucks, a dump truck and a bulldozer. The Army and MOP teamed up to find him what he needed. The wet season is still thrusting its head about, but Ticas is optimistic.

"We're going to finish before they let them [the accused gang members] out this time. We'll be done by October."

August 21, 2012

The well is becoming a metaphor for the country. The deeper you dig, the worse things get. The longer you wait to solve a problem, the worse the problem becomes.

The well has flooded. The rains came and flooded everything. When it was all ready to go, only eighteen more meters left to dig of "the damn well," as Ticas now refers to it, it flooded.

The rains fucked up the good summer stats, too. With consistent showers over three months, Ticas only dug twenty-seven yards. Thirty-seven in total.

This is what happens when you let a problem fester: The solution doesn't stay the same. He has all the tools that he needed before. But now he needs a new tool: something to pump out the water.

And yet, Ticas is optimistic. He thinks he'll hit the bottom in a month and a half, and that by October DNA tests will prove that the gangsters are guilty. He's excited that they might find even more bodies down there. He heard that an informant, who used to be part of a gang of kidnappers, said that when they get to the bottom "they're going to be surprised."

August 29, 2012

El Niño gets creative when talking about the well. For example, about the dead at the bottom he tells me, "Those who are in the well didn't die from drying out." Later, in a more reflective mood, he asks himself: "Imagine if someone decided to build a house here, and wanted to clean out the well." It poses one question: How many unknown wells are there? Nestled into our country's cornfields, how many bodies are turning into compost? And how many bloody stories are hidden in the shadows of the jocote trees?

September 3, 2012

A week ago Ticas got a pump to suck out the water. He drains the hole and starts digging again, but it's hard going through all the mud. He's only descended a single yard all week. There are seventeen more to go and just a month and a half until the trial.

Ticas has a new plan: Dive back into the well and figure out exactly what the wall is like that they're going to have to break through. They could try to open a hole in the wall and scurry in like moles to see what's what. He, the detective working the case and a lab technician will be the moles. Each of them will use a different color rope to drop in. That way, Ticas explains, "if there's a disaster, they'll be able to recognize us: I'm red rope, the detective is yellow, and blue for the technician."

October 30, 2012

Ticas is working other cases now. Other cadavers. He's dug up a few young men from Soyapango, in the middle of the country, a few women from Santa Ana, in the west. Meanwhile, the rains are soaking everything in Turín. It's impossible to dig. The pump came in too late. Everybody is asking for their machines back. The backhoe, the dump trucks—they're all returned.

All work at the well in Turín has come to a standstill. Nobody is digging up the dead.

The six gangsters, after being locked up for two years, waiting for something that would never happen, are due to be released.

Ticas, once again, is frustrated.

"Imagine if each of those we let out kills somebody else, or maybe two other people. How many would that be?"

Then he repeats that he would have liked to have dug it all himself with a pick and a shovel.

Maybe he's hit on something: That's who we are as a country, a man with a pick and a shovel trying to dig up our dead, and yet unable to dig deep enough to save them.

Early February 2013

The regional chief of the prosecutor's office, Mario Jacobo, confirms that representatives of the state asked for provisional dismissal of charges for those accused of dumping the bodies into the well. He says it's a strategy in order to get another year to keep digging, that they've been able to pin two of the bodies onto six of the gangsters, and that they're positive there are at least five bodies in the well, if not many more. He hopes that by the end of this month they will get to the "exact point where forensic investigator Ticas wants to be." *After over a year of work*, he would have been able to add.

The chief prosecutor says that provisional dismissal is a "strategy," but in Salvadoran courts many describe provisional dismissal as "dismiss me and never see me again."

February 2, 2013

Media latches back onto the story with headlines like "Twenty Bodies Found in Turín Well" and "Getting to the Bottom of Turín Well." Articles describe a change that people have been unable to explain: The depth of the well is not the same as it used to be; it is now only forty-two meters deep. Water has been leaking in from somewhere. Maybe the digging cracked into a new vein of ground water. Whatever happened, Ticas is now only five meters from reaching the supposed bottom.

In one of the articles, the head of the MOP, Gerson Martínez, is interviewed about his agency's role in the excavation: "The MOP has an agreement with Public Security to collaborate as much as possible." He later adds: "It is a contribution, on the part of MOP, to combat the impunity in this country."

February 27, 2013

El Niño gave testimony yesterday against nineteen members of the Hollywood Locos Salvatrucha clique for committing acts of murder, though none of it relates to the well. Prosecutors are claiming all that's left to do is get to the bottom of the well and determine a court date for the accused, but nobody knows if they will still be in custody at that point, after two and a half years in prison and still without being taken to court.

El Niño says he's tired of going to court and talking so much. Yesterday he identified the accused by nickname: Danger, Maleante (Bad Boy), Gallo Callejero (Street Cock), and Patas (Paws). He says he doesn't know who the other witnesses may have named.

March 30, 2013

Ticas is only four meters from the bottom, four meters away from digging down forty-two meters to the bottom. Almost there, he feels a new fear: that he himself will die inside the well. The digging isn't dry anymore. It's more like digging through a muddy swamp. It's not raining, but water is coming up from below. A subterranean seep, leaking from the walls, bursting with every scoop of the shovel. Despite the danger, and the fear, Ticas is also thrilled, seeing light in the damp darkness.

"We expect to find a tall, thin man from Santa Ana who was thrown in along with his laptop."

His new hypothesis is that they will find the first body at a depth of thirty-nine meters and the last, which they have located with prods, opening small holes that are quickly filled back in with water, at a depth of forty-two meters. Below that, as Ticas reports, "Who knows?"

This is Plan B. Or maybe it's actually Plan C. Or maybe even Plan Z. It's all that's left for him. From the wall of dirt directly in front of Ticas to the well shaft where the bodies are, there are eight more meters. Eight meters straight ahead. Ticas now wants to start digging from above again, from about thirty meters down, digging a five-meter-wide hole heading diagonally into the well shaft. Then, once the prosecutors find him scuba gear, he can drop right into the dark swamp at the bottom of the well, right into that soup of earth and bones.

April 1, 2013

He still hasn't reached the bottom. Today marks 805 days since authorities discovered bodies in the well. Twenty-eight months. This is what we know: At the bottom of the well there are bodies. Maybe ten, maybe twelve, maybe as many as twenty. But definitely at least there are four.

Entering into the small city of Turín, in western El Salvador, if you continue on past the dirt street, cross the train tracks, pass the mud house and continue on through the cornfield, you'll come to an open field with a jocote tree, and next to the tree is the well. At the bottom of the well there are bodies. This is all we know.

7

The Most Miserable of Traitors

July 2013

Without these murderers, hundreds more murderers would be walking the streets. Without these rapists, hundreds more rapists would be stalking the nights. The plea-bargain witness: criminals the state pardons in exchange for their testimony. Their lives in grave peril, many of these men and women are battling the most dangerous gangs of the continent. Nobody but the state backs them up, and often the state becomes their enemy.

The tiny room is in the back. Through the metallic door you can see the sky is threatening to storm, and the heat is a force—a presence—all its own. You can feel it: the heat cramping every corner of the room. That's what the room is, a place that locks in the heat, a place where Abeja (the Bee) used to be locked up. Who would've guessed that he, Abeja, that irreplaceable snitch, the informant of one of the most wanted gangs in the country, would end up, in his attempt to save his own skin, melting away in that tiny room?

To get to the tiny room you have to leave behind the capital of El Salvador, drive down a highway, get stuck in a knot of exurbs, roll back onto another highway and take it almost to the border of the state of Chalatenango and Honduras, ask someone for directions, and then ask another someone, and then a third, until somebody finally tells you how you get to the hidden town of Agua Caliente. At this point you have to stop and ask yourself if your little car will endure the grind of a dirt road full of rocks and chunks of asphalt. You have to burrow into the hills that line the narrow (and fierce) wedge of the Salvadoran north. You have to admire the extravagance of that purple palace crowning a hill in the middle of the rural landscape, its architecture straight from the dreams of Walt Disney. You have to wade through your own doubt: Could that cluster of houses be Agua Caliente? You ask the old campesino what he thinks, and you hear him say that he isn't sure, that he thinks it might be just a little further ahead. You go on. You get to a sign that reads, humbly: "Welcome to Agua Caliente." And still you go on, because there's no other choice but to go on. You ask one person and another person and a third until someone knows where you can find the police post. You have to smile politely at the deer-in-headlights look of surprise that people give an outsider who's going around asking for the police. You pass by the town's tiny park and hook a left as passersby stare and drop their jaws, and then you get to a point where the town runs out of road and smacks into the woods. You convince yourself that one of those tiny rural houses left in the nothing must be it. You backpedal. You ask around. You see big eyes, open mouths. Then, finally, you find the half-built police post.

The police have a pet: a turtle that appears and disappears into a patch of trees framing the entrance. The police post is a three-story house of concrete blocks, the top story left unfinished, without a frame or windows or doors or paint. The front door is open and there's a friendly woman on the first floor who bids you good evening and has no ready answer when you ask to speak to whoever's in charge. "Let me see who's around," she says.

Twenty minutes later a young man comes down from the second floor, looking surprised. He invites you to his office, a stuffy room with no computer and a diagram sketched on the wall of the limited organizational structure: Chief of Post slash Customer Care slash Patrol Officer slash Second Patrol Officer slash Third Patrol Officer.

"How can I help you?" asks the officer.

"I understand that Abeja was held in this post, that he escaped from here."

He lets out a groan. "I thought, since we're so far away, that the capital's media wouldn't touch the story."

"Well, we got the news, and I came to see where exactly you had him. It's probably a delicate matter?"

"Yeah man, it's a real delicate matter. Because this isn't a good place to detain a person like him. There are plenty of good places, designated by law, over there in the capital."

"You knew who Abeja was snitching on, right?"

"Well ... the kid was here ... We didn't know everything there was to know about the situation, but we knew it was delicate."

"And someone like him, here in this area, now that he's escaped, what do you think awaits him?"

"I would think that for someone like him, out there by himself somewhere, it's death that awaits him."

It's Sunday, May 27, 2012, and the police have called every possible media site to El Castillo, the police headquarters of San Salvador. They have something important to show the cameras. Wedged between three large heavily armed officers in balaclavas, José Misael Cisneros stands with his hands cuffed behind him. The thirty-six-year-old man is better known as Medio Millón (Half a Million), and if you've come across any police intelligence report about organized crime in the last eight years, you've surely seen his acne-scarred face. Medio Millón was one of the first Mara Salvatrucha leaders in El Salvador to be named on the US Treasury Department's "blacklist"—included on June 5, 2013. By April 2015 the list contained ten Salvadorans, of whom only Medio Millón is not an active, non-incarcerated MS member. Other members of the list include some of the most notorious clique leaders, including El Diablito de Hollywood (the Hollywood Devil), El Trece (Thirteen), Cruck Colocho de Western (Curly of Western Avenue) and El Viejo Pavas (Old Turkey).

Even surrounded by cops in the heart of El Castillo, Medio Millón looks fearless. He's been on the run since September 14, 2010, when he escaped the 100 policemen sent to capture him. The police attribute their failure to leaked classified information. They're convinced that Medio Millón is the mastermind behind the country's cocaine exports, and that his armed wing is part of one of El Salvador's largest cliques, the Fulton Locos Salvatrucha of the Mara Salvatrucha, which was originally founded in California's San Fernando Valley. According to the police, the clique has 200 members and collaborators in the town of Nueva Concepción alone, which neighbors Agua Caliente and is where they had initially sought to capture the kingpin, Medio Millón.

The police handed their findings over to the Public Prosecutor's Office (PPO), who pressed charges against Medio Millón, against eighteen other Fulton gang members, and even against three police officers from Nueva Concepción. The PPO called three witnesses to court who testified that the gang members and police officers had been close to murdering them under Medio Millón's orders. The PPO also called forward a plea-bargain witness to explain that Medio Millón would routinely hire gangbangers and police as hit men. And yet, on September 18, 2012, the Specialized Trial Court of San Salvador said they didn't believe the witnesses' accounts to be true and thus ruled the defendants innocent of all charges.

But the PPO wasn't left defenseless, nor was Medio Millón set free. With a few punches left, the PPO pressed new charges against Medio Millón, now accused of conspiring with the Fulton Gang, along with forty-seven other Fulton members who were accused of multiple homicides. The PPO argued that at least some of those murders had been committed with a military weapon that Medio Millón had gifted to one of the clique leaders—alias El Simpson. Their evidence was the testimony of yet another plea-bargain witness. On June 5, 2012, Medio Millón was called to court again, and this time the Specialized Trial Court of San Salvador agreed that there was sufficient evidence for a trial. Things were marching along thanks to a gangbanger kid who was willing to spill it all, explaining how the murders were executed and even sketching the scene of Medio Millón strutting down the hill, circled by his bodyguards, handing an AK-47 over to El Simpson. Everything was moving forward because the Salvadoran state had Abeja.

"Where are the cells? Where do you keep the delinquents?" I ask the young officer at the police post of Agua Caliente.

"No," the officer responds. "I mean, we don't have cells, we just have this back room to lock up drunkards and keep them from fighting in the streets. Sometimes we lock up people who commit serious crimes like robbery and extortion, but we end up sending those over to Nueva Concepción where the station is bigger and actually has jail cells."

The tiny back room. The boiling back room.

"And what did Abeja do while he was here?" I ask.

"Nothing. He'd just spend his time locked away," the officer says.

"How much time did he spend here?"

"Some fifteen months."

"And you'd never let him leave for anything?"

"No. I mean if he wanted a soda or something, he'd tell us and we'd do him the favor of getting it for him at the store. But since he hardly ever had the money, well, he hardly ever asked."

In late 2011, Abeja, a twenty-something-year-old kid, sat in front of prosecutors from Chalatenango and, for an undisclosed reason, admitted to being a member of the Fulton Locos

Salvatrucha. He said that his clique dedicated itself to extortion, murder and drug trafficking in the states of San Miguel, Santa Ana, Sonsonate and Chalatenango. He told them many secrets, secrets that spanned sixty-three typed pages. Secrets that the prosecutors gave titles to, including: "Case Closed on Old Street," "Homicide on Don Yon Plaza," "Case of Carmen Guerra." The prosecutors believed Abeja's secrets would help them jail forty-seven gangsters, including Medio Millón. The prosecutors typed in their report: "These facts come from the testimony of the plea-bargain witness, hereafter called Abeja."

I ask the officer: "Did you get more boots on the ground when Abeja was brought out here?"

"Nothing. The unit that brought him, they forgot him. Months passed without them coming back."

When the Salvadoran state deems a criminal's testimony to be credible and potentially useful in bringing charges to other criminals, they stop labeling them as a criminal and corner them into becoming a so-called "plea-bargain witness," a status they sell to the informant as the only way to avoid charges of homicide. The state stopped chasing Abeja and began to rely on him. They promised not to lock him up, but rather to escort him to the Department of Victim and Witness Protection of the Executive Technical Unit of the Justice Sector (UTE), where he'd meet other people like himself, people who had committed crimes and then betrayed their cliques, ratting them out. They offered him protection, food and a roof over his head, at least while the trial lasted. But because Abeja decided he didn't want to go to the UTE, he was handed over to the police instead and promised a box of food once a month.

"What did Abeja eat?" I ask.

"Oh, who knows? They only sent him a box of food once in the fifteen months. Sometimes we gave him some of our food. Sometimes he spent a day or two without eating."

For the local police officers, the star witness in the famous case of Medio Millón was little more than a nuisance. Not only did their guilt sporadically compel them to fork over part of their lunches, but they could no longer use the second floor as a space to relax. The police office of Agua Caliente has thirteen officers. But to say thirteen is really to say five. Usually, four of them are outsourced to another unit. Maybe they're sent to guard a construction site on a highway or to search for bodies on a nearby mountain range. Four others are on vacation. Only five officers are actually here, and they divide themselves into two shifts. The ones on shift right now are patrolling, taking care of complaints. Officers not on shift rest on the second floor, with their eyelids closed, and, when Abeja was here, with their ears perked for any sign of the hungry kid locked up in the back room.

On January 17, 2011, a woman came to the Ombudsmen for the Defense of Human Rights (PDH) in Chalatenango. What this institution does best is issue reports—on everything, sometimes even on the air that blows into their office. About the woman's visit, an officer wrote: "A woman who wished to remain anonymous came into this delegation saying she had a family member detained in the PNC [National Civilian Police] Post of Agua Caliente [the boiling back room] who had recently been released, but she was actually worried about another young man who is still detained. She had gotten into the habit of bringing food to both inmates, but now that her family member has been released she feels sorry for the other inmate who will have no one to bring him food, as he seems to have no family whatsoever and has been locked in that cell [the boiling back room] for a long time."

The next day, two officials from the PDH drove out to the police post and asked for the kid, using his full name (because even though we'll go on calling him Abeja, the woman and the two officials knew the plea-bargain witness's full name and even wrote it in their reports). Abeja muttered that he was grateful for the woman's kindness.

"But you knew what type of witness you had, how important it was that he testify? You knew that he couldn't possibly want to stick around in those conditions?" I say to the officer.

"We knew what he was like. We knew he'd get bored, but there was nothing we could do."

Abeja is not unique. The ugliest thing about all of this is that Abeja doesn't stand out. There are many like him. He, along with all the other plea-bargain witnesses, are criminals we depend on. They're a good part of what fuels the judicial system of El Salvador, of all of Central America. Each year, the UTE assists more than 1,000 people in El Salvador. In the seven years since the Special Law for the Protection of Victims and Witnesses was passed, the program has housed people who betrayed their criminal organizations to get out of prison, or because they hoped for a better life, or because they were victims of those organizations. Assisting all those people who survived the crush of violence includes supplying them with toilet paper, housing needs and baby formula. Most of these people, the great majority of these people, according to data put out by the UTE, have witnessed a homicide or were nearly murdered themselves.

A smaller percentage of these witnesses, about fifty a year, are plea-bargain witnesses who have decided to betray their gangs. Most of these witnesses agree to be interned in safe houses; others, like Abeja, prefer not to. And many more are never granted the status of plea-bargain witness, but are nevertheless kept in rural police posts where they dole out information while locked in tiny rooms or cells, in a state of limbo between being jailed and being sheltered. Only a judge can grant plea-bargain-witness status. As Mauricio Rodríguez, the director of UTE's Department of Witness and Victim Protection, told me, it can take months for an informant to be declared a plea-bargain witness. While awaiting the judge's decision, UTE can't do a thing for that person.

Many of us celebrate the fact that Viejo Lin, the national kingpin of Barrio 18, is now behind bars, but few of us remember Luis Miguel, the plea-bargain witness who incriminated him. For many of us, it's a relief that Chino Tres Colas (Three-tail Chinaman), another kingpin of the same gang, has joined the likes of Viejo Lin, but few know about Zeus, Apolo, Orion, Aries and Neptune. The trial of the thirteen gang members accused of twenty-two homicides in Sonsonate made national news, but no one thanked Raúl. Those gang members were known as the Baggers because of how they'd wrap the limbs of their victims' bodies in black bags. No one thanked Zafiro and Topazio for solving the Massacre of Las Pilitas. No one thanked Daniel for explaining how Los Sicarios, a clique made up, in part, of police officers, operated in eastern El Salvador. On Monday, May 28, a large number of the Salvadoran population saw Medio Millón handcuffed on national news, but no one saw Abeja go hungry in the tiny, boiling room of Agua Caliente.

Murderers, rapists, slayers. Witnesses, respondents, confessors. Few understand the overlap of these categories as well as Israel Ticas, the man who exhumes the dead from the ground, the only forensic investigator in all of El Salvador. From the year 2000 until today, Ticas has exhumed 703 bodies.

It's hard to find a good time to talk with Ticas. He tells the story he wants to tell, and the little ditty playing along with the cartoons on the TV in the small restaurant where we're meeting is going to have to be the background music.

First, the numbers. Cold and grim: Most of the 703 bodies Ticas recovered were thanks in part to the help of plea-bargain witnesses. Twenty-seven bodies from the bottoms of twelve wells. He was tipped off to eight of those wells by neighbors who'd noticed a fetid stink in the air, or simply by catching someone in the act of throwing over a body. Thanks to plea-bargain witnesses, Ticas was tipped off to another four wells. Thanks to plea-bargain witnesses, Ticas has recovered sixteen of those twenty-seven bodies.

Now, his words. Perhaps the worst part of this story. "One time I pulled out a boy about five years old and a girl about eight. The witness said they promised the girl that they wouldn't kill her little brother if she let herself be raped by fifteen men. They raped her and then killed them both. It was in Ateos, in 2006. I found the two bodies hugging."

"Do you feel the witnesses are sorry for their actions?"

"No. They're totally calm. I admire that about those fuckers. They're not even embarrassed. I remember a white guy who died of AIDS. He got to be so nice after he got sick. His wife was the last body he threw into that well. I asked him, 'So you killed your wife?' 'Yep,' he said to me, 'the Maras told me she knew too much. I told her she had to die. She got on her knees and asked me if she could please say good-bye to our three kids. We went to the house and she kissed each one on the forehead. Then I brought her back here, she was begging, telling me I could tell the Maras that I'd already killed her, that she could flee the country. I told her that an order is an order. I beheaded her and I threw her head over while her body was still squirming.' That's how I found her, on top of another nine bodies. 'You'll find a knife in her vagina,' the witness had told me. And that's what I found."

"Have you gotten any therapy?"

"Nothing."

"What do you think of these plea-bargain witnesses?"

"They're important to my work because they tell me what I'm going to find under the ground, they tell me what happened. They're invaluable. I've worked with some thirty witnesses who have given me details, and then I verify if it's true, and that's evidence, that's on the record."

Few could start with the story of the eight-year-old girl and end with what he sees as the importance of these miserable traitors who participated in the murder of that same eight-year-old girl, but Ticas understands this country. One of the girl's rapists is now free; fourteen others are behind bars.

In the restaurant, the cartoons drone on.

This is another restaurant, another conversation. On the other side of the table sits a longtime police investigator who's been shuttled from one division to another. This officer has participated in police raids based on information gleaned from plea-bargain witnesses. They betray; he raids. Without them, he would've had to endure long stretches with very little to do over the course of his policing career.

"For me, just hearing them talk gives me the runs," he says about the witnesses, for whom he feels not an ounce of gratitude. "They're sons of bitches, they're police-slayers. Any chance they get, they escape from the safe houses. They'll go on extorting people from inside the safe houses. Just fifteen days ago one of them escaped. He called and said he'd come back but only if we brought him his wife. The fucker. I'm not going to spend my time looking after that lazy fucker's wife."

Police don't like to talk about, as the cop termed them, "gangbangers who want to save their own skin." In fact, even on an institutional level they don't like to talk about them. I spent weeks asking the police communications department to talk to me about plea-bargain witnesses, but after several tries the department told me it was impossible to find anyone willing to talk, especially if I was planning on bringing up Abeja.

Plea-bargain witnesses, especially former gang members, have to deal with the fact that their cliques have committed many crimes against the police. In other words, their guardians will often have a profound hate for them. Sometimes they're even forced to testify about the complicity of the police. Abeja did exactly that in Medio Millón's trial.

Their supposed anonymity (many police officers know them

intimately) is like a bad and dangerous joke. Giving them a code name is often just a court formality, nothing more. It doesn't protect them.

I spent hours talking with a key witness, Liebre, also known as El Niño Hollywood, a hit man of the Mara Salvatrucha who unabashedly told me what his gang name was and what his previous gang name had been before that, even giving me the go-ahead to publish names. El Niño, from the Hollywood Locos Salvatrucha clique, was the principal hit man for Chepe Furia (discussed in Chapter 1) and had survived a murder attempt at the hands of a gang of ex-military agents who came looking for him at the police post where he was being held. Luckily, the local police managed to stop the hit men. When I first met with El Niño, one of his attackers had just been granted status as a plea-bargain witness; in exchange for his testimony he'd been forgiven any charges related to his attempted murder of El Niño.

El Niño's also received death threats coming from inside the prison of Ciudad Barrios. Local police officers, so El Niño tells me, have invited him out of his cell on the condition that he murder someone for them in a ploy to get him out so they could kill him. Thanks in large part to his testimony, Chepe Furia, leader of the Hollywood Locos Salvatrucha of Atiquizaya, was condemned to twenty-two years in prison.

El Niño lives among a handful of officers who hate him, in the middle of a zone largely controlled by the clique he came close to obliterating. El Niño's situation, as we'll see, isn't very different from what Abeja lived through.

On a dark and cloudy evening, El Niño curls up on his porch in front of a car-tire-turned-coffee-table, where he sets the dollar sweet bread his wife brings out to us.

I ask him what he most misses of his former life, and he tells me he misses hunting lizards and crabs near the river. If he were a free man, he says, what he would most like to do is simply go to the park with his daughter. His two-year-old daughter observes us from afar, waiting to be fed the boiled *güisquiles,* served with salt and lime, that her mother has set out on the tire. That's what El Niño would like to do—if he were free. Because even though he's not locked up, he feels locked up. He knows there are people who want to kill him, and the tiny shack where he lives is only, as he says, "a golden cage."

El Niño is sick of the state telling him he's been exonerated. He's been living as a plea-bargain witness for three years, and he's put clique leaders, as well as dozens of hit men, behind bars. He knows that without his help, Chepe Furia, Liro Yocker (Little Joker), El Extraño (the Stranger), El Maniático (the Maniac) would not be locked up, because the only thing the state has against them is his testimony.

El Niño pauses before answering. Though he speaks in gang slang, the content of his words is the product of pure reflection. He seems to turn to stone before responding.

"How has the state treated you?"

"It's fucked up. Sometimes they give me eggs, but the problem is that I'm constantly asking the police for money for tortillas. For my little girl, the UTE only sent one package when she was born: some clothes, shoes, towels, diapers, little things like that, basic things. But that was the only time. She can't use any of that anymore because she's grown now. I haven't been able to buy her a little dress. If I were out of here, I could make $40 a day no problem."

"What happens if your little girl gets sick?"

"They've never offered medical help. I've had to go out to get it. When my girl got sick I spent $20 at a clinic in Ahuachapán. One friendly cop gave me $5. Another time, when I had to take her to a hospital, another cop gave me $5. That's all the help I had."

"And what else are you lacking?"

"No shoes. No clothes. Everything I have has been given to me. One time some agents bought me some used clothes. But they should have just left me to fend for myself. I'd be better off. Milk, sometimes there's some in the UTE food box. They told me they were going to give me $9 a day. One time they even sent me a box with no beans."

The monthly UTE box is nothing luxurious. It's supposed to include four pounds of beans, some rice, pasta, salsas, salt, sugar, oil, toilet paper, soap, toothbrushes.

Rodríguez, of the UTE, told me that this was typical. Every year he has to deal with the government's penny-pinching. The UTE budget is about $4 million a year, but after accounting for the paychecks of the many police officers hired to guard the safe houses, after accounting for the more than 1,000 witnesses, the food boxes and all the white-collar protected witnesses who demand better housing, the budget simply doesn't cut it.

"There are people we house in $500-a-month apartments because they demand those conditions," Rodríguez explains. "Sometimes I have to beg doctors to give me baby formula for free." And then there's months when the government refuses to pass a budget. "That's absolute hell because we have to deal with the fact that we simply can't pay rent, and we have to see how we'll find the money to send everyone their food boxes." Rodríguez remembers when they were trained by the US Marshals Service to implement the directives of US courts, including the overhaul of the witness protection program. A marshal explained to Rodríguez that in the United States, witness protection involved moving the witness and their families to another state, giving them at least a year of job training, housing, food, a monthly income and changing their identity. Rodríguez smiles, imagining what he could do with such resources. By law, the UTE cannot hand out cash, it cannot change a witness's identity, and only in very special cases can it continue to offer protection once the witness has finished his or her court process. In most cases, after giving testimony, the protection is over, the food box is done. Though the food boxes seldom come anyway.

"If you could only see the safe houses," Rodríguez says, "if you could see how we manage to cut corners. We plant vegetables in makeshift gardens on rooftops, we buy them plastic pools to raise tilapia. We do it all."

Back to my conversation with El Niño.

"You don't think you'll sink back in the game?"

"I can't say. Even here, I've been offered to do some jobs."

"What do you think we Salvadorans owe you?"

"I've risked my life. I got off the streets and got a fuckton of hit men off the streets with me. That's why there's a hell of a lot of people who want to kill me now. Police, gang members. I don't know who works for who here. I don't want to be in danger no more, I have my little girl to think about. Society doesn't care about my safety, they only care that I've testified. They should stop and think. They should say to themselves, 'Ay, things could go really bad for this roach. He has his little girl. He has his woman. Let's at least give him a little job.'"

It's June 21, 2013. We're at the City Hall of Ilopango, a suburban city of San Salvador, along with four leaders from various Barrio 18 cliques. The government and the gangs have just made a truce, and Barrio 18 cliques have come together to yell at city officials who have been creating more community projects in zones dominated by the Mara Salvatrucha. Barrio 18 is starting to get desperate.

The clique leaders agree to sit down at a table in City Hall and answer some questions. The first is simple and direct: What is a plea-bargain witness? The lead spokesman, who wields his political power from behind prison bars, says: "They're liars who incriminate people who haven't ever been involved. It's nowhere near justice. Because of a witness, ten, twenty people are accused, and many weren't even involved." Another of the gangsters speaks up: "[A plea-bargain witness] is a traitor, a snitch who endangers our family."

Surely, if we weren't at City Hall, if we were on their turf and sitting around shooting the shit, their words would be far less measured. Now, in their roles as negotiators of "the truce," they're riding the brakes throughout the conversation.

"And," adds the chief spokesman, "the police are always fucking with you to say more. They tied me up, hit me and left me in Alaska [MS turf] for them to kill me. All this because I said to them: 'Kill me, I'm not a little bitch, I won't tell you a thing.' The police threaten you with death but that doesn't mean you talk."

I ask a question even though I feel I'm already hearing its answer in their voices. It's one of those questions that, for obvious reasons, sounds pretty dumb: "Would you forgive a plea-bargain witness?" The gruffest of the bunch answers: "I'll put it this way. If someone did it the first time, they'll do it again, and if he didn't already spill a fuck-ton of blood, he'll spill it the next time."

We have time for one last question. "Is the state able to keep the witnesses anonymous, or do you guys usually find out who betrayed you?" The four exchange looks and smiles. The leader responds: "It's as if someone in your family started a rumor. You know who started it, when they started it and how they started it." The gruff one has something else to say, the words already in his mouth: "You always know, because you can see their family start to disappear, and the one who got the 'status,' sooner or later, he's going to disappear, too."

"No, we don't have a cell. That's why he couldn't have broken through any bars. This isn't a cell, it's just the little room at the end of the first floor. Just above the septic tank."

Under Abeja's room was a tank of shit.

The guy speaking is the chief of the police post of Agua Caliente. I finally got him on the phone. I gave him my cell number, but because the police post's telephone can't call cell phones, he wasn't able to call me back. The chief of investigations of Chalatenango had lied to me. He'd told me that Abeja had broken through the bars of his cell and escaped. It was a lie. There was no cell and no bars. And because the post isn't fit for an inmate, the police simply outfitted the room—a place to temporarily lock up a drunk—above a tank of shit.

"We'll sometimes lock up a binge drinker but only so they'll stop bothering people. We hold them two, three days and then let them go. But we never keep murderers here. It's dangerous for us and dangerous for them. That kid (Abeja), when they brought him here, they told us they'd only keep him here one night, but they left him here fifteen months."

Abeja didn't escape from prison. Abeja escaped from a tiny, boiling room above a septic tank in a police post that, with luck, is staffed by two officers at a time.

The circumstances of Abeja's transfer to Agua Caliente seem accidental. Agua Caliente is the city in which Medio Millón, the man against whom Abeja testified, was born. Agua Caliente is ruled by the Fulton Locos Salvatrucha clique— forty-seven of whose members Abeja was testifying against. That's to say, of the 262 municipalities in El Salvador, the state chose to lock Abeja up in the town where Medio Millón was born. The PNC has dozens of delegations staffed with police. The PNC has at its disposal, and only a half hour away from this police post with its septic-tank stink, a real police office with a real jail cell, several patrol cars and more officers. But the PNC decided that it was best to travel the unpaved road, get lost in the Salvadoran north, drive over dirt and rocks and dirt and rocks for half an hour and keep Abeja in the town in which Medio Millón was born. The state thought it was best to keep their key witness locked up above a septic tank without any food.

And there are—surely there are—people who enjoy the thought of Abeja—an ex-gang member, a murderer, a rapist and an extortionist—writhing with hunger in a boiling, shit-stinking room. But because Abeja left, because Abeja is no longer with us, no one will be able to tell the jury that the body found on July 3, 2010, in the village of Ex Ira, was Francisco Domínguez; no one will be able to say that Jessica took him home with the promise of sex and then, when Francisco had stripped down to his red boxers, in came El Tigre, El Simpson and Abeja, who strung wire around his neck and shoved a gun so deep down his throat that blood shot out of his nose. No one is going to tell us that El Simpson ordered Chino killed because he wanted to quit the Fulton clique, because he no longer wanted to be a hit man. No one is going to be able to say that that's why he was shot to death in a ditch near Nueva Concepción. No one will talk about how Doña Carmen Guerra was murdered because she had a "close relationship with the police." No one will remember that the gang member known as Monge—no one else will even know his full name—asked Doña Carmen Guerra for a cup of water, which she gave to him, and for which he thanked her with several .38-caliber shots. No one is going to say how a girl threw herself on top of Monge, begging him to stop shooting at Doña Carmen Guerra. No one will talk about the murder of Isaías Alcides Carrillo, the vegetable vendor who was shot in the head. No one will talk about the M16 still on the streets, or the 9 millimeter, the .38-caliber, the .357.

No one, of course, will be able to say that "at about noon, in comes Misael, alias Medio Millón ... In rolls a gray 4Runner truck, along with a bodyguard ... I was there, and El Simpson and El Rayder, who tells El Simpson that Medio Millón would be coming by with an automatic from Nueva Concepción. And Medio Millón is the first to get out, then the bodyguard, and Medio Millón has two 9 millimeters and the bodyguard has an AK-47 that he gives to El Simpson. And Medio Millón says: 'Here it is, we've already come to an understanding.'" No one will tell us any of these things.

No one will tell us these things because the person who was

going to tell us got sick of going hungry, of feeling overheated, of getting no more than shit stink in return for his testimony. No one will tell us because Abeja got sick of all this one day in June and unhooked a couple three-inch rods, opened the half-broken doors to the balcony, crawled up a space about the size of an elevator chute and climbed to the third floor. He left behind the septic tank, hopped over the next-door neighbor's fence and ran.

"I think," the officer says, "that if he has any enemies out there, they'll probably boot him into the next life."

8

El Niño Hollywood's Death Foretold

November 2014

Miguel Ángel Tobar, known as El Niño Hollywood, ex-member of the Hollywood clique of the Mara Salvatrucha, was murdered on November 21, 2014. A key witness for the state, having helped send more than thirty gang members to prison, he was also a murderer. Even as they promised to protect him, state officials always knew that it was only a matter of time before he'd be murdered. This is the brief story of a man I knew was going to be killed.

Since 2009 Miguel Ángel Tobar knew that he was going to be murdered. Sometimes he thought it'd be the Salvadoran police. Other times he thought it'd be members of Barrio 18. Usually, though, when he thought of his impending death, he was convinced members of his old gang, the Mara Salvatrucha, would be the ones to kill him.

At thirty years old, Miguel Ángel Tobar was convinced he wasn't going to die of a heart attack, from a fall or from old age—definitely not from old age. Sometimes, he thought he'd be gunned down on a dusty trail in the western Salvadoran state of Santa Ana, or maybe Ahuachapán. From 2012 on, as far as I know, he was always conscious of "the Beast" that followed him. He referred to the Beast as violent death that didn't take you from this life, but tore you from it. He talked about it because he knew it, because he had been the one to execute it so many times. He talked about it all the time. Which is why, a year ago, he went to recover a 12-gauge shotgun from where he'd buried it on an empty plot of land. He'd stolen the gun from a gas station security guard during a robbery, which the police had ordered him to carry out, in a town called El Congo.

Tobar felt he needed more backup, and so he got his hands on another gun, a .357 pistol, though the police confiscated it when he was walking outside of his shack in the Las Pozas neighborhood of San Lorenzo, in Ahuachapán state. The Beast always close at his heels, he crossed undetected into Guatemala at the beginning of 2014 and paid $20 for a *trabuco*, a hand cannon—two tubes of metal that, when slammed together, shot out a 12-gauge shell. Though Tobar knew he'd someday be murdered, he wanted to avoid being cut up, tortured or hanged. He was hoping for a single gunshot.

He was so confident he'd be killed that he didn't mind openly talking to me about it. Ever since I met him one January, two years previously, I'd been trying to stop by and see him at least once a month. I paid him a routine visit on Tuesday, March 14, 2014. That day in March he felt like he was closer to death than usual. The night before, someone had told him that a couple of young men had strolled into the neighborhood looking for "the gangster living around here." Tobar and I talked inside a pickup truck with tinted windows. I kept the motor running the whole time.

"Hey man, there's a problem," I told him. "You're always changing numbers so it's hard to find you. You need to give me the numbers of some of your family members so I can call them to get ahold of you."

"Yeah OK. In case something comes up ... I mean, so they can let you know when they get me: 'Hey, they killed El Niño.'"

He always referred to himself by the nickname he used when he was still in the gang: El Niño of the Hollywood Locos Salvatrucha clique of Atiquizaya, or, simply: El Niño Hollywood.

On Friday, November 21, 2014, it wasn't one of his family members who called me. It was a neighbor. I got a call at 3:43 in the afternoon telling me that what we'd all been expecting to happen had finally happened. "Hey, bad news," the neighbor said to me. "They did it to El Niño in San Lorenzo."

Miguel Ángel Tobar was a killer.

If you asked him how many people he'd killed, he'd tell you: "I've wasted … wasted about fifty-six. About six women and the rest men. I'm including faggots as men, 'cause I've killed two faggots."

A killer.

In police files there is evidence of thirty homicides in which El Niño participated as a member of MS, which is, according to the FBI, the most dangerous gang in the world. The gang was founded in the late '70s in Southern California but was then uprooted, along with 4,000 of its members, and sent to Guatemala, Honduras and El Salvador as the region descended into civil war in the late '80s. Today, in El Salvador alone there are an estimated 40,000 members. What the United States tried to flush away has rather multiplied.

Miguel Ángel Tobar was a killer.

He was ruthless. In 2005, working with other gang members, he killed a twenty-three-year-old man known as Caballo (Horse). Caballo had done something idiotic: He'd tattooed a "1" on one thigh and an "8" on the other, even though he had two letters ("M" and "S") already tattooed on his chest. Somehow, Caballo pulled off being a member of rival gang Barrio 18 when it made sense for him and then passed himself off as a member of MS whenever that made sense for him. Tobar found out his secret, lured him into a rural area of Atiquizaya, along with some other MS members. And then he killed him. Before he died, however, when he was limbless but still breathing, they managed to torture him for a few more minutes. When the body of Caballo was found he had no arms or legs left, no tattoos. That was the day when Tobar, who was then known in his clique as Payaso (Clown) thanks to his long, large-mouthed and impish face, changed his name to El Niño, because as they were ripping out Caballo's heart, he had an epiphany— the act seemed like the birth of a baby. Of a *niño*.

Miguel Ángel Tobar was a killer.

Everybody's always known it. The police knew they were dealing with a killer when they first approached him in 2009 for help in solving crimes committed by members of the Hollywood Locos Salvatrucha. They never thought otherwise. In fact, the chief of police who came to his shack in Las Pozas on the day he decided to turn against his gang needed to take the necessary precautions. El Niño was armed that day with a .40-caliber pistol and a .357 and had been smoking crack. And yet El Niño still agreed to go with the chief of police to the police station in El Refugio.

El Niño felt fenced in. Members of his clique were beginning to get suspicious that he was the one who'd murdered the three gangsters from the Parvis Locos Salvatrucha clique (from a neighboring city of Atiquizaya) who had killed his brother. In the heart of every gang is a mangrove tangle of intrigue and conspiracy. El Niño's brother, known in the clique as El Cheje (Woodpecker), was murdered in 2007. Since then, little by little, and without telling other members in his clique, El Niño was getting his revenge. He killed Chato, Zarco and Mosco (Shorty, Blue and Fly), each with one shot to the head. The fourth, Coco, fled to western El Salvador after seeing his friends drop, one by one, shot in the head by the brother of his victim. And yet Tobar was much more than a murderer. He was a key witness for the police and the attorney general's office to arrest more than thirty members of the Hollywood, Parvis and Ángeles cliques of Santa Ana and Ahuachapán. It was his testimony that led a judge to sentence the two leaders of the Hollywood clique to twenty-two years in prison. One of the leaders, El Extraño (the Stranger), was a thirty-year-old man from Atiquizaya. The other more well-known gangster, Chepe Furia, was described by the ex-minister of security and justice, Manuel Melgar, as having raised the gang to the ranks of an organized crime group. Today, thanks to El Niño's testimony before a judge in San Miguel, Chepe and El Extraño are both serving twenty-two-year sentences for having murdered a police informant in Usulután State on November 24, 2009.

Miguel Ángel Tobar was a killer.

And yet, without his help, thirty other killers would be running loose in El Salvador. And probably—most probably—he was killed for lending a hand to justice in El Salvador. He probably would have put another eleven men behind bars—men allegedly responsible for dumping their victims' bodies in a well in Turín—but he wasn't able to testify before he himself was killed.

On November 21, it wasn't just a killer who was killed. A state-protected plea-bargain witness was killed. The state had given him a new name: Liebre (Jackrabbit) or sometimes Yogui. That was what they called him in the case files and in court when he appeared with a balaclava on his head and in a police uniform too big for his small, stout frame. Still, Miguel Ángel Tobar was murdered while under the state's protection.

The turned-over bicycle, the puddle of blood that poured out of his head—just thirty steps from the San Lorenzo police station, off of Portillo Street. It's 8 p.m.

It's Friday, November 21, 2014.

San Lorenzo is north of Santa Ana, passing the park in the town center and heading twelve miles up a two-lane road that runs through the valley of Atiquizaya. I arrive with my brother, Juan, who'd been visiting El Niño with me since January 2012.

The police station on the edge of the city is a small building illuminated by just a few streetlights. At this hour, most of the streets are already dark. Residents in San Lorenzo go to sleep not long after the chickens. There's nobody out but a few young people, talking in the plaza, who turn to notice when our truck passes.

Two policemen, neither of whom seem frightened, stand outside the station as we pull up. If a pickup with tinted windows stopped next to a rural police station at night almost anywhere in El Salvador, most cops would have their guns in hand. If they don't, as they don't here in San Lorenzo, it's because they don't think that the country has reached a critical point of violence. And, to them, it hasn't. In San Lorenzo, which has a population of about 10,000, there were, according to police statistics, zero homicides in 2013. In 2012, there were two. In 2011: zero. So far in 2014 there's been one homicide, which occurred two hours previously: the murder of Miguel Ángel Tobar, otherwise known as El Niño Hollywood. Since June of 2012, this is the first recorded murder in the city, which makes San Lorenzo stand out in the country.

After a brief chat with the policemen, it's clear that El Niño was recognized in the town as someone destined to die. "He was problematic," one of the cops says to me. "A delinquent. Just this year he had a problem with a colleague from the Santa Ana Division of Criminal Investigation (DIC) who was having some drinks in this boy's neighborhood."

Everyone in the neighborhood knew El Niño. As homicide statistics prove, San Lorenzo is not a city with a gang problem. El Niño himself described it as a place of robberies not perpetrated by gangs but by groups of truck thieves. It was a thruway, and not a home, for gangsters moving between Atiquizaya and Guatemala. When El Niño first arrived, in the middle of 2014, word soon spread that there was a gangster, or a man who turned against his gang, or maybe even a leader of a gang who was now living in Las Pozas. Rumors flew. The first time I visited him, as we chatted in the truck with the motor still running, some curious locals stopped by to get a look at who had come to visit the infamous Niño Hollywood. Street salesmen, neighbors, even a few students from the small school in the dusty Las Pozas neighborhood came by to snoop and sightsee.

The police hated him for the simple fact that he'd been a gangster. He spoke like a gangster and caused trouble like a gangster. He was also irreverent and smoked a lot of pot.

A number of cops also hated him because he was the plea-bargain witness in a case against two Atiquizaya policemen: José Wilfredo Tejada, on the Atiquizaya homicide unit, and Walter Misael Hernández, on the extortion unit. These two policemen had ordered the arrest of the young man who was murdered by Chepe Furia later that same day. El Niño had seen the victim with Chepe only a few hours earlier, and his testimony not only tied up the case against Chepe but outlined the police's involvement in the murder.

El Niño lived with his eighteen-year-old girlfriend and their two-year-old daughter, Marbely. The family got by on what work El Niño could find, which mostly entailed growing marijuana or trafficking small amounts from Guatemala to sell to the few users he knew who lived in the area. He also received a largely insufficient food box from the Executive Technical Unit (UTE) of the Justice Sector.

The UTE supports 1,000 people a year, most of them victims or witnesses of crimes. Only about fifty a year are, like El Niño, protected plea-bargain witnesses: murderers, thieves or coyotes involved in crimes and protected by the attorney general's office. The setup is simple: protection and support in exchange for testifying against your former criminal accomplices, typically fellow gang members. It was through UTE that El Niño was provided with his shack and his monthly basket of supplies: four pounds of beans, four pounds of rice, pasta, salsa, salt, sugar, oil, toilet paper, soap and a razor. That was it. In order to buy more food, clothes, plus milk for his daughter, El Niño started selling marijuana.

After January of 2014, the aid basket stopped coming. There was no explanation or warning; it just didn't come anymore. El Niño still needed to testify against the police and the suspects concerning the well in Turín—which he himself had used as a mass grave for his victims' bodies. But it wasn't the only thing that stopped. His $60 stipend stopped coming as well.

In March, El Niño decided to leave behind his pregnant girlfriend and daughter and find a safer place to live.

At first he stayed in a small, abandoned hut (built years ago by a local farmer) on a nearby hillside. He kept his 12-gauge shotgun—the one he procured during a robbery he committed on behalf of the police—nearby for protection. El Niño had infiltrated a group of his gang members and was planning on informing the cops, minute by minute, as he and his fellow gang members proceeded with the crime. He held up his end of the bargain. He sent text messages as he and his accomplices were on the way to the gas station, but the police never arrived, and so he went through with the robbery and stole the security guard's shotgun, along with some money. He later buried the shotgun for his own future security, and then recovered it shortly after leaving his shack. That was around the same time he'd invited three men, three *ganyeros* (potheads—a word derived from "ganja"), to leave Las Pozas with him. The *ganyeros* had problems with a few MS members who would occasionally come to Las Pozas to make sure their rivals, from Barrio 18, hadn't taken control of this no man's land. In Las Pozas, disputed territory, you can see tags of both the 18s and the MS.

El Niño and his three refugees took turns sleeping in the hillside hut: Two rested while the other two kept watch; they only went down the hill if they needed something.

The first time I visited him outside of El Refugio, El Niño told me to wait for him in the shade of a huge ficus tree along the side of the road to San Lorenzo. It was Barrio 18 territory. As I waited for El Niño, a few boys eyed my pickup

Kevin Ignacio Vasquez Maldonado in the arms of his mother, San Pedro Sula, Honduras

Schoolchildren examine the blood left by the killing of a seventeen-year-old boy in Ciudad Credisa, El Salvador

A noticeboard of missing persons at the Institute of Legal Medicine, San Salvador. The bodies of those who die violent deaths in the city are taken here, and families looking for missing relatives frequent the institute.

Israel Ticas, "forensic archaeologist," exhumes the bodies of several gang victims

Vultures in a graveyard, Guatemala City

El Mezquital, a Guatemalan gang neighborhood

Funeral for Carlos Sorto Alfredo Ramirez, July 29, 2012, El Salvador. Ramirez was a Barrio 18 gang member shot dead by police.

Ramirez's eighteen-year-old girlfriend, eight months pregnant, weeps over the coffin

Pictures here record the location of prisoners in the Izalco prison, El Salvador. This medium-security institution houses Barrio 18 members exclusively.

The Cojutepeque prison, a former barracks housing approximately 1,200 inmates in a space designed for 300

La Esperanza, a prison known as Miami, has become a symbol of the deficiencies of the Salvadoran penitentiary system. Overcrowding not only forces prisoners to endure medieval living conditions, but stymies any attempt by the authorities to control them.

The former library of La Esperanza is now a cell of stifling humidity. Inmates are allowed out for twenty minutes each day to exercise.

In San Salvador, gang members of the Mara Salvatrucha (MS-13) and Barrio 18 conducted a symbolic disarmament to show their willingness to make peace

Migrants traveling in the space between wagons. In the south of Mexico, it is common for hundreds of undocumented people to ride a single train.

Guatemalans Melisa and Beverly, twenty-four and seven years old respectively, in Arriaga, Oaxaca, on their way to Ixtepec. Intercepted in Tapachula, Chiapas, they had to bribe agents from the National Migration Institute the equivalent of about $100 to continue their journey.

Erotic dancing at the Calypso Club, Cacahuatán, Chiapas. Many of the Central American prostitutes working this area are victims of trafficking.

on the side of the road, seemingly in the middle of nowhere. Then, suddenly, El Niño burst onto the street. He had a short machete in his hand and his hand cannon and five 12-gauge cartridges on his belt. He was wearing the same balaclava that he wore on top of his head like a hat during the first trial. He jumped in the backseat of the pickup (my brother Juan was in the passenger seat) and started frantically looking around, obviously frightened. "Hit it! Hit it!" he said. "Step on it!"

I hit it.

As we were passing through Atiquizaya El Niño scrunched down in the seat as far as he could, covering his face. We checked into a seedy motel on the Santa Ana highway, closed and double-locked the door, and only then did he relax enough to talk.

Little by little, measuring the risks in Las Pozas, he had decided to go back to his mother's house, where he had been born and raised. Living on high alert, he had set up a system with his *ganyeros* to maintain a constant lookout for anything unusual.

It became a lot harder to find him after he moved out of El Refugio. He'd ditch his cell phone every week. To sell marijuana in town he'd travel through the backcountry to Guatemala. Soldiers and police stopped him a number of times. They confiscated his weapons. Once, they arrested him while he was fishing, finding two joints on him. The police took him to Atiquizaya where, despite having told them that he'd retired from the Central Locos Salvatrucha clique, they locked him up in the dungeon (as they sometimes call the jails) with MS members. That was October 2013. He told me that a cop passed by his cell and said: "This is El Niño de Hollywood, the man who put Chepe Furia into prison." Luckily, he'd hidden a pocketknife blade in his sock. He holed himself up in the corner of the cell and the other gangsters—whom he described as very young—couldn't work up the courage to attack the notorious ex–Hollywood Loco. All the while, brandishing his blade to keep the young gangsters at bay, he was under protection of the state. Or at least on paper he was. Finally, the local police were given the order to release him.

El Niño was what he was: a criminal who'd lived a hard life. Set free, he fought in cantinas and once, when a drunk policeman came by his house and started insulting him—calling him an "asshole, a Mara traitor, a faggot"—El Niño whaled on him, knocking the cop unconscious. Hours later, the policeman was shot twice by a 12-gauge shotgun. He lived and later accused El Niño. Three witnesses I spoke with, however, told me that two other men were responsible. El Niño didn't have his shotgun at the time and insisted that the shooters were "two Barrio 18 idiots" who, according to him, were passing by the Santa Ana police station when they saw a drunk cop and decided to take advantage of the opportunity and kill him.

At the end of our visits, he would usually say good-bye in the same way: "Alright, well, let's see if I'm still alive the next time you come around."

The police described the murder scene in the following way:

El Niño was riding a bike on Portillo Street, which connects with a number of dirt paths that lead to Las Pozas. Two men, about forty years old, both fat and with crew cuts, swerved at him in a tuk-tuk. He ditched his bike and started running. The first of six bullets hit him from behind. The first drops of blood specked the pavement only a yard away from where his bike came to rest. El Niño kept moving forward as they shot him two more times, once in the back of his head, right behind his ear, and the other in the ribs. More blood dripped onto the pavement about fifteen paces away. Another fifteen paces and he fell face down. He was able to turn around to fight back, but the shooters quickly pumped three more bullets into him. Head and chest. The shells are there, next to the pool of blood on the red-spattered pavement. After the body was taken away, the scene looked as if a dying animal had dragged itself across the ground. The shooters fled not into the hills, but directly into San Lorenzo in the same coughing tuk-tuk they'd come in on. Though the crime scene was about fifty meters from the police station, an officer didn't arrive until about twenty minutes after the shooting. There was never any search for or investigation of the killers.

I imagine El Niño shaking on the pavement, blood coming out of his mouth. I knew him. I know that he fought like mad. They'd already tried to kill him once before. He fought like a cornered animal, with everything he had. He always said that his time was coming and that there was a slim chance the Beast would kill him peacefully. "No way, that would be weak," he would say. And he said it because he knew it, because he had been that beast himself.

Earlier that Friday, November 21, the day of his death, El Niño had gone to San Lorenzo to register the birth of his second daughter. At three months old, they named her Jennifer. Jennifer lost her father the same day that he legally recognized her as his own.

Nobody, not a cop, a prosecutor, a judge or a UTE official, lifted a finger to keep El Niño safe. Nobody ensured that his food box was delivered. All of the policemen I spoke to about his case, over the course of two years, knew that El Niño was going to be murdered. They talked about it like it wasn't a concern or a failure on their part.

In March of 2014 I published the chronicle "The Spine of the Mara Salvatrucha" on *El Faro*, where I am a reporter, a profile of El Niño that my brother Juan and I co-wrote. About a month later, my brother Carlos, also a reporter for *El Faro*, told me that Raúl Mijango had sent him a message. An ex-guerilla commander, Mijango was one of the principle mediators in the March 2012 truce signed between the Salvadoran gangs that drastically reduced murders throughout the country. Though the truce is now falling apart at the same speed that homicides are on the rise, Mijango is still recognized as the principal contact for the gangs. The national kingpins of the gangs, all imprisoned in Ciudad Barrios, are in charge of setting their organizational policies. Mijango told my brother that our chronicle on El Niño bothered many of the gang leaders, as it exposed inside information on how they ran their gangs. My brother asked Mijango, considering that the publication had put El Niño at increased risk, if there was anything that could be done about his situation. Mijango's response was simple: "No, there is no solution."

Everybody knew he was going to be murdered. I even knew it.

In early 2013 I was talking to El Niño in his shack over a plate of boiled *pipian* (Salvadoran squash).

"Do you feel used?" I asked him.

"Everybody's gotten something good out of my case but me. All the big shots in high society have gotten gains. How much was Rambito's murder worth? Chepe Furia paid $11,000 to set up Rambito. I haven't gotten anything."

"But what are you giving us? How do we know you won't go back to killing when the state sets you free?"

"They haven't given me any other choice. There should be a work program. We'll give you a shot at testifying in court, they say to me. I haven't gotten rid of my tattoos because they haven't offered me protection, and at least with them I can gain some respect. The information I've given is valuable. I said it was me. I pulled the trigger. The other people did this and that. That should be worth something."

"You think you'll go back to your past ways?"

"I can't rule it out. If they offered me something else ..."

The gangsters that threatened him in the Ciudad Barrios prison in 2011 were wrong. They told him they'd leave him smelling of pine, referring to the coffin they assumed he'd soon be filling. El Niño was wrong, too. He told them they didn't know what they were talking about, that coffins are made out of mango and conacaste wood.

The coffin El Niño was buried in was made out of teak. It's the cheapest material available in these parts. The mayor of San Lorenzo donated the coffin after receiving a request from El Niño's father-in-law.

The wake, on Saturday, November 22, was modest. About thirty people, friends of El Niño's mother, sang evangelical hymns. One of the hymns was about the two sides to life: the heavenly refuge and the infernal waters. There was *atol* (a sweet, corn-based hot drink), coffee and sweet bread. El Niño's mother sat slumped and defeated in a plastic chair next to the coffin. She didn't cry. This wasn't a first for her. In 2007 the Maras had killed her other son, Cheje, a gangster in the Parvis Locos Salvatrucha of Atiquizaya. She just sat, slumped and silent, staring out from her plastic chair. El Niño's widow was breast-feeding in the corner.

Outside of the cemetery there was a party going on. Las Pozas was in full celebration. There was a stage, a disco ball shooting out colors, and speakers playing reggaeton at full volume in front of the school. Only about a hundred yards away from the wake, the party music was competing with the funeral hymns. The annual neighborhood festival had long been scheduled and organized by the mayor of San Lorenzo. They weren't going to stop it for one death.

Sunday, November 23, noon. The Atiquizaya Cemetery. El Niño's burial.

The grave is a hole in the ground right next to a steep slope marking the edge of the cemetery. El Niño's father-in-law dug the grave himself. There are about thirty people, most of them invited by the pastor of Las Pozas church. About five grave sites over, a group of young gangsters are throwing dice. The gravedigger sitting next to the security guard tells me, referring to the gangsters, "They are the ones in charge here." The area is controlled by Barrio 18. My brother Juan and I seem to be unsettling the gangsters who are keeping watch. A gang member walks up from the steep hillside. Two more break off from the dice game and head over. Then another one appears, laughing, cocky, just as the mourners start throwing dirt onto the coffin. The newcomer looks like a caricature of a gangster: a wide-brimmed fedora, an oversized white shirt tucked into baggy black pants, and white tennis shoes. He walks behind us, spits and takes off. Another one comes up the hill. Two women start singing a new hymn. El Niño's mother now starts to cry. Soon she's wailing. It goes on for five minutes. We decide to leave as the men shovel the last of the dirt onto the grave site. It seems like the gangsters are about to do something. We're almost surrounded. El Niño's girlfriend and her father can feel the tension. They try to hurry things along. We tell the widow that we'll see her at the cemetery's gate, that it's best if we leave. A man cuts a twig from an izote tree (the Salvadoran national tree) and sticks it in the ground where someday, maybe, someone will plant a cross.

My brother and I are leaving through an alleyway when we notice that a tall, dark young man, about twenty-five years old, is following us. He asks us to stop. We ignore him. Behind us the burial party starts to stream out of the cemetery. The tall young man stations himself at the cemetery gates along with another man, watching the line of poor grievers stream out. We quickly shake hands with the widow and her father.

Inside the cemetery, without a cross, without a mausoleum, without a gravestone, there is a small pile of dirt with an izote branch stuck into it. Underneath lies Miguel Ángel Tobar, El Niño of Hollywood, a man who everybody knew was going to be murdered.

9

The Massacre of Salcajá

September 2014

Guatemala: the "golden door" for drugs passing through Central America. June 2013: Eight policemen in the city of Salcajá are murdered. The mutilated body of another policeman is discovered soon after. A hunt begins. While following this search for reestablishing some sort of dignity in the small city of Salcajá, I find I am witnessing the complicated chess match that is Central American narcotrafficking. This is not a war. High officials such as the minister of government aren't even sure if arresting the drug barons helps. The barons themselves play the game, and if they are arrested or extradited, the game gets even bloodier.

That Thursday, June 13, 2013, in Salcajá, nobody thought it odd to hear explosions. Locals had been setting off fireworks all day in celebration of San Antonio de Padua, who, even though he isn't the city's patron saint, is typically bombarded with fireworks and prayers every June 13 in this small agricultural city in western Guatemala. That June 13 was especially festive, as there was also a wedding in the central church, right in front of the mayor's office and police station in the central plaza. The wedding party was setting off their own fireworks. Which is why nobody even flinched when more explosions rang out at 8:17 in the evening. The first bang came from a gunshot that killed, with one shot to the head, a police officer who was walking down the street on his break. There were seven more to go.

Not even to Miguel Ovalle, the mayor of Salcajá, did it seem strange to hear explosions just outside his office that evening. He remembers pausing in the middle of brushing his teeth during a break from a council meeting. "Fireworks," he thought, continuing to brush. But then—more explosions sounding—he paused again. The noises seemed more powerful than before. "Fireworks," he reassured himself. When he was done brushing he left his office, walked through the second-floor lounge and then froze upon entering the room full of terrified council members. Three of them had walked outside for a smoke break and had witnessed two double-cab pickup trucks and an off-road SUV pull up next to the police station.

"Mr. Mayor, they came and killed all the police," one of the councilmen said.

Mayor Ovalle thought that it was a joke. "Is that so?" he replied.

The councilman told him to look out the window, from which there is a view straight down to the street in front of the police station. Mayor Ovalle approached. He saw the bodies of two policemen sprawled on the ground in a puddle of their own blood. The three trucks were still outside.

His next thought was: "Now they're going to come for us. They won't want to leave witnesses."

There were footsteps coming up the staircase outside the office. The council members and the mayor dove for cover, crouching in the corners, convinced that in a few seconds they were going to be lying in their own puddles of blood.

Instead, one of the men who had gone down to smoke, and who had been frightened and temporarily paralyzed by the gunshots, walked back into the office. Mayor Ovalle remembers that he looked green in the face. That was when they heard the three trucks start up and speed away.

"The meeting is over," the mayor said. "Go home to your families."

He knew, however, that he couldn't just go home. He washed his face and sat tight for about fifteen minutes. When he started coming out of his stupor, he made a phone call to the governor of the state of Quetzaltenango and told her: "They showed up and killed all of the police. You need to come. You need to see this. Talk to whomever you need to, but come."

When he hung up he found himself again in his empty mayor's office, across a narrow street from a police station where a group of hit men riding in luxury trucks had just murdered eight officers and, he would later learn, kidnapped the police subinspector. He wondered for a moment if it were all a bad dream, a strange hallucination provoked by a headache and all the fireworks set off for San Antonio de Padua Day. But no. It was no dream. He decided to go home.

In the days following the massacre, the city of Salcajá became the center of Guatemala. All major national newspapers ran headline stories about the police killings. There was speculation that Subinspector César García, who was kidnapped instead of killed, provoked the massacre by pulling over the son of one of the major drug traffickers for reckless driving a few days previously. The young man complained that he was stopped and even went as far as self-identifying as the son of the trafficker. That didn't stop García from arresting him, which, according to the theory, brought on the wrath of his father. Various national media outlets ran with the hypothesis. And, though it turned out to be wrong, the mistake says a lot about the state of Guatemala.

Ninety percent of the cocaine that arrives in the United States passes through Guatemala. The country is a huge port of drug exportation. "The Central American Office" is how narcos often refer to the country. A week after the massacre, the official version of the narco's son's arrest sparking the incident was accepted across the country. Eduardo Villatoro Cano, better known as Guayo Cano, was named as the father of the young reckless driver. Forty-two years old, Guayo Cano was originally from the state of Huehuetenango, which borders Mexico. He began his criminal career in the mid-'90s, working as a coyote for migrants. His zone of operation was around the city of La Democracia, a common waypoint for migrants crossing into Mexico at the Guatemalan city of La Mesilla. Guayo Cano began at the bottom, but his cruelty and boldness let him rise quickly in the ranks, fighting long battles with adversaries and making contacts with both Mexican cartels and other narcotrafficking groups throughout Central America. The state's hunt for Guayo Cano after the massacre of Salcajá covered the entire Mexico-Guatemala border region. The minister of government even gave the search for him a specific name (supposedly without irony): Operation Dignity.

A vulnerable state, attacked in the seat of power (across the street from the mayor's office and inside the police station), seeks to restore its massacred dignity.

A month and three days after the massacre, Operation Dignity had captured ten alleged members of Guayo Cano's group. On July 16, they captured a man they claimed was a commander in the group, Francisco Trinidad Castillo Villatoro, known as El Cebo or El Carnicero [the Bait or the Butcher], as he was on his way to a horse race. El Carnicero, the police claimed, was one of the assassins who attacked Salcajá on that bloody Thursday of San Antonio de Padua.

On July 16, surrounded by twenty-two journalists pushing microphones, cameras and recorders into his face, Minister of Government Mauricio López Bonilla opened up to reporters with lightly masked rage. He was upset, and maybe even felt humiliated. "He is a killer, a murderer, just like the others. A butcher. His job is to butcher people. Seriously, these people barely resemble human beings. They're animals, and I don't mean to disrespect animals, but these narcos are the most brutal people we've ever come across—they're responsible for many murders. We are going to clamp down on all of their possessions. We won't even leave them televisions to watch the news on. This is a message to all the narcos who are going around murdering people: You better soak your beards [prepare for what's coming] because we will not let this sort of thing stand any longer."

Two weeks later, two more men, Rax Pop and Pop Cholom, both indigenous, were arrested and accused of working as bodyguards for Guayo Cano. Police arrested them in a raid in El Naranjo, another common waypoint along the Mexican border for migrants, drugs, weapons and all sorts of contraband. Next to fall was thirty-four-year-old Pop Luc, accused of being the author of multiple assassinations. Minister Bonilla explained that after two months serving in the military, Pop Luc deserted and began his criminal career in a gang run by Juancho León. In 2008 in the Guatemalan state of Zacapa, along the border with Honduras, León was killed in a shootout at the lake resort La Laguna. According to military and intelligence authorities, the Mexican cartel Los Zetas was contracted by Guatemalan cartel leaders to kill León, who had become a prominent trafficking competitor and bandit. After Los Zetas completed their mission, they decided to stay.

Eighty-three days after hit men turned the Salcajá police station into a morgue, Operation Dignity had a breakthrough. On October 3, 2013, as he was walking out of a hospital in the Mexican city of Tuxtla Gutiérrez, Mexican police, acting on behalf of a formal request from the Guatemalan government, captured Guayo Cano. Minister Bonilla explained that the suspect—who looked significantly less fat than in the photos distributed by police—had been leaving the hospital after getting liposuction, part of his strategy, which included face surgery, to change his appearance. When Guayo Cano, serious and even haughty looking, accompanied by his cousin who was also accused of taking part in the massacre, exited the official Mexican airplane to be handed over to the Guatemalans, he claimed that he had been in the hospital for appendicitis. He also explained: "Everybody knows that in this business there is no forgiveness ... I don't know anything. I'm no snitch ... Talk or not, they're gonna wreck us either way ... And everybody already knows who's working behind me."

Eighty-three days in, the statistics of Operation Dignity were as follows: sixteen arrests, forty-three raids, US$117,226 seized, the decommission of thirty pistols, twelve rifles, nine machine guns, three shotguns, 4,412 rounds of various calibers, sixty-five vehicles, fifty-six cell phones, eight military uniforms, ten balaclavas, six bags of caustic soda, one ounce of cocaine, sixty-seven fighting cocks, sixteen deer, forty-three purebred horses and four wild birds.

Guayo Cano thought that he could poke the state in the eye and that nothing would happen. Then Operation Dignity dismantled his organization. The state won the game ... but the game had only begun because Guayo Cano made a bad move, he shook up the chessboard, and everybody saw it.

This is when the next major wave in the fight against drug trafficking began in Guatemala. According to the US State Department, as of 2013, 600 tons of cocaine were passing through the country each year. The massacre of Salcajá and the subsequent fallout are good guides to understanding the chess game of criminal politics in a country in which there are some winners, some losers and some who never even get to play—they lose before they even start.

We are in a small, spartan room inside police headquarters in Guatemala City. One table, two rolling chairs, two glasses of water and a recorder. In front of me, in a brown shirt and tennis shoes, and with a friendly smile on his face, is one of Guatemala's chief investigators, a man integral to many of the arrests of the Guayo Cano group. This man was one of the few charged with restoring the dignity of the country. In order to complete the mission, however, he knew he'd have to perform some pretty undignified tasks. He assures me that it's typical in this kind of case. The investigator first arrived with a small team, four other men, all riding in the same double-cabin pickup. They left the capital city one morning very early, around three or four, heading for La Democracia, the city where Guayo Cano's convoy of hit men supposedly were based. They didn't tell anybody else, not even other policemen, and they had excuses prepped if anybody asked them what they were doing in Huehuetenango. Even though they would be working out of a new police station, they didn't want to sleep there or hang around too long anywhere in the state. They drove back to the capital—an almost four-hour drive—every night, not wanting to mix with other cops working in the region controlled by Guayo Cano. If, on some nights, they had to stay in Huehuetenango, they slept in cots at the police station and told no one. They all knew, as every policeman in the region knows, that talking with colleagues about a narco investigation could be the same as signing your own death sentence.

The investigator was meeting me to give me advice about my upcoming trip to La Democracia.

"Getting to La Democracia from Huehuetenango," he told me, "is a little complicated. The whole route is under control of the narcos."

"And," I asked, "if I just show up and start asking around about Cano's continued control of the region?"

"That's dangerous."

"They'd know I'm in town?"

"Let me tell you something. We've only been working in La Democracia for a little bit. Besides our first raid, we've only been there one other time this year. We go in and we get out. We don't linger. I don't recommend that you go."

"According to you, what happened that night in the Salcajá police station?"

"What Cano wanted to do was start a fight against the state. He was motivated by rage. [He wanted] to kidnap a cop and kill him like they had killed some of his own. According to what we know, there were between twelve and fifteen people in three vehicles. The vehicles were very similar to government vehicles, which was probably why the policemen weren't alerted sooner, and the hit men wore Army uniforms. They came in like soldiers, pointing their rifles. They yelled that they were performing a military operation and told everyone to get out. The cops started running, but the hit men knew the layout of the station, it was very well planned, they knew where the exits were, where the doors were. They went straight for the office where the subinspector was and pulled him out."

"What happened to him?"

"They took him alive and drove him to Huehuetenango. Two days later we found some of his body parts. They dismembered him. They turned him to soup and dumped what was left into the river in La Democracia."

Subinspector César Augusto García was the commanding officer of the station in Salcajá. The hit men didn't murder him like they murdered his colleagues. Instead, that San Antonio de Padua Day, they took him away alive.

For weeks the media was highlighting a YouTube video, claiming it had been posted by Guayo Cano's people and showed them murdering García. Various politicians referred to the video as accurate. In the video you can see a thirty-something man tied to a chair. He is brown-skinned, has Asian-like features and short, military-cropped hair. He is already bloodied and seems to no longer have a tongue. The man grunts something like a death rattle. Men off camera giggle. "Your time has fucking come," someone says. The camera moves to focus on the man's left hand. Other hands appear on the screen, one of them with a knife; they start cutting off the victim's fingers. Later, a man with his face covered walks behind the victim, lifts his head up and decapitates him with a knife. Many people assumed the man was the subinspector from Salcajá. It says a lot that even politicians bought the story without proof. It turns out that they were wrong, though García probably did suffer a similar fate.

Two days after Guayo Cano's men struck at the dignity of Guatemala, lifeguards and policemen found scattered human remains on the bank of Valparaíso River in the city of La Democracia. They found a five-by-five-inch piece of cranium, two fingers, a strip of skin, and human intestines.

According to the investigator, the forensic evaluation revealed that a number of these body parts were removed from the victim while he was still alive. Later, they found the victim's shirt.

He hadn't just moved a few pieces; Guayo Cano had thrown the entire chessboard into the air and then spit in the face of his opponent. But what was it that so infuriated him?

I asked the lead investigator in the case to explain who Guayo Cano was in the criminal world.

"In 2007," he began, "he was a humble worker. He started as a coyote, just like his brother. A third brother worked for a narcotrafficking band under someone named Romero. This brother brought him along, starting Guayo off as a chauffeur. Then this Romero figure was killed and Guayo was left without a job. Through a contact he got another job working for a Mexican named Gabi. Guayo gained Gabi's confidence and people started getting to know him. Then Gabi was killed. By this time, however, Guayo had good relationships with two other groups from Zacapa and Izabal [both on the border of Honduras], who were suppliers and had connections in Mexico. One of those, known as the Doctor, was from Tuxtla Gutiérrez, Chiapas. Guayo started working with the Doctor in 2008. Then Chicharra came in and tried to impose a $50,000-a-month tax on Guayo for working in his zone. Guayo didn't want to pay. As Chicharra is the leader of one of the most ruthless criminal groups around, Guayo Cano left for Mexico. He was schooled by the Doctor and the Gulf Cartel. He even got a lot of help from Los Zetas when he was beginning to outfit his own group. He was in Mexico about three months. Then he returned to Guatemala and hooked up with his brother, the coyote. With assistance from Los Zetas he decided he wanted to avenge the death of Gabi, who was killed by Chicharra in Agua Zarca. The hit was set up by Guayo with help from Los Zetas, or maybe it was the other way around. It was revenge. Guayo was going to join [Los Zetas], but in the end he didn't."

This is a typical story of a hotshot Central American drug capo, someone who counts in kilos instead of grams. They are epic tales of storied bad guys with cute nicknames who parade around half-imagined kingdoms where they are the center of everything and get to make all the rules. These are strange and impenetrable worlds filled with code words and carnage, in which players function as if it were just another day at work: One coyote initiates another, who, months later, kills a boss and then joins up with Los Zetas to stage a massacre.

The fight in Agua Zarca, a neighboring city of La Democracia, was a five-hour gun battle that raged ten miles up and down the highway surrounding the town. Seventeen people were killed. The fighting was sparked during a horse race when two competing trafficking groups, one Mexican and the other Guatemalan, threw themselves into a battle as if they were in the streets of Baghdad. The groups used high-power rifles and even grenade launchers. In the end, the Mexicans were forced to flee back across the border. According to the Guatemalan police investigators, the Mexicans were Los Zetas members with the backing of Guayo Cano, and the Guatemalans were part of Chicharra's band. No authorities had the courage to enter into the fight as it was still raging. Instead, they waited an entire day for reinforcements to arrive and only then began their investigation. La Democracia, Agua Zarca, the cities were the dominion of the mafia. The state, when it did show face, was the intruder.

According to the investigator I spoke with, Guayo Cano's decision to collaborate with Los Zetas was in response to the $50,000 tax Chicharra had tried to impose on him. After the battle in Agua Zarca, which lasted nearly five hours, there was a sort of secret meeting between the opposing sides. The investigator, who told me he learned the details from one of his informants, explained it to me thus: "There was a meeting between Chicharra and a few of Cano's lower-ranking officers in La Democracia. Cano was there as well. Chicharra is the elder. A bunch of the narcos met. They said they made a contract, formed an alliance, no more violence between them. Chicharra would buy his drugs from one of the smaller players. He gets to decide who traffics how much and who gets control. Cano is the armed wing, acts as protection, but won't attack [Chicharra] anymore."

Those were the terms of the ceasefire in Huehuetenango, the contract between the sides who governed the region. There was no good reason to invite the Guatemalan government to participate.

In this austere room, the investigator and I continue our conversation.

"What area did Chicharra control?" I asked.

"Agua Zarca."

"And how many men did Guayo Cano have?"

"Let me think. Between drivers, hit men and collaborators that we're aware of, I'd say about twenty-five."

"And Chicharra?"

"He was at another level. He had around fifty men. His brother, El Zope [the Buzzard], is in prison. Chicharra, not sure. Some people wanted to bring a case of tax fraud against him. But the charges didn't stick, and they eventually pinned them on Guayo Cano instead."

"Chicharra is more powerful than Cano?"

"It's a bloody business, and he [Chicharra] controls the drugs. He pulls the strings, even Cano's strings. He has control by deciding how much product passes."

The weaker Central American players in the drug business act basically like a tag team. One of them is killed or extradited to the United States and then another tags in until he is killed or extradited. The war against drugs, seen from this perspective, is infinite. This war, if you want to call it by the name ex-President of Mexico Felipe Calderón used, has a long list of enemies waiting to be tagged in. It's a self-generating list.

Just in the state of Huehuetenango you can see a clear example of this tag-teaming. El Zope, or Walter Arelio Montejo Mérida, was extradited to the United States in March 2013 to be tried in the District of Columbia for drug trafficking. El Zope had been tagged in by Otto Herrera, the top Guatemalan drug lord of the past decade, who was caught and arrested in Mexico in 2005. He later escaped from prison but was then recaptured in Colombia in 2007 and extradited that same year. In 2013, after having served his time, he was freed from prison in the United States. Herrera had used Salvadoran ports, working with Eliu Martínez (a Salvadoran trafficker who would also end up extradited and sentenced to twenty-nine years in US prisons) to traffic up to five tons of cocaine, which he later sent north to the United States.

In sum, Herrera tagged in El Zope and El Zope tagged in Chicharra, who now has the space to run free after his biggest competitor committed a grave error (murdering eight cops in the Salcajá police station on San Antonio de Padua Day) and was taken out of the match.

Guayo Cano didn't understand the rules of the game. He wasn't even tapped out by another player. He didn't face extradition, which is the grand tribunal of the match. Instead, he was disqualified by the referee for thinking that nobody would notice if he did whatever he wanted in the ring. Even though the ref is half-blind and hardly has any standing or authority, Guayo Cano made such a spectacle that he got thrown out.

Cano was infuriated that the subinspector of Salcajá had robbed him.

I asked the investigator if the eight murdered policemen worked for Guayo Cano.

"More like they did something that went against Guayo Cano's interests. For narcos, drugs and money are a commitment. If a shipment starts moving, it better arrive. Those are the rules. You get a package from Zacapa or Izabal and then you transfer it and take the money to La Mesilla or some other part of Huehue."

"And what about the theory that the cops were robbing money or drugs?"

He explained to me what police had discovered of the subinspector's involvement in the drug world: He had received payment to selectively interdict a shipment.

The shipment "was probably money. That money was definitely robbed in Salcajá. It came up from Zacapa. The subinspector didn't know what was in the car, if it had thousands of dollars or kilos of cocaine. He just got paid to stop it. We don't know who was driving. The money belonged to Guayo Cano. Who contracted the subinspector? We don't know. We don't know if he was paid in dollars or quetzales, but he received $50,000. I think they were quetzales."

"And what was in the car?"

"$740,000."

"And stopping Guayo Cano would open more space for Chicharra?"

"If Guayo Cano lost ground, who else could fill that space, especially if everybody else is small-time compared to Chicharra?"

"I'd like to say something I've noticed," I told him. "In Guatemala, or in Central America, there are only two ways to stop a drug lord: The gringos come in [for extradition] or the drug lord does something stupid like Guayo Cano. Otherwise, it's smooth sailing. What do you think?"

"That's what it seems like."

"Did you feel your life was in danger while investigating this case?"

"Yes. I felt moments of psychosis. We think about twenty policemen have been killed while working cases related to Guayo Cano."

"I need to get to La Democracia," I said, "and I need some advice about how to do so."

"My advice is that you don't go."

"If I rent a car here in the city and drive to La Democracia, would they know about it?"

"Yes."

My idea of getting to La Democracia remained just that—an idea. I never would make it. In Salcajá I couldn't find anybody—not an investigator, an activist, a prosecutor or an official—who would assure me I'd be safe in La Democracia. Nobody knew a contact or could think of a safe way to ask questions. The only help I was offered came from a detective: "I can collect your body afterwards."

La Democracia, I was starting to realize, is completely run by the mafia.

Operation Dignity was an illusion. It was gazing into a fun house mirror. The Guatemalan state looked tough in taking down Guayo Cano. But the region Cano brutally ruled over remains dominated by the same forces, or maybe by a force even more brutal than him: Chicharra. The case of Guayo Cano followed the most basic of rules: action (forceful), then reaction (necessary). The state reacted, but La Democracia remains in the hands of the mafia.

Openly recognizing its own limited capacity, the state tolerated the mafia's control. In the case against Guayo Cano, the Public Ministry heaped on two other murders of state officials.

In December 2012, Yolanda Olivares, another judicial official and two employees were driving between La Mesilla and Huehuetenango City when a truck full of heavily armed men stopped them. The armed men shot up their vehicle and then, with the passengers still inside, burned it. Prosecutors later hypothesized that the men worked for Guayo Cano.

An optimist might say that even if he hadn't murdered nine policemen, Guayo Cano would have eventually been captured for the earlier murder. A pessimist would probably say that if he hadn't been that stupid, Cano would still be trafficking drugs into Mexico without a problem. A realist would say that ten months had already passed since the killing of Olivares and three others and nobody had done a thing to hunt down the murderers until after the massacre on San Antonio de Padua Day.

In the end, Guayo Cano never achieved anything close to the status of any of the major Guatemalan drug barons. He never gained the prestige of names such as Lorenzana, Overdick or Ortiz López. All of the barons would end up captured, but none would face charges in Guatemala. They would all be extradited. The difference was that none of them committed a massacre inside a police station across the street from the mayor's office.

In April 2013, when she was still general prosecutor of Guatemala, Claudia Paz y Paz and I spoke of drug barons, arrests and the future of the country. Paz y Paz didn't try to sell me the story of a strong state. In fact, she told me that it was impossible to know what would have become of the judicial branch in Guatemala if the drug barons hadn't set up shop in the country. She seemed to have the same kind of hope a castaway has when he sees a bird in the sky. She gave me an example.

"In the Walter Overdick case they raided his house in Alta Verapaz and detained his son, who is now in jail, as well as his wife. Overdick went on a local radio station, this was about five years ago, and said that if they didn't let his wife and son go he was going to kill the judge. They let them go. This wouldn't happen anymore. Now, we've even caught Overdick himself. A tribunal asked for him to be extradited and we shipped him out. What changed? That those judges [who were threatened by Overdick] lived in Alta Verapaz, they lived in the place where he ruled everything. Now those cases are tried in Guatemala City and in courts for high-risk cases. The prosecutors in Alta Verapaz didn't have the right conditions of security, same with the city of Zacapa where Lorenzana ruled, or in Huehuetenango with Montejo, or in San Marcos where Chamalé was."

The castaway's bird is tired and trembling, but it's still a bird. It still signals land. Overdick, also known as El Tigre, who was first an enemy and then an ally of Los Zetas in Alta Verapaz, was extradited to the United States on December 10, 2012. Waldemar Lorenzana, also known as El Patriarca (the Patriarch), the supposed right-hand man of Mexican drug lord El Chapo Guzmán, seventy-six years old and a melon farmer, was loaded onto a federal plane and extradited to the United States on March 19, 2014, to be tried in New York City. Juan Alberto Ortiz López, also known as Chamalé or Hermano Juan (Brother John), the strong man of the Pacific, after ruling a whole strip of coast for ten years, was extradited on May 22, 2014, to be tried in Florida.

The barons who don't act like human butchers are assimilated into the system. They are part of the Guatemalan state, which is why the state doesn't chase them—it'd be like a dog chasing its own tail. Except that when the United States gives the command, the tail gets chomped. The three major barons represented over forty years of large-scale drug trafficking, and still not one of them, at the moment they boarded their planes surrounded by DEA agents to be tried as criminal masterminds, were facing a single charge in Guatemala. They left their country with clean records.

During another conversation in her office, in June 2013, Paz y Paz reformulated the same question I had asked her before—why Guatemala didn't attempt to prosecute the drug lords, why they let El Patriarca Lorenzana be tried elsewhere and only went after barbarians like Guayo Cano.

She told me: "You should be asking me if I would have arrested him if we had wanted to try him in this country."

But I didn't ask her. It was obvious to me what her answer would have been: No.

I'm sitting down in a fast-food restaurant in Zone 1 of Guatemala City. Accompanying me is a policeman who was part of the team working with the DEA to capture, among others, Walter "El Tigre" Overdick, Eliu Lorenzana and his father, Waldemar. Two televisions are blaring, and a gaggle of little kids are scampering around the place. Nobody is close to us. Maybe other customers find it odd to see the three of us (the third is an ex-prosecutor) whispering over a voice recorder placed in the middle of the table. The official, who wishes to remain anonymous, was probably the most important player in Guatemala in the recent fight against drug trafficking.

We're talking about the untouchables, those above Guayo Cano. The ex-prosecutor tells me that evangelical churches and law offices are the most common money launderers for Guatemalan drug traffickers. The capos keep their distance from Guatemala City because they don't want to clash with the "historical families, who have the capital divided up by zone; this zone is for this family, this zone for the other, each with their own business." He speaks to me about brokers, "lawyers or businessmen who act as the intermediaries between the two worlds, because none of those families want a yokel in a cowboy hat walking into their office with his boots smelling of cow shit. But the family does want to do business with the yokel in the cowboy hat. And so: the brokers."

I stop him to ask a question.

"I don't understand why, if the criminal network remains, you even want to try to capture capos like Overdick or Lorenzana."

"Look," the policeman responds, "it's not about wanting to capture these people or not. The state is more scared of these people than they are interested in them. The ones who are interested are the gringos, and the gringos just want them as trophies, even though they know another [capo] is just going to fill in the gap. They just want to send a message: 'We're working on it.'"

According to the policeman, the capture of Waldemar Lorenzana on April 26, 2011, perfectly exemplifies how it isn't a question of capability, but of will. No longer whispering, as all the other tables are unoccupied, he explains: "Without the gringos the man would be free. Without the massacre, Guayo Cano would still be trafficking. The ones who go down are either idiots or have caught the eye of the gringos."

The capture of El Patriarca didn't even entail a raid. There were no soldiers involved. All that it took was a little will—for extradition. Four policemen, including two women, went to the small melon farm on the outskirts of the village of Maribel, in the Teculután region of Zacapa state. The officers wore old cowboy hats, work shirts and heavy boots. They hid their pistols in their boots and left their watches, rings and gold necklaces at home. Three days in a row they ate beans, eggs and tortilla breakfasts at a rural food stall close to the melon farm. From their position at the stall they were able to keep an eye on who came and who went from the village, all the while passing themselves off to the woman who ran the stall as melon workers. And they ate on credit, paying off their meals every third day, because a melon worker who doesn't eat on credit is like a Don Quixote who doesn't have a mustache. They told the woman they would pay off their debt as soon as they were paid. She said that *el señor* came to pay his workers on Saturdays, around two in the afternoon. He comes, she told them, in his gray pickup, always at the same time. That same Saturday they started tailing the gray pickup, following it with two cars. By the following Tuesday, when Lorenzana stopped to talk to someone, the officers saw that he was riding shotgun. They arrested him (he was unarmed) along with his grandson. They took his phones and the truck. "If we had left the fool with his phone, he would have made one call and we would have been murdered on the spot." Instead, the policemen, two officials from the prosecutor's office, a drug baron and his grandson took off in a caravan back to the capital, heading straight to the Tribunal Tower. On the drive, the policeman tells me, Lorenzana tried to pay him off: "Stop," he said. "I'll have them bring you a million dollars, cash, you could do whatever you want with your life and I'll take it easy." They didn't accept the money, but the fact that he even offered says a lot about Guatemala. Later, on the same ride, Lorenzana tried a new tactic: "Save your life. Don't throw it away." He was threatening them. Still on the same ride, the policeman received a call from a police colonel, who told him that they needed to let Lorenzana go, that the arrest warrant was invalid. He didn't listen, but the call says a lot about Guatemala.

From the Tribunal Tower, ten officers transferred Lorenzana to the maximum-security prison in Fraijanes. "You're not going to believe me," the policeman says. "Do you know how many cars were following us? About forty, filled with armed men with, according to the official story, legal weapons. They were hoping to free him, but since we put him in a patrol car instead of a truck, they didn't know what vehicle he was in. There were a fuck-load of cars following us, but orders were not to start a shit show." The ex-prosecutor adds: "If they started the fight and he tried to escape, you'd have to halt the extradition process and charge him for crimes committed here. Nobody wanted that."

I ask: "If that had happened and they took him to a court

for high-risk cases in Guatemala, what do you think would have happened?"

"He would have been acquitted," they both answer, nearly at the same time.

"After making a few calls?" I ask.

"Ha," the ex-prosecutor answers. "With just one [call]."

"But then why was there so much energy to try Guayo Cano for the Salcajá massacre here in Guatemala?" I ask, expecting another ironic reply.

"Because Guayo Cano isn't anybody. He's an annoying flea, nothing more, a flea on the skin of Chicharra, who himself is a flea on the skin of Lorenzana."

Guatemalan logic, or maybe logic in the entire northern triangle of Central America, is that there is no tolerance for either fleas or for elephants if the United States says so. But there is tolerance for a whole range of fauna that is in no risk of extinction. What seems to happen is that when the elephants are extradited, little fleas seem to proliferate.

Journalists adapt. When a journalist is talking to a government official, especially someone in high office, the journalist expects lies, cover-ups, hedging and evasion. And yet expectations are always broken. For the past few months I've been coming repeatedly to the office of the minister of government to interview Mauricio López Bonilla, a man who may dodge questions—a politician is a politician—but when he answers, he answers straight. Only with these kinds of politicians is it worth trying to have a conversation. With the rest of them, it's better to go for interrogation.

It's March 2014. I'm sitting down with Bonilla in his office. He only has fifteen minutes so there's only time for one good question. I decide to explain to him my analogy of the elephant and the flea. He responds quickly, promising me another interview later. This is what he rapidly sums up for me about Guatemala's drug war.

"It's a shame. We know that we have corrupt police, which is who we've been focusing on, not on Guayo Cano," Bonilla begins. "Last year through the first few months of this year, more than 360 Guatemalan policemen have been charged with crimes. Illicit association is what we've brought against most of them."

He continues: "It's impossible to fight against everyone all the time. It's bad strategy. We have an eye on a lot of people, but we have our priorities."

Guayo Cano's police file goes back to 2009.

Bonilla continues: "Yes, I wanted to leave a message about Salcajá. If you're going to drop a bomb like that, you become a priority. Neither your sons nor your grandsons are going to be able to traffic drugs. But even then, as always, some other group will benefit."

Maybe the sons or grandsons of Guayo Cano won't be able to come near a gram of coke, I think, but the sons and grandsons of Chicharra are probably jumping for joy.

What he says next is worth hearing: "Before the government entered this fight, there were ten or twelve criminal organizations with operating capacity in the country. Today there are fifty-four, all of them well armed. The arrival of Los Zetas was a major factor in this atomization. Before, the leaders were illiterate, but strategic. The leaders now are killers and butchers. The Americans swept up the generals and left us with the soldiers. Parallel to this phenomenon, after the peace accords [ending the Guatemalan Civil War in 1996] we started disarmament but didn't find a substitute to fill in the role of state power. During President Berger's time in office [2004–08] we downsized to 15,000 soldiers. At the time of the accords we had 30,000. Everybody here knows who the narco standing on the corner is, or who is running packages through the villages. The question is who he's working with. Assassinating nine policemen is idiotic. We have a clear agenda to persecute the groups that rise to power and represent a threat to the state, but with the animals, we go head on and with all we have."

There is little doubt that at this point in the war on drugs Minister Bonilla would be in agreement with his predecessor, Carlos Menocal. Both right-leaning Bonilla and moderate/left-leaning Menocal see the overstepping of the US as a Damoclean sword hanging over the whole country. Bonilla is an ex-Kaibil combat veteran who thinks in terms of strategic offensives for infiltrating guerilla camps. Menocal is an ex-journalist who currently works as a legal consultant.

I meet Menocal in another restaurant in Zone 1. He's also in a hurry, needing to get back to a hearing, and we only have a half hour to talk.

He tells me he agrees that even when the drug barons leave, their business remains. He also thinks there's no way around it. Guatemala, he tells me, is a place where the barons started working with Colombian drug lord Pablo Escobar and turned the country into the "Central American Satellite Office." It is a country where government officials "agreed five years ago to capture the big fish in order to maintain harmony with the United States." This is what Bonilla means, Menocal explains, when he refers to "the sword of Damocles: They either seize enough goods or they are disqualified and accused of a whole range of things." The government compromises on education, health, security, even going to great lengths (sending undercover policemen to work on melon farms, eating eggs and beans for four days) in order to capture a big fish like Lorenzana and send him north.

It's a quid pro quo agreement with the United States. I want this and I'll give you this in return. As simple as that.

Menocal tells me that during his term in office he had a list of sixteen "extraditables," of whom he caught twelve. It was one of his priorities to crack down on states that weren't complying with his requests. Despite his success,

Menocal wasn't happy with what he got in return for his work.

"I see the cooperation with the gringos as an actual gift compared to the money they spend on fighting with the narcos. Even still, you can't deny that the gringos have an obvious agenda. Not even Sánchez Cerén [the current president of El Salvador] would deny it. We're like the ham in the sandwich: To the south you have a series of countries producing the narcotics; to the north you have the highest-consuming country. There are 20 million drug consumers in the United States … In Guatemala, for every $10 supposedly spent on security, $4 goes to fighting the drug war."

For Bonilla, it's a "perverse circle," the extraditions leading to the atomization of violent groups like that of Guayo Cano in the interior of the country. During another interview with him in a Guatemala City hotel in June 2013, Minister Bonilla told me: "There was a regional summit here and Secretary of State Clinton came down. She said that for every $3 we put in [in the fight against drug trafficking] they would put $1. It's a bad joke, because in the end we're putting money that we could have used for education, health, many other things."

The arrest of the Guatemalan barons isn't anything more than fear of the sword hanging over the state's head. It's more survival than it is strategy. The battle against drug trafficking in Guatemala is not a decision grounded in sovereign agency. It is a battle they are thrust into.

Central America, especially northern Central America, especially Guatemala, is not a place where money dedicated to security isn't needed elsewhere. Before leaving our interview, Menocal puts a few last brushstrokes on his portrait of the country.

"From 2008 on, about 256,000 illegal arms have come into the country, according to what we're seeing on the black market. The coyotes here have a very powerful structure in place that leads to further crimes, including human trafficking.

We've even seen a case of Jordanians coming here and tricking young girls to go back with them to Jordan. And the gangs are moving beyond extortion ... They just shut down a clique that had 2.5 million quetzales (about $330,000) in its accounts."

What it all points to is that the Lorenzanas of Guatemala will keep being extradited, while the Guayo Canos will remain.

It's June 19, 2014, a cloudy day in Salcajá. This is a town of small tile-roof houses, asphalt streets, corner stores and a central church. I'm in a tiny shop-cum-restaurant next to the police station where the eight cops were massacred. On the table in front of me is a plate of enchiladas; on the television the Costa Rican soccer team has just tied 0-0 with England to qualify for the 2014 World Cup in Brazil.

I spent last night in Xela, the state capital of Quetzaltenango. To execute his massacre, Guayo Cano swung into town from the neighboring state of Huehuetenango. In Xela I met a local politician in a bar. We sat at the most remote table in order to talk more comfortably. Nervous, he had agreed to meet me only after a family member convinced him. But after I told him what I wanted to talk about, even the dark bar didn't seem to give him any comfort. After some pressing, I convinced him to order a tea and chat. When his cup was empty, he told me, "There's a lot to say about that [the Guayo Cano case], but it's not smart to talk. I'm sorry."

Earlier today I visited with the substitute for the police subinspector who had been butchered and kidnapped by Guayo Cano. His name is Milton García Paniagua. We met in the police bunk room, in the second story of a building a block away from the station where the massacre occurred. City officials relocated the station after the incident. Now the old station—prime real estate next to the mayor's office, the church and the central plaza—is vacant and, seemingly, cursed. No businesses have tried to rent the building.

Paniagua laid on the table a piece of paper with nine bullet points. He had prepared what he wanted to tell me. When he noticed that I was trying to read what he'd written, he covered the paper and only glanced at it as we spoke: "We are here to serve our citizens ... what happened was an isolated incident ... a lamentable act." He basically said nothing.

Later I convinced another policeman from Xela to sit down with me, also on condition of anonymity.

He finally shows up in the small store/restaurant dressed in civilian clothes and, without a word, takes a seat next to me.

"It's hard to be a cop here," he says. "You're corrupt as soon as they see you."

We talk at length, watching the game and eating *garnachas* (a fried Guatemalan tortilla covered in beans and cheese). Just a moment of our long conversation should serve to relate what the man told me.

"Four of the massacred men were corrupt," he tells me. "The others died for nothing. There are plenty more of them [corrupt officers] there. Remember that the first checkpoint to try to catch Guayo Cano wasn't even put in place until almost three hours after the massacre. Funny, right? Just enough time for them to get back to La Democracia."

I ask him if he is currently working with corrupt police officers.

"Yes."

"And you know their names? Who they work for?"

"Yes."

"Will you tell me?"

"No."

"Why not?"

"Lead." The lead of bullets.

"Fine," I say. "I still want to go to La Democracia. Do you work with anyone who's not corrupt and who could get me there safely?"

"Don't go."

And then, finally, I left it at that.

10

Men Who Pull Out Nails

May 2011

Amid chaos, killing is the rule. Three armies are fighting for control of the Salvadoran prisons. The government, an impotent spectator, watches as body piles upon body, massacre follows massacre. Whoever runs this underworld runs the whole market. And yet, if you are inside, your history will hunt you—hunt you like a dog to the very end of the world.

"Any minute we're going to have a massacre in Apanteos. We're just waiting to see how it starts. And you know what's the worst? With the resources we have, we can't do anything to stop it." He was talking to the four journalists surrounding him. He'd insinuated as much about the pending massacre before, but this time he came right out with it. When we were saying good-bye at the door of his office I asked again, "And this is on the record?"

"Of course," he said, "We can't be responsible for what we can't avoid."

Typically, politicians in the security sector of the most violent country on the continent like to keep their comments vague, skirt the issues, euphemize, *soften* (that's the verb for it) their comments. Normally they claim ignorance, they hide, excuse or even *shy away* (that's the other verb) from the real issue.

But that afternoon in his office, Douglas Moreno, warden of the Apanteos prison in Santa Ana, a city in western El

Salvador, didn't lean on the typical diplomatic vocabulary. When this happens, when you're not expecting it, the words can sound even stronger, they can resonate even more emphatically: *mas-sa-cre.*

A massacre in Apanteos. It's what Moreno predicted in September 2010. A massacre among the 3,700 inmates jammed into a space built for a maximum of 800. A bloodbath in a compound 2,900 inmates over capacity.

My question was whether the prediction was based on intelligence gleaned from his insight into what was bubbling up from behind the bars, or if it was a threat for anybody getting close to the prison: a family member, a lawyer, an inmate representative or even one of the prisoners themselves.

The next day I went to downtown San Salvador to meet with someone very close with common prisoners, otherwise known as "civilians," inmates who are not gang members, ex-cops or ex-soldiers. My contact, or rep, was an ex-con, as are most prison reps—guides who help lawyers and family members, and sometimes journalists, to navigate the world of El Salvador's prisons.

We met in a Chinese restaurant that had nothing Chinese about it except for the letters on the sign and the porcelain cat on the counter. I ordered fried chicken; the rep ordered fried beef. We both drank horchata. This was our third meeting, but the first since I had heard Moreno's prediction. We got straight to it.

"So," I said, "Everybody's expecting a massacre in Apanteos?"

"Pretty much. I already told you that it's a time bomb, about to blow the fuck up."

"Is there anything that can be done?"

"Separate all of them. That's it. The final nail was when they started moving in the gangsters."

In June 2010 more than 100 female members of the Mara Salvatrucha were transferred into Ward 1 of Apanteos, a prison that was supposedly reserved exclusively for "civilian" prisoners. That was when the alarms started going off in Wards 5, 6, 7 and 8. One after another the prisoners were revealing themselves to be active members of the Maras, or at least sympathizers: They claimed that they had family who were gang members, that they came from gang neighborhoods, that they were past members. Allies: the category of which a legitimate gang member would say, "We let them walk among us."

The arrival of the MS *jainas* (Janes, a derogatory and commonly used term for female gang members) set off a domino effect that nobody in the prison expected. The following day it was revealed that five of the eleven wards of Apanteos prison were run by the MS gang. Inmates who had previously declared themselves to be civilians, so they wouldn't end up in a gang prison, were coming forward to admit their affiliation.

"And that," my informant told me while sitting in the "Chinese" restaurant, "didn't make them very happy." I wanted to know which "them" he was referring to, but we had finished our plates, there was nothing left in our glasses but the thick dregs of horchata, and the conversation, I knew, was over. I'd gotten used to the way it works with questions about the prison system: Behind every answer lies another question. Behind every act there is a hidden motive. A story to explain every story. There were massacres before this massacre. In other words: You're always standing on only the tip of the iceberg.

If you were a film director looking to cast somebody to play the warden of a Salvadoran prison, Orlando Molina, the director of Apanteos prison, would probably be high on your list. A commanding presence, short and strong looking, and with a thick mustache, he speaks intelligently and rapidly about his prison. Actually, he doesn't just tell you something, he reports it. According to Director Molina something doesn't happen; rather, an "occurrence takes place." He doesn't talk with Juan or Pedro, but with Guard So-and-So, or Señor Journalist. In my first visit with him in September 2010, he "afforded me" the pleasure of introducing me to the "penitentiary center." Speaking loudly, he listed off the basic stats: "Ward 1, 176 females from MS; Ward 2, the sick, minor crimes and seniors; Ward 3, inmates with medium-term sentences; Ward 4, long sentences and serious crimes; Ward 6, intake and adaptation to the prison; Ward 7, sentences from three to thirteen years; Ward 8, from three to twenty years, including 269 MS males; Ward 9, minor crimes and processing of inmates without convictions; Ward 10, inmates without convictions for serious crimes; Ward 11, special sector, unadapted inmates, challenge inmates, high-threat inmates. Listen. I'm not calling them bad, everyone here is bad. I mean challenging inmates.

"From Ward 3 to 8 we have the gallery, the central wing made out of cement and iron, divided by walls and bars where the inmates can shout insults or greetings from one cell block to another. Wards 9 and 10 are set off a bit from the central wing, and Wards 1 and 11 are completely isolated."

"Director Molina," I formally addressed him, "I would be pleased to speak with the representative of the challenging inmates of Ward 11."

He took off his hat, scratched his head, swiveled around in his chair and called his boss, the warden, on his phone: "Yes, yes, that's what he wants. OK, I'll do it, boss. Yes, yes, at your orders.

"We'll pull him out, but remember that these people are sharp, and they have plenty of time to think about what they'll say to you, to put on their best and nicest face, and that who you talk to might not be the actual leader, but their spokesman."

If the inmates in Ward 11 wanted to show their friendliest face, I'd need to reconsider what "friendly" meant. A wiry man tattooed from shoulders to wrists and with rings around his eyes that nearly made him look like a raccoon was led out to speak with me. He was the representative of "the Rebels." Representative is an informal position that formally represents the ward. As another prison official told me: "If the representative doesn't give you permission to enter the ward, only the Police Unit of the Maintenance of Order [riot police] can get you in."

The rep from Ward 11, who didn't want me to publish his name, listened to my introduction and then launched into a speech about the "inhumane" conditions inside the prison. After about five minutes of listening politely, I had to stop him and explain that I didn't want to talk about conditions. It's not that there isn't need for a serious investigation into a prison system built to house 8,080 inmates that actually has locked up 23,048. The conditions are indeed abysmal. But it doesn't take talking to a prisoner to hear about the conditions because the director of prisons himself will tell you stories of prisoners sleeping on their feet, of a stench so bad it will make you vomit, of prisoners who hunt cats to make soup, of sickness for which there are no doctors or medicine, of extortion, of rape committed with penises, with bottles, with bats and with knives, of inmates who have gone crazy behind bars … There are many stories. "Inside [the prisons] they violate human rights that haven't even been invented," a colleague of mine told me after spending months immersed in the world of Salvadoran prisons.

The rep bristled when I cut him off.

"What do you want to talk about then?" he asked.

"People are saying that a massacre is about to explode in here."

"Yeah, and they're saying it's our fault?"

"No, they're saying that there are issues between the new inmates."

"There's an easy solution," he tells me. "Pull out the new inmates, take them to one of the gang prisons. Pull them out of Ward 8 tomorrow and that's that. We can't live with them.

173

They make us pay them; they threaten us. We can't play sports anymore because we run into them, we can't go to the sick room because we see them there. We can't go to programs, see a movie, nothing, because when we try we get jumped."

"Are they fighting you for control of the prison?"

"No, you don't get it. It's not about control, it's about peace—that's why we want them out. They want control. Yesterday they took twenty-five of our friends out of Ward 8 and they all got jumped. Remember that there are people in here sentenced for killing some other shitheads out there, and remember that they don't hesitate to get revenge, and remember that in here you pull out all your nails and everything gets accounted for.* So, why don't they just take them away? If they know that this is a time bomb. Or do you think they forgot about the massacre of 2007?"

The rep from Ward 11 referred to the gangsters as shitheads. The rep from Ward 11 has been locked up for more than ten years. The rep from Ward 11 knows that in prison there is time to collect on your debts, to pull out your nails. He remembers the last massacre.

In prisons you pull out nails. In prisons you bear your scars. It's inevitable that somebody, or sometimes many people, pay for their nails and their scars with their lives. The last massacre in a Salvadoran prison, in January 2007, was in Apanteos.

At five in the afternoon the "civilians" of Apanteos heard gunshots from the guard towers. Gunshots and then more gunshots, every five minutes, interspersed with noises of struggling coming from the wall, behind which were 500 members

---

* *Translator's note*: In Central American gang slang, "to pull out nails" or *arrastrar clavos* means to be indebted to someone because of something you've done to them. It is akin to retribution or revenge coming to you. It is a threat, the future cost of your action, the inertia of violence, another spin in the cycle of death. To pull out a nail is to bear judgment or condemnation.

of Barrio 18. None of the civilians had any idea what was happening. Both the rep from Ward 11, another anonymous inmate, as well as one of the guards shooting from the tower, all of whom were in Apanteos during the 2007 massacre, described the same thing.

The noises increased to a thundering in Ward 7. "Pum, pum, pum. Without end," the anonymous inmate described to me. "The walls were shaking. Gang members on the other side were ramming it with their cots, and we knew that sooner or later it would fall."

There were fewer civilians in Ward 7 than gang members on the other side of the wall. The inmates in 7 weren't all friends either, which made it hard to get the story straight. Some of them, supposedly, crouched in the corners with their heads between their knees. Others sat on their beds as if they were going to try to sleep. Others, those "who knew about their nails," once they heard the shots, the "pum, pum, pum," paced nervously outside their cells. The noises continued for two hours. And then the wall fell.

Another prisoner I spoke with told me that in that precise moment everything slowed down. The banging stopped and an overwhelming silence reigned as hundreds of gangsters started pouring through the hole in the wall. "Knives, shanks, clubs, at least two pistols." Gangsters would soon break through the other walls and have the whole compound to themselves. Only a few civilians tried, in vain, to run. Run where? Though the interior walls had come down, they were still locked inside the prison. "Like crazed ants," one inmate described it to me.

The gangsters patrolled the wards in groups of at least thirty, each group leader walking ahead with camera phones. The mobs would stop in front of each civilian they came across, most of whom waited like a child being scolded by a teacher, staring at the floor. They pulled heads up, pointed their phones at faces and then sent the files. Then they asked, over the phone, "This one?" If the voice responded in the negative, they marched on. If the voice said yes, the group "fell on them like hungry hyenas after a dying horse. All you could see were chunks of flesh flying through the air."

From seven that night until nine the following morning, the 18s swept through every ward, lifting each head to their camera phone and, according to the official record, devouring twenty-seven men. "There were more," another man, locked up in a different prison, told me. According to him (he also wanted to remain anonymous) there were inmates who were reduced to nothing but blood. A man turned into a puddle. "Like four of them, when they [the 18s] found out what nails they carried, they turned them into ground meat in the shower room. Little pieces that they flushed down the toilets."

What sparked the massacre? According to my source, who shrugged his shoulders and responded as if it were an every-day, almost natural occurrence: "Because they were pulling out a nail. A big nail."

That other nail was another massacre. The Mariona prison massacre of 2004.

In August 2004 Mariona prison was filled with both Barrio 18 members and civilians. Many of the civilians had joined ranks with the prison gang, La Raza. It all started, according to three inmates I spoke with who survived the massacre, when the 18s bought, from guards, some boards that construction workers had left inside the prison grounds. A board in the hands of an inmate can quickly become a weapon. A man known as El Viejo Posada, a well-respected civilian inmate in the gangster family line of mythical barrio names like Trejo, Guandique and Bruno, ordered his second in command, Racumín, to take a message to the 18s: "Give up those boards or we're going to play soccer with your heads."

They never gave up the boards. El Viejo Posada ordered their own civilian weapons to be distributed: mostly shanks and sharpened pieces of cots. Silently, with the help of guards who opened cell-block doors, they entered into Wards 1 and

2, where the 18s were waiting for them with their boards. It was hand-to-hand combat. There were dead on both sides. It wasn't certain who won, but most think it was the 18s. One of the witnesses I spoke with, who was involved in the fighting, told me that El Viejo Posado "turned himself in to the guards so the 18s wouldn't kill him. He shit and pissed himself, handed over the .38 he was packing and turned himself in." After "the gizzard," was over, which is what prison brawls are called in El Salvador, authorities counted thirty-two dead. But, according to my source, it was "more, much more. Thirty-seven if you count those chopped up in the showers." Much of what goes untold in prison massacres is flushed down the drains.

After the 2004 massacre many of the inmates were transferred out of Mariona, most of them going to Apanteos. Which is where the rematch of 2007 took place.

An eye for an eye. A massacre for a massacre. In prison life, memories aren't forgotten. Nails are carried and then pulled out. Scars are revealed.

In 2007 the 18s in Apanteos still remembered that on the other side of the wall there were those who pulled out their nails and they were ready to deal out their revenge: "They are the men who have the blood of homeboy on their hands. They know we're coming." Hyenas after a dying horse. "It was like a witch hunt," one of my sources described it to me.

And the maxim repeats itself: Behind the story is a story. Behind the massacre is a massacre. The iceberg has a base, and to get to the bottom you need to go swimming.

It was the same every time. Director Molina responding to a request of mine: pulling up his hat, rubbing his forehead, murmuring, "OK, OK, that again, Señor Journalist."

This time I was asking that he pull the rep everyone wanted to talk to from Ward 8, the MS Ward. Director Molino made a call to a guard on his radio and asked if he could pull him out "without causing a brawl." The guard said he could do it, and fifteen minutes later a short, dark-skinned man sat down across from me. The man looked like he had lived a hard forty years, resembling a bricklayer or a construction worker more than a gangster. Besides asking that I not use his name, he spoke freely and got right to the point.

"The problem here is that inmates in Wards 9 and 10 are from the 18."

"And you're from the MS?" I asked.

"What happens is that if you live where the MS lives, everybody says you're MS, and then you carry your nails and they want to fuck you up. But all you want to do is live a life with your lady, nothing else. I don't even want to be from here."

"Are you MS?" I asked again.

"It's like this. You live where they live. You see them around. You got family, and maybe you work up a little sympathy, but that's not the problem. The problem is not with the MS, it's with the 18s who are hanging around with the Transfers, the group in control in Ward 11."

I would later learn that the rep from Ward 8's son and brother are both members of the MS and that he himself is serving time for a crime committed with two active members of the MS who are locked up in a prison dedicated to MS members. And yet the rep from Ward 8 wouldn't admit affiliation. The group he referenced is a relatively new name on the map of power within the prison system: the Transfers Band.

The Transfers proto-gang was formed in the mid-2000s when civilians realized that the program of separating gang members from non–gang members was more half-lie than half-truth. The massacre of 2004, which greatly weakened La Raza and reduced them to control just a sliver of Mariona, as well as the massacre of 2007 in Apanteos, were key moments in the formation of the Transfer Band. The inmates murdered in 2007 had mostly been relocated from Mariona (after the 2004 massacre) to Gotera, and then from Gotera to Apanteos, where they were locked up next to their enemies from Barrio 18—nothing but a single wall separating them. As opposed to the well-organized 18s, the new transfers barely knew any of the inmates in the prison. Thus they became the dying horses trying to outrun the pack of hyenas.

With the memory of the murders still fresh, civilians in Apanteos met with the Transfers Band after the massacre. The logic was simple: They wanted to talk with inmates who had power in the prison system, inmates who, despite claims that Apanteos had only one noncivilian ward, were already organizing there. They started getting the word out, forming groups, setting rules so that when they pulled out their nails with the gangsters, when they drew their scars with the 18s, they wouldn't be alone; they would be part of the Transfers. They achieved unity, expanded and soon started dominating drug trafficking inside the prison. A leader emerged, a man with various names: Miguel Ángel Navarro. Ex-PNC [National Police]. The Animal ... but more on him later.

Before I finished my interview with the skinny construction-worker-like rep from Ward 8 I asked him the same question I had asked his enemy a few days before, the rep from Ward 11.

"Why do you want to run the prison? What's the business advantage?"

He smiled at me.

"There's none," he said. "None. We just want to grow old in peace."

The inner workings of the prison reveal a simple problem: When inmates tell outsiders that all they want is to grow old in peace, the finger always points to somebody else; it's the fault of the MS, or Barrio 18, or the Transfers, and never their own fault, the fault of MS members themselves, or Barrio 18s, or the Transfers.

The ward reps only want to talk about hellish conditions, never about their fight for power. And it's true: The conditions are hellish. Conditions inside these prisons are out of this world, criminally awful, and yet in that hell, the fight is always about power.

I spoke with warden after warden, prison researcher after prison researcher, even guard after guard, until finally I found what I was looking for. The Worm, a rare bird of an inmate, had spent the last eight years locked up in five different prisons, getting a taste of wards specific to MS members, 18s and civilians. The Worm didn't belong to any group. If he had to fight for one side, he'd pick the Transfers first, then the 18s, and if there were no other options, he'd resort to siding with the MS. He's a survivor, and he knows how and when to affiliate himself. The Worm, too, wants to grow old in peace, and he knows how to do so: Keep a low profile, as low as the dirt— become a worm inching through the soil, silently, underneath the world of the beasts. Watching them from below.

The first thing I asked him to do was to draw me a map, to lay out the power dynamic—the inmate's version of what Director Molina had given me. Rail thin, toothless and squatting on his haunches, the Worm described to me the lay of the land.

"What's important to know is that in Apanteos the Transfers are in Ward 11 where they're joined up with the Machine and Mao Mao [other prison gangs, originally from El Salvador, and without strong national presence]. The Transfers control 11 and two other wards, 5 and 6. The 18s have 9 and 10, along with La Mirada [an affiliated gang centered in eastern El Salvador, originally from the Los Angeles suburb La Mirada]. The MS have 8, plus they've infiltrated some other wards. All of them lose their shit when they run into each other. The ones in 8 [the 18s] are against everybody else, and are trying to figure out what to do."

"How come?" I ask. "What do they want?"

"They want to be able to do their business in peace, and they want other people not to do business. You have to realize that everything here is connected, a prison is just one piece of the puzzle. It's part of the plan to spark a brawl, part of the plan to charge rent [for access to beds or other parts of the prison], even if it's just a little, to inmates outside their gang or to unaffiliated people like me. Part of the plan to take all this up the chain of command. If you don't have power, nobody is going to hear you. The more prisons you control, the more they're gonna listen."

"Who's the leader?"

"If you're looking for the leader, he's right here. It's the Cobra, from 11, but if you want to know who the leader-leader is, ask for the Animal, who's in Zacatecoluca. He's the one who says sneeze and everybody sneezes. That's the prison where all his dogs are barking and where everybody else gets dog-bit."

All the people I spoke with, the director of prisons, the rep from the Transfers, the rep from the MS, Director Molina, the Worm, all pointed to the imminence of a brawl in Apanteos. They all knew it. Even the most humble inmates cooped up behind bars knew it. And yet the Worm helped me understand how deep the base of the iceberg went, and how little of it we could see. The coming massacre had nothing to do with fights or personal vendettas; it had to do with power structures, with dominoes set up to knock down entire prisons so someone could win central control of the criminal world in the entire country. From behind bars in a super-max prison is where the Animal and the Little Devil (the national leader of the MS) issued their orders, and it was in Apanteos where the dogs obeyed and got ready. Some started infiltrating enemy wards. Others were honing strategy, working up steam to prepare for the onslaught. And the system, incapable of doing a thing, sat back and watched.

At noon on November 24, I made a call to the warden of Apanteos, Douglas Moreno. He answered from what sounded like the middle of a construction zone. Metallic thundering drowned out most of what he said.

"Warden," I said, "they're saying that the battle has begun."

"It's … give … -iot."

Another thunderous bang.

"Warden, what's going on?"

"Hold on," he yelled. "They're … Wait, wait! They're already fighting."

The line cut.

At eleven in the morning the MS and their allies from Ward 8 decided that enough was enough. For the past three days the civilians in the prison had been trying to clean things up. They swept up anyone they thought was an MS member, delivering them to the guards and asking, "You going to take them where they belong, or should we kill them?" Soon, they retook control of almost all the wards in the prison. Almost 100 inmates were rounded up and stuffed into Ward 8. That morning, Ward 6 did the same thing, presenting twenty-five suspected gang members to the guards and threatening to kill them if they weren't taken away. The problem was that Ward 8 was already bursting at the seams. There wasn't room for a single new inmate, let alone another ounce of anger.

Moreno himself went to Ward 8 after guards informed him that inmates there were planning an offensive against Ward 6. "They're throwing everybody from all the other wards in here with us, and it's not right," the construction-worker man I had spoken with a few weeks ago yelled at Moreno. As he issued his complaint, other inmates from his ward had already gotten onto the roof in preparation for breaching other wards. Moreno, as he would later explain to me, then went to Ward 6. There the argument was pretty simple. An inmate named Molina Ruíz told him: "We can't live with the MS. That's it." Next Moreno went back to his office to try to think it out. And that was the moment I called him. The thunder was already sounding in the prison. The MS had begun their invasion of Ward 6. The first to die was the last man to speak with Moreno, Luis Antonio Molina Ruíz, forty-one years old. He was serving time for embezzlement, a nonviolent crime. Next, the long-awaited riot spilled over into Ward 7. Inmates were finally pulling out some of their nails.

Next to fall was an inmate from Ward 8: twenty-five-year-old Victor Kennedy Menéndez, stabbed in the heart. In my conversation with the Worm five days later, he told me about the first murders: "The first two were civilians, but connected to the Transfers. The guy from Ward 6 [Molina Ruíz] they killed because he talked to the director. The guy from 8 they killed because he'd infiltrated the gang members, and it was time to pull his nail."

Guards had succeeded in evacuating most of Ward 6 before MS members had gotten all the way in. As Moreno knew that things were about to explode after talking to Molina Ruíz, he ordered the immediate transfer of all civilians to other sectors. Molina Ruíz, however, didn't get out in time. "I'd just gotten out," Moreno told me, "when they killed him." Besides the two deaths, twenty-two other inmates, those who weren't evacuated in time, were injured. They were stabbed, beaten and clubbed by MS members, or by their allies, though in the moment there was no difference between the two. If it weren't for the rapid exodus of inmates, the day would probably be remembered for twenty-four deaths instead of just two deaths and twenty-two injuries.

Lucky timing, slow-moving MS members and an ineffective attack saved the prison from a different kind of massacre. The Worm summed up the day for me: "The nail is still in there. It's definitely gonna happen again. Soon."

Maybe it won't be until Gotera prison (where over 200 gang members were sent from Apanteos after the riot) over-fills enough that the gang wards start leaking into the civilian wards. Or maybe it won't happen until the remaining gangsters in Apanteos come into contact, once again, with the civilians in Ward 6. Or maybe it will happen tomorrow. Nobody knows. For now, the nail remains in place.

On November 30, a thirty-six-year-old man was stabbed to death in Zacatecoluca maximum-security prison. His name was Miguel Ángel Navarro, otherwise known as the Animal.

The TV news bits about the stabbing were thirty seconds or shorter; newspaper articles were half a page or less. Articles said that he was stabbed, that he was serving time for armed robbery and illicit association, and the likely motivation was a fight between rival gangs. None of the stories mentioned that he was found dead in the cell of his spokesman and second in command, Iván Buenaventura Alegría, also known as the Rapist of Merliot, who had been sentenced to 107 years of prison in 2001 for raping eight women. Nobody seemed to question the idea that it was a fight between rival gangs even though the cell in which the Animal was found was in the lower floor of Ward 3, which is where the civilians were located so that the MS from Wards 1 and 2 and the 18s from Ward 4 weren't next to each other. Nobody put two and two together or thought that the murder might have something to do with what had happened in Apanteos. Nobody mentioned that pulling out a nail pulls out other nails, that the Animal was the head of the Transfers, the man who, if he ordered that they sneeze, every single civilian in the Zacatecoluca sneezed. The Animal, according to two separate sources I spoke with, was the man who gave the order for the civilians in Apanteos, where he himself had previously served time, to start kicking the MS out of their wards.

In April 2010, nine different civilian prisons erupted, vying for control of the country's gang operations. After the dust settled, six gang prisons had affiliated themselves with Apanteos. The fighting was popularly attributed to the inhumane living conditions in the prisons. And yet all of my sources, from the man I met in the Chinese restaurant, to the

Worm, to a fired ex-guard from Zacatecoluca prison, told me that something else was going on: In April of the same year, prison authorities transferred the Animal from Apanteos to Zacatecoluca.

The iceberg is always deeper than it seems.

The director of Apanteos prison, Molina, agreed to meet me again on Wednesday, December 1, one day after the Animal was found in a cell with seventy-two stab wounds in his face, neck, chest and back. Molina doesn't seem to smile much, but when you get close to asking the right question, he'll give you a bit of a smile.

"They killed the Animal, Director," I said. "It seems as if what started in Apanteos between the MS and the civilians was settled in Zacatecoluca."

I got him to smile.

"You think so? The world of prisons and inmates is complicated in this country, isn't it?"

He didn't want to elaborate. But the Worm assured me that behind the bars there were only two options for inmates: One, that they kill MS members in revenge for the earlier Apanteos massacre, or two, that they kill the civilians trying to climb up the ladder of the Transfers who were against attacking the MS. The ex-guard from Zacatecoluca I spoke with, who was the first person to find the Animal's bloodied body, told me: "An inmate, scared for his life just because he was locked up next to the Animal, assured me that it was Abraham Bernabé Mendoza, El Patrón, who wanted to take over ... Supposedly someone in the MS ward sent the order to El Patrón, in Ward 3."

Maybe both of the Worm's options played out.

Before the Animal was killed, both cameras were covered in the outdoor patio where inmates, in groups of twelve, were let out for their forty minutes of fresh air a day. The Animal was killed between 11:00 and 11:20, and the murderer had to be one of the other eleven inmates who were given access to the patio and the door to the Animal's ward.

I asked Director Molina if he had known that there was going to be a massacre in Apanteos.

"Yes, we knew something was going to happen, but we didn't know when."

Prison officials recognize uprisings as part of life. You can predict prison massacres like you can predict storms: The horizon darkens, the barometer drops. Stopping them is a different story. All that matters is when the clouds break.

The director paused, considering the situation outside of his prison: "The problem isn't if it's going to happen or not. The problem is with the system itself, that it's broken. This is why there are going to be more."

"More massacres?"

"Maybe. But that's not the point. We've been suffering the aftereffects from years and years of abandonment. Problems with administration, lack of capacity, security, infrastructure, finances and corruption. Where do you want me to start? All this has real consequence. The system decided to pack all the gang members together so they wouldn't be killing each other. But now they don't all fit in gang-only prisons. In the west the gang members won't even let any more of their own members into the prisons. So they're sending them to civilian prisons, where the civilians have started organizing. And now there are even more groups who all want the same thing: power, power, power. The questions are: How many groups have formed? What can we do with them? If there's not enough room to keep them separated, do we put them all together?"

"I imagine so," I said. "If they don't fit, they don't fit."

"Well, yes. I suppose so."

In Apanteos there are 240 MS gang members or allies in Ward 6. Another 250, those most directly involved in the riot, were transferred to Gotera prison. But even after the transfer, almost all the other wards in Apanteos remain in conflict with Ward 6. Soldiers were brought in to guard the perimeter walls, but these are the least important walls in the prison. Inside, as Director Molina told me, "Things are still balancing out, being negotiated, because there's always going to be tension."

The seemingly infallible memory of past offenses, combined with overpopulation, makes up what is essentially a permanently ticking time bomb.

According to the Worm, "Your nails don't disappear in here. Eventually you have to pull them out."

They are already starting to pull out another nail.

Part 3. Fleeing

There are those who believe that in this corner of the world there's nothing left for them. There are those who are willing to launch themselves into a new inferno by crossing the border, by fleeing.

11

The Tamed Coyotes

March 2014

Why did Los Zetas massacre 268 people, most of them migrants? Stories of Salvadorans killed in the bloodbath of Northern Mexico, an account from a veteran coyote and some uncovered documents all point to the fact that the massacres were meant as a lesson to coyotes: Pay or stay out.

The lay of the land has changed. Coyotes no longer rule the road.

The coyote returned much sooner than expected. Normally, he'd be gone more than twenty days, but this time he came back only five or six days after having crossed Mexico's southern border. That's why Fernando, the coyote's driver in El Salvador, was surprised to receive his boss's call. It was August 2010 when the coyote asked his driver to pick him up at the Salvadoran border town of San Cristóbal. He was alone, without his six migrants. The coyote—so Fernando later explained to investigators—was nervous, refusing to explain what had happened and offering nothing but excuses: "A dog bit me." A few days after, Fernando would know for a fact that no dog had bitten the coyote. It had been a far bigger beast.

On Wednesday, August 25, 2010, Salvadoran newspapers blared the headline: "Seventy-Two Bodies Found at Tamaulipas Ranch." In the early morning of August 23, a disoriented eighteen-year-old Ecuadoran with a bullet wound through his neck stumbled up to a marine checkpoint in Northern Mexico. He said that he had survived a massacre perpetrated by Northern Mexico's crime lords, Los Zetas. The marines traveled to a cluster of towns called San Fernando and from there they journeyed to a village called La Joya. In the middle of nowhere, on a narrow dirt road, they were met by a storm of bullets. Three gunmen and one marine died in the crossfire. The surviving hit man fled. The marines trekked on to a warehouse where they saw a snake of bodies coiled against a cement wall, bunched on top of each other, swollen, deformed, tied up. Massacred.

Thanks to the testimony of the surviving Ecuadoran, a boy named Luis Freddy Lala Pomadilla, every Salvadoran newspaper picked up the story of the massacred migrants. Little by little, day by day, the facts were confirmed: Fifty-eight men and fourteen women, migrants from Central America, Ecuador, Brazil and India, all on their way to the United States, were massacred by Los Zetas.

Fernando, the driver, tells me that on the day the headline was printed around the world, he got a call from the coyote.

"I'm out of here," the coyote said. "If the police come, tell them you don't know me."

"But why?"

"Remember: You don't know nothing about me!"

Fernando is the name given to the coyote's driver as a key witness in the trial against six Salvadorans accused of human smuggling. Fernando and the coyote had known each other since they were kids. They were neighbors when Fernando lost his job and accepted the coyote's offer to work as his driver. Fernando told the judge, prosecutors of the anti-trafficking unit and various agents of the Elite Division Against Organized Crime (DECO) that his job usually entailed picking the coyote up, driving him to meetings with potential clients, driving him to meetings with other members of their organization and driving him to the Guatemalan border. Until August 2010, his job did not entail keeping his mouth shut in front of the police.

In December 2010, the police showed up. They arrested Fernando as well as a 33-year-old man named Érick Francisco Escobar. According to the Public Prosecutor's Office (PPO), the police, Fernando, and other witnesses, Érick is the coyote in question.

Police investigators had located the victims' families and obtained seven corroborating testimonies. One of the witnesses, a man whose son was shot to death by Los Zetas in Tamaulipas, was the only witness who said he was able to recognize Érick. And he did. He pointed out the coyote who had guided his son to his death.

Fernando was also accused of belonging to the human-smuggling ring, but after a few weeks in the San Vicente penitentiary—where he was forced to sleep sitting upright next to a toilet—he decided to tell investigators what he knew.

Three months after the first round of arrests, the police detained a man who had managed to stay under the radar. Carlos Ernesto Teos Parada is a large man from the town of Tecapán, leader of the first division soccer team Atlético Marte and owner of several city buses. According to investigations as well as Fernando's declaration, he was the leader of the pack of coyotes of which Érick was a member.

Sabas López Sánchez, a twenty-year-old kid, and Karen Escobar Luna, twenty-eight years old, were also from Tecapán. They both ended up in the snake of corpses found in the abandoned warehouse in Tamaulipas.

Fernando's declaration allows us to imagine that the migrants, at least the six traveling with Érick, spent their last days hanging from the back of a train.

Fernando painted a picture of two migrant routes through Mexico. One of them starts in Chiapas, where hundreds of thousands of migrants pour into Mexico every year after dipping their toes in the Suchiate River that divides Guatemala and Mexico. Through a stretch of 175 miles where the train doesn't run, migrants will walk through shrubland and then take *chiapaneco* buses or shared taxis until they get to the city of Arriaga, where they'll crawl onto the back of the steel beast for an eleven-hour ride under the unforgiving August sun to the city of Ixtepec, Oaxaca, where they'll switch trains, catching one that runs much faster, forty-five miles an hour for six to eight hours, to the city of Medias Aguas, Veracruz, where the trains coming from Oaxaca and Tabasco meet and continue north on the same track to Mexico City. From there, the migrants go on to the cities of Ciudad Victoria, Reynosa, Nuevo Laredo, where they cross the Rio Grande, outsmart the US Border Patrol and finally, with tremendous luck, reach the vast state of Texas.

Fernando knew Érick to be a man of vices. A drinker and coke user. He liked, as the witness put it, "to fly."

In the world of coyotes, snorting coke is as drinking whiskey is to the world of gamblers. Nothing special. And it wouldn't be an identifying trait, we wouldn't have even noticed, if what happened hadn't happened.

Fernando told prosecutors how one day Carlos Teos and Érick got together in the town of Usulután with some other members of their coyote group. This was about a month before the massacre. Teos doled out instructions. He spoke of the migrant route, of making new contacts, ordered some of the members to pay their dues. Fernando noticed the dull glint of a firearm and followed all orders. Teos came back with a wad of bills and gave Érick $3,000, enough money to cover several trips north.

The families of the six massacred Salvadorans say they had arranged to pay Érick between $5,700 and $7,500. They paid half up front and were to pay the other half once they reached the other side, the United States, soil they never set foot on.

After the meeting, Fernando drove Érick to Constitution Boulevard in San Salvador, to a barrio called La Granjita (the Little Ranch), run by an old Salvadoran gang by the name of Mao Mao. The barrio is often referred to as La Pradera (the Prairie) because of an eponymous motel in the area. Érick was looking to buy some coke and do some lines in the car.

The lines of coke would be a typical part of the story for any coyote, a simple curiosity, had Fernando's story not ended as it ended.

On the road, one of the women traveling north with the coyote called a family member, who later testified against the coyote. The prosecutor's report paints the woman as having sounded upbeat:

"I'm in Mexico and I'm with the guy who's going to take me. I'm fine. Tell everyone I say hi. I'll let you know when I'm in the United States."

Another migrant called his father from the road.

"Who are you going with?" his dad had asked. "Are you with Érick?"

"Yep, he's still with us. He's waiting for us."

What happened hadn't yet happened. These small events hadn't yet resulted in the coiled snake of bodies.

On August 11, according to various reports, six migrants left El Salvador and were massacred thirteen days later on an abandoned ranch in Tamaulipas.

Fernando says the group stayed in two hotels a few blocks away from San Salvador's international bus station. Some of the migrants stayed at Hotel Ipanema, others in Hotel Pasadena. Both are short-stay hotels that charge $17 for a double bed. They're used by truckers, migrants and coyotes.

The investigators were able to get a search warrant for Hotel Pasadena. Among the guests were a ten-year-old and an eighteen-year-old about to start their journey north with two coyotes: a recent deportee from the United States and a cop. The investigators detained both coyotes. They also found a Guatemalan man by the name of José María Negrero Sermeño. The investigators radioed the man's records to be checked, and they soon found that he had an arrest warrant (issued by a Salvadoran judge) for human smuggling. When they seized his multiple phones, they found the numbers of police officers, migration officials, Central American border patrol agents and various governmental officials. When they reviewed the man's previous calls, they found that he'd been in communication with Érick and Carlos Teos.

The ill-fated migrants got onto an international bus traveling toward the capital of Guatemala. Érick gave the bus driver $120. According to Fernando, that was $20 per migrant to be used by the bus driver as collateral in case any police officer noticed that the migrants had a guide out there somewhere. Érick, Fernando and another man—Carlos Arnoldo Ventura, who would later be sentenced to four years in prison for smuggling—drove to the border. Fernando remembers Érick calling Carlos Teos. The two men chatted about possible routes and dates.

Case files state that Carlos Teos—who had a US tourist visa—left El Salvador almost a week after the migrants. Fernando says Teos's job was to welcome the migrants in the United States, guide them to their families and charge for the second half of the trip. Teos would sometimes exit El Salvador through a checkpoint and sometimes not, though he would never enter through a checkpoint. Teos's bank records show that he's the kind of man who goes from having no cash to close to $10,000 in less than a month; the kind of man who goes from having $85,000 one day to $94,000 three days later.

The last thing Fernando knew of Érick is that he had crossed the border without passing through a checkpoint and boarded a bus with his migrants in Guatemala.

~

And then Fernando received Érick's call. A call that came much too soon.

"I'm out of here," the coyote said. "If the police come, tell them you don't know me."

For a few weeks the coyote disappeared. When he resurfaced, so Fernando says in his declaration, Érick shared with him a small detail that would completely change his story.

Érick told Fernando that he had overspent his money. To pay for his vices, Érick blew the money he'd reserved for Los Zetas. Érick—so Fernando said—knew the magnitude of his actions, he knew he had spent money he needed to have, money that was not negotiable, and that's why he abandoned his six Salvadorans.

When the investigator tells me that Carlos Teos and Érick were acquitted by a deputy judge of the Specialized Sentencing Court of San Salvador, his voice breaks. I can almost hear a sob in the back of his throat.

Despite Fernando's testimony, the call records, the eyewitness account of the father of one of the massacred boys, despite the fact that the same evidence and the same testimony prompted another judge to convict two other members of the group, the deputy judge in this case acquitted Érick and Carlos Teos.

"It was a total surprise, we'd already been celebrating … It's so sad. We all looked at each other in disbelief."

The Public Prosecutor's Office has appealed and is awaiting the criminal court's decision whether or not to reopen the case and assign another judge.

Meanwhile, the only thing left of the victims' families was the testimony they themselves gave. Every one of the family members who spoke in court received a death threat. Someone called each of them and told them that they would be disappeared, murdered. They related the threats to the prosecutors and then fled for their lives.

~

Thanks to an Ecuadoran kid, much of the world learned what happened on that abandoned Tamaulipas ranch.

On September 14, 2010, eighteen-year-old Luis Freddy Lala Pomadilla of Riobamba, Ecuador, spoke via video-call with a prosecutor from Mexico City. Pomadilla is one of two survivors, though the boy stresses that there may be another survivor who he saw escape the ranch one night, albeit followed by a thunderclap of gunfire.

The Mexican prosecutor was more interested in getting names and aliases out of Pomadilla. He asked for El Coyote, El Degollado (the Beheaded), Chabelo, El Kilo, Cabezón (Big Head) and El Gruñon (the Grouch), a known member of the Guatemalan special-op military unit with historical ties to Los Zetas, the Kaibiles. He also asked for the names and aliases of five more Salvadorans. He asked if any of these men were known to be Zetas. Pomadilla said they'd all kept their distance; he could barely remember El Kilo—Martín Omar Estrada, later captured and condemned as ruler of a Zetas zone of operation in San Fernando. Pomadilla—just like the six Salvadorans, he was abandoned by his coyote—remembers that it was some eight Zetas, all armed, driving a white double-cabin pickup and a four-wheel-drive Trooper, who stopped the three buses full of undocumented migrants approaching the US border. He remembers that he was taken to San Fernando and ordered to sit against a cement wall. He remembers that one of the Zetas asked if any of the men and women in the group wanted to be a Zeta. He remembers that only one migrant kid raised his hand and said yes. "But they killed him all the same." They killed him and seventy-one more. Pomadilla, who had been taken for dead, remembers gunfire ringing for three solid minutes. The cacophony came from a single gun. Seventy-two migrants had been shot dead.

Los Zetas are, as a military colonel once described them to me, a gang of cavemen. The colonel was charged with overseeing a state of emergency in northern Guatemala in 2011.

As the colonel put it, the Zetas shoot first, then torture, then murder, and then, if anybody is still alive, they ask their victims to please follow orders.

The cavemen in them, however, don't overshadow the mobsters in them. One interest is present in absolutely every operation this gang has masterminded since I've been following them since 2008: profit. Why would they kidnap seventy-two migrants, take them to a forgotten, rural ranch and massacre them? What could they have gained?

The main theory of the Mexican authorities is that Los Zetas killed the migrants because they'd refused to join them. One of the women, guided by Érick and murdered at the ranch by Los Zetas, was merely eighteen years old and from the Salvadoran state of Libertad. Does that fit the profile of somebody usually recruited by Los Zetas?

The story of the six Salvadoran migrants who were murdered, who paid with their lives for the small infraction committed by their coyote, speaks to another strain of logic. Those who don't pay can't cross. Migrating through Mexico has a cost, and those costs are set and collected by Los Zetas.

The coyotes and migrants who want to avoid paying their taxes will have to confront the cavemen. What message could be more powerful than seventy-two corpses coiled against a cement wall?

Perhaps Los Zetas hoped to send their message to coyotes and migrants in one blast. But in order to be sure, in order to understand just how the mafia was able to change the coyote rule book, we have to sit down with one of those stealthy guides.

There are few better places to find a good coyote than the Salvadoran state of Chalatenango.

There are six empty pint glasses and a plate of appetizers that the cheese-and-cigarette trafficker is picking and poking at. We're seated in the restaurant of a small hotel on the outskirts of the capital of Chalatenango, which is really just a small town with a bank and a smattering of fast-food restaurants. The cheese trafficker, whom I met thanks to an intermediary, says this restaurant and hotel are owned by a famous coyote from Chalatenango. The coyote looks nervous as he approaches our table, though you can tell he's interested in who I am and what I'm doing at his restaurant. The cheese trafficker, thinking better of introducing us, falls silent.

The round-bellied trafficker seated beside me buys cheese for pennies in Nicaragua and brings back hundreds of pounds of it hidden behind false doors in cargo trucks. He also coordinates truckloads of Chinese and Russian cigarettes packaged in mislabeled containers headed to Ocotepeque, Honduras. Once the trucks cross the border, they take the labels off and sell the cigarettes at half the price of other brands. In many stores in Chalatenango you'll be more likely to find Modern than Marlboro.

As the trafficker's plan has backfired, and for some strange reason he seems intent on helping me in my search for a coyote, he slaps off his hat, takes a deep breath, narrows his eyes, and says: "You can turn over a stone here and find a coyote. The problem is that the young ones, the new ones, are more skittish, and they don't like talking to journalists. This guy might blow us off, but why don't we try with someone higher up? I'm grateful to him because he's the one that showed me the ropes of cheese trafficking. He's the coyote who teaches everyone else how to work. He's the first coyote of Chalatenango."

It's Friday, and the cheese trafficker says to give him the weekend to talk to this lord of coyotes.

The lord of coyotes is big and tough as nails. He amicably welcomes us into his home in Chalatenango, sending for tilapia, rice, tortillas and beer.

The cheese trafficker has succeeded in convincing his boss that in exchange for his stories and explanations, in exchange for his testimony, I'll keep his identity secret. The coyote trusts me. And that's why, on this October evening of 2013, the conversation moves along without hesitation.

The coyote is sixty years old. He got in the business of taking people to the United States in 1979. In his first attempt to cross into the United States, he paid 600 colones—which at the time was about US$240—to a Guatemalan coyote. The trip ended with him being locked up in Tijuana. While serving time in various detention centers he got to know another Guatemalan coyote. This lord of coyotes, who was a twenty-something-year-old kid at the time, offered to find him new clients in El Salvador. In those days, so the coyote remembers, his job was not demonized. Coyotes weren't detained simply for being coyotes, and they certainly weren't put on trial, as happened to Érick, in the Specialized Court for Organized Crime. This coyote felt so comfortable with what he was doing that in order to promote his business he opened an office in the central Salvadoran city of Cuscatancingo and published ads in the classifieds section of various newspapers announcing "safe trips to the United States," along with a business telephone number. A few months later, when he had already learned from the Guatemalan everything he needed to learn, the coyote branched off and started his own business. People would call his office and ask how long they'd have to walk. The coyote would explain that they would travel through Mexico by bus, and that they'd cross the border through Mexicali, San Luis Río Colorado or Algodones, and that they wouldn't walk more than an hour. And that's how it was. When the coyote had about fifteen to twenty people, he'd start the journey north. The largest group he crossed was thirty-five people. Crossing Mexico, the coyote remembers, could be a pleasant trip. "People only had to get off the bus to take a piss," he remembers. Everything would already be taken care of at the migration checkpoints, and they'd only have to pay a few dollars at each checkpoint.

In the mid-'80s, after the National Guard searched his office, mistaking his business for a guerrilla unit, the coyote decided to take a few years off, alternating long stays in the United States with sporadic jobs crossing small groups of migrants.

Then in 2004 the coyote started working again. Business, however, had gotten more difficult, and it was about to get worse.

"Everything was changing. There was more security in Mexico, and suddenly it was a crime to be a coyote in Guatemala. So the price for a coyote went up to $6,000 per person. Few things were the same."

Traveling coyotes, those who guided their migrants throughout all of Mexico, had become nearly obsolete.

"By this point the job had more to do with coordination, and that's how it still is. A coyote in Guatemala is in charge of organizing a group of people on the southern border of Mexico, then there's the guy who takes them to Mexico City. He's usually a Mexican. He's paid anywhere from $1,200 to $1,300 per person. In Mexico City, another guy takes them to the US border. That guy charges $800, and you have to pay him another $100 for securing the housing and food for the little chickens. So to get from here to the US border, a migrant needs to put in some $2,500. Then, to get into the United States, to go to Houston, for example, coyotes charge $2,000. Some ask $2,500 just to get across the border. Then they keep them there, detained, in safe houses. I wire them money from here, and they start letting people out of the safe house one by one. They'd charge $500 just for the vans that drive people to the safe houses. Now they charge $700. So for each person, the coyote in Guatemala is making $1,000 to $1,500 in profit."

One can cut expenses in Mexico, but that requires methods that, for this coyote, are "inhumane." For example, squeezing 120 migrants into a cargo truck routed to the US border without stops. If you have the right contacts at the Mexican customs office, they can flag the truck as being full of fruit when in reality the truck is full of dozens of people suffocating from heat and lack of oxygen, without deodorant or perfume, without watches or cell phones, without anything that could beep and give them away. There are coyotes who can save a few hundred dollars by stuffing people under the false bottom of a banana truck and making their migrants ride lying down for more than twenty hours until they reach Mexico City.

The coyote says the price of guided migration has gone up in the past five years, and that no one priding himself on being a good coyote should take a migrant to the United States for less than $7,000 dollars.

"There are more risks now," the coyote says, and with a finger in the air he traces the letter Z.

"When did you start to pay off Los Zetas?" I ask.

"We started working with them in 2005, but it wasn't obligatory yet. Having a contact with Los Zetas was like a guarantee for safety, so we'd seek them out. The Mexican coyote would organize all that and make contacts with the police. Later, around 2007, Los Zetas started to squeeze the undocumented migrant directly. They didn't care whose migrants they were. They started charging $100 per person. It's only gotten worse."

Los Zetas, who were initially the armed wing of the Gulf Cartel, branched off around 2007. Maybe the migrant tax was initially like a bonus to their salaries, but it later became guaranteed income, their low-hanging fruit.

"A hundred a head, that's what Los Zetas charge to let you cross Mexico?" I ask.

"Now it's $200. A coyote should include that sum in the initial quote they give to migrants. The risk is higher, that's why the price has gone up, the coyote doesn't want to risk his life for $1,000 in profits."

"Do you have an understanding with Los Zetas?"

"We give the money to the Mexicans, it's the Mexican

coyotes who take care of these things. I don't know any Zetas. If someone here says he knows one of them, he's a liar. That Mexican contact might be paying $100 and charging me $200. That might be going on. But we have to pay up."

"Or?"

"Well, look what happened with the massacre in Tamaulipas, they owed them, and these guys didn't give a damn whose migrants they were. To them it was just a message: Someone forgot to pay, so this is what has to happen. And now that coyote has to pay the consequences. No one rounds a group of people up just to send them to their deaths, a coyote just wants to make money and gain credibility."

"But there are coyotes who still travel through Mexico with their migrants?"

"A good coyote won't travel with his migrants. That doesn't exist anymore. No one will put himself through that risk. Maybe they'll leave them in Ciudad Hidalgo [on the southern border of Mexico]. Everything is done piece by piece; one has to coordinate. OK, there are the madmen on the train. The train guys charge some $4,000 to $5,000. But those are the *polleritos* [a chicken man, referring to a guide leading and traveling with *pollos*, or migrants, as opposed to a coyote] who take two, three people. Some of them actually want to go north themselves, and they've already made the trip before, they know a little about what it's like to ride the train, so they pick up a couple more people and they all go together. But that's how people get kidnapped. If you always pay $200 per person, they won't bother you, but if you go all by yourself ... well ... then. That's when the Zetas get angry: 'This guy is going to cross and not pay anything,' and then they double down and charge up to $5,000 a head. If you work with those Mexican contacts who know the Zetas, then you're guaranteed that your migrants will cross Mexico, no problem. I mean, this group is in with the military and police. An officer will even detain you, check to see if you've already paid Los

Zetas, and if you've paid, they'll let you go right away. If they realize you haven't had contact with Los Zetas, then they'll squeeze you, and you're not going to go to jail, they'll take you straight to them, to Los Zetas. That's why people get disappeared. Mexico isn't a problem if you've dealt with Los Zetas. But if not ..."

By nightfall, I say good-bye to the coyote, leaving that "if not" hanging over our heads. For the six migrants who left with Érick, that "if not" led to a storm of bullets in an abandoned warehouse. For others, the "if not" can lead to worse. If you've paid your due to Los Zetas, you're fine. But if not ...

Sometimes Bertila forgets what she's talking about. She also eats very little. Over sixty years old, Bertila weighs less than 100 pounds. On March 27, 2011, her son Charli disappeared as he was traveling from San Luis Potosí, Mexico, to the northern border city of Reynosa. Since then, Bertila eats hardly anything and sleeps poorly. She dreams, though. She dreams that Charli is not dead, that he's come back home, and she says to him in her dream, "I thought something bad had happened to you." And he responds: "To me? Nothing's happened to me."

Sick of earning $4 a day in his maquiladora job, motivated by the impending birth of his first daughter and persuaded by an offer of a loan from a coyote—which he planned to pay off after a few months of working in the United States—Charli decided to leave behind his house in Izalco (in western El Salvador) and migrate north. He left with a coyote and four other migrants.

I'm seated in a patio in the village of Izalco with Bertila, Charli's mother, and this is what, from under the weight of her pain, she tells me.

Charli, his coyote and the other migrants left on a Monday ready to ride a combination of buses and trains to the US border. By that same Friday, however, the coyote was back in Izalco with all his migrants, except for Charli. In Oaxaca state, migration officials had detained the entire group, except for Charli, and deported them. Charli continued north by himself.

He reached the northern Mexican state of San Luis Potosí and stayed four days at the house of some distant relatives who had settled there years previously. That was where he contacted his family for the last time, speaking not with Bertila, but with Jorge, his brother, who worked as a day laborer in Oklahoma. Jorge told me over the phone that Charli had had his doubts. By this point the coyote from his village had set off again from El Salvador with his four migrants. This would be their second attempt. Charli, so Jorge remembers, told the coyote that he was thinking of going north to Reynosa on his own where he could look for another coyote to help him cross the border. Jorge tried to find the female coyote who had guided him a few years back. She worked by using other people's documents and crossing people through border checkpoints, or by leading her clients straight across the Rio Grande. The difference between the two options was half a grand. She charged $2,500 for false documents and $2,000 for the trip across the river. But Jorge couldn't find her, and Charli was getting impatient. Even so, he told his brother, the coyote from their village had warned him: He'd told him not to move, to wait for him. He told him that the road north was full of Zetas, that they'd sniff him out. They were on the hunt for migrants who walked alone.

Jorge had some idea of the dangers ahead. Just a few months before, a cousin of his had gone to the United States and told him he'd miraculously made it alive: "He told me Los Zetas would kidnap a coyote's migrants if he didn't come to them first, that they were always looking for any coyote who refused to pay. My cousin had to travel with one of those coyotes, and when he realized Los Zetas were looking for him, he had no choice but to run from his group. Luckily, he was able to hide."

And yet, to wait in Mexico as a migrant is to wait in limbo … in an interminable hell.

Charli decided to catch a bus headed to Reynosa.

On April 6, 2011, the authorities of Tamaulipas state announced that they'd found eight mass graves in a village called La Joya, outside of San Fernando, the same town in which, just the year before, Los Zetas had massacred seventy-two migrants in an abandoned warehouse. The graves were full of fifty-nine rotting bodies. Some of their skulls had been bashed in.

At first, the state authorities tried to minimize the situation, labeling the dead as "members of transnational criminal organizations, kidnappers and victims of highway violence."

But the bodies wouldn't stop sprouting from the ground.

By April 8, eight bodies were reported to have been found; by April 15, the toll was 145 bodies in thirty-six separate graves; by April 29, the governor of Tamaulipas announced that 196 people had been found murdered.

We realized only too late that we could have done something to stop the carnage, that the least we could've done was take preventative measures after finding the seventy-two bodies in 2010. The US National Security Archive declassified a series of cables sent from various American officials working throughout Mexico to Washington, DC. The communiqués, primarily sent from Matamoros, a border town close to San Fernando, stated that between March 19 and March 24 of that year, almost a month before any of the mass graves had been found, droves of hit men were pulling over buses en route to Reynosa and kidnapping their passengers. The state knew about it.

This same route, despite his coyote's warnings, is how Charli traveled. It's the route that thousands of migrants from all over the world take to arrive at the last stage of their journey: the US border. Those kidnappings were not random or isolated; they had become the norm.

Though an interdisciplinary commission was charged with identifying the discovered bodies, many of the bodies were actually identified thanks to mothers of the disappeared. They traveled all the way from Central America to offer blood samples for the DNA tests.

One of those mothers was Bertila. One of the bodies identified was Charli.

Bertila, now seated at a *pupusería* table on the patio of her house in the village of Izalco, has one foot in this reality and another deep in the sea of her thoughts. Her gaze seems to lose itself inward, and she often forgets what we're talking about. It's as though a movie were continuously playing in her mind's eye. Invariably, that movie is a tragedy. She dreams of police officers handing her a box or a coffin, or whatever it may be— the packaging changes—with Charli's bones inside.

In December 2012, almost two years after her son was kidnapped and murdered by Los Zetas, Bertila received notice from Mexico's attorney general that the body in row 11, lot 314, section 16 of the Municipal Cemetery of the Cross in Ciudad Victoria belonged to her son Charli.

To describe the suffering of a mother whose son has been murdered and disappeared, whose bones she'll never be able to bury—almost three years after that barbaric tragedy, Bertila still hasn't received Charli's remains—is a dangerous challenge. What adjective could describe Bertila's feelings? What adjective could approximate her pain? The only thing I can think to write is that Bertila doesn't wholly live in this world, that in her mind a terrifying dream plays and replays, disconnecting her from this world.

All I can write are her own words:

"Sometimes I forget that I'm talking ... sometimes, when

they would ask me if I knew something about Charli, I felt that I was being punched ... from the inside ... I was falling, for a long time I was falling ... I threw myself on his bed and I stayed there. Two years, seven months and ten days have passed. The bones ... well, I'd find a little peace with them. Though maybe I'll never find complete peace. But that would fill my life a bit, because sometimes this thought terrifies me ... Whenever it rains hard I imagine that the bones might wash away and I'll never be able to find them. That has me ... every time I hear of a hurricane in Mexico, that there's a storm, a tropical storm, I think about that. It's a deep anxiety when I see that everyone is able to bring flowers to their dead or bring their loved ones over to meet them ... I can't even receive mine ..."

Again, the question: Why kidnap Charli and others like him? Why waste the gas and the men, why risk getting caught to detain a bus of migrants? Why bother to take them to different towns outside of San Fernando? Why murder with such brutality? Most of the bodies have no bullet wounds. They died by brute force, with hard, sharp objects, with sticks and machetes. Why all the carnage?

Why did this happen to Charli? Why did this happen to the six migrants traveling with Érick? Why did this happen to seventy-two people in 2010? Why did this happen to 196 people in 2011?

The coyote of Chalatenango tries to answer these questions.

We agreed to meet a second time at his house in Chalatenango, but at the last minute, the coyote changes plans. He says he's working on one of his ranches, that we should meet on the highway in front of the Fourth Infantry Brigade. He tells me to turn on my emergency lights, pull over to the side of the road and that when he passes me, he'll honk his horn.

He arrives. One of his laborers is driving. The coyote is drunk.

In theory we'd go to one of his ranches, but I end up following him to his house. We sit down in the same spot as last time. It's hard to get the conversation going because he wants to talk about other things. I concede. For a while we talk horses, whether the Appaloosa is better than the Morgan, whether the Spanish is better than the Peruvian.

One of his men brings out a tray of beer.

It's been an hour and we still don't talk of migrants. We're in an alleyway with no exit. I ask questions and he answers with disconnected, rambling thoughts.

Finally, when I've understood that the conversation should end, that he's tired, that his eyes are closing for want of sleep, I raise my voice and say:

"I don't understand the massacres, the deaths, the craziness of Los Zetas."

He finally seems like he's about done talking and raises his voice to a pitch to answer my question.

"It's obvious. They've made their threat clear to those who don't want to pay. They [the massacres] are just messages. I recommend people study the situation before they go north. Is your coyote going to pay or not? If he's not going to pay, may God be with you."

12

Men Who Sell Women

October 2012

A woman who tried to migrate tells the story of how she ended up, at the mercy of Los Zetas, in a brothel in Northern Mexico. A group of Guatemalan traffickers uses bloody rituals to show their victims, some of whom are minors, that trying to escape leads you down a painful path to death. A Salvadoran charged with selling a woman in Southern Mexico may be freed after serving only two years in jail. Weak governments confront groups of organized crime that are ruthless, bloody and persistent.

The barbaric act of trafficking women and girls for sexual exploitation is a barely understood phenomenon in Central America, pushed into the shadows of other crimes given more attention.

The prosecutor asks. Grecia answers.

"What part of the body?"

"On my calf. They took us to a place where they tattooed us. They fed us and had us smell some chemical that put me to sleep. When I woke up, I had the tattoo. My leg was hurting and was bleeding, not a lot, but dripping a little. It's a butterfly on a branch, together they form 'Z.' That was the difference, it meant I was theirs, I was merchandise."

Grecia's gone. Twice she testified how an organized crime group used her body as a receptacle for whatever they pleased. She told her story to the Salvadoran government and the

Mexican government. Then she left. She no longer lives in El Salvador. She's a refugee now. For her safety, few know where she's made her new home.

I know she's twenty-nine years old, is married and was unemployed when she decided to migrate. She has three kids. The eldest is six years old, the next in line is three and the youngest is ten months. Though I've never heard her speak, I'm listening to Grecia's words. They come from a voice recording I myself made. It took me fifty-two minutes to read aloud into my recorder the written declaration she submitted to a Salvadoran judge.

In a hearing before her assailant at the Ninth Circuit Peace Court of San Salvador, at 9 a.m. on July 2, 2010, the witness known as Grecia answered the questions of prosecutors and defense lawyers: What happened to her? How did she survive?

The prosecutor asks. Grecia answers.

"Why were you called before this court? You were called before this court so that justice could be served in regard to the crimes of kidnapping, rape and human trafficking that were committed against you. When did you set off for the United States?"

"April 13, 2009."

"Why did you decide to make this trip?"

"Because of the economic situation in my country."

"Who were you traveling with?"

"With Mr. Ovidio Guardado."

"Describe Mr. Ovidio's physical appearance."

"He's a male of about sixty-nine years of age, with white skin, short, graying, wavy hair, five feet eight inches tall, no teeth. He has a scar on his head."

"What did this man do?"

"He lied to me. He never told me he was a coyote. He told me we'd go to the United States, and then once we were in Mexico he revealed his true plan."

"And what was his plan?"

"His first plan was to rape me, but, given the circumstances, he wasn't able to."

"How many people were with you when you first set off on this trip?"

"Only Mr. Ovidio."

Ovidio is a brown-haired, wrinkled, sinewy-limbed campesino; he's like a dried up, leafless tree that'll stay standing for years to come. Ovidio is a relative of Grecia's husband. He's the neighbor of Grecia's mother and mother-in-law. Grecia trusted him.

As with Grecia, the initial hook for most sex-trafficking victims is the hope to be free of poverty. Made up of twelve men and one woman, the Barberena trafficking ring uses this hope to its advantage. Until 2006, the Barberena ring operated from the eponymous municipality in the state of Santa Rosa on the Pacific coast of Guatemala. Known for the bloody rituals used to terrorize their victims, they were nonetheless able to buy the sympathy of a Salvadoran judge, who has absolved many of their members of all charges. But there's ample time to delve into these wonder-inducing aspects of the Barberena ring; what we need to focus on right now is how they would lure their victims.

The Barberena ring operated out of a bar called El Pantanal (the Marshland). Their method of deceit was simple. They would send an expedition of Salvadoran men or women who, after years of being forced into sex labor (one survivor was enslaved for seven years) were all struggling with various forms of mental illness.

They would send these men and women to villages and hamlets in the border states of Santa Ana and Ahuachapán. They would go door-to-door claiming to be employees of supermarkets or restaurants that were newly opened in Barbarena and in search of personnel. They would offer $70 a week, plus compensation for moving costs, and then $50 up front to seduce those who remained doubtful.

Northern Central America is a point of origin, transit and destination for victims of trafficking. While Guatemala has the greatest percentage of trafficking victims in Central America, many of the victims also come from Nicaragua, El Salvador and Honduras. Because of the thousands of migrants they continuously produce, all four countries push a steady stream of their people into the hands of Mexican traffickers. The experts—NGOs, prosecutors, police, international organizations—explain that proximity to Mexico and the enormous flow of migrants walking through Guatemala make it an ideal place for traffickers to set up camp.

The scammers who comb through towns and villages and hamlets are not armed with sheer luck, going door-to-door until someone opens and drinks in their drivel. Rather, many of these scammers settle down in an area, become part of the community, get to know their neighbors and appear to be good Samaritans. Using false names, they throw down roots. Silvia Saravia, who offers emotional help to victims of trafficking for the Salvadoran Public Prosecutor's Office, says that the scammers know so much about the women they traffic, that they even know whether or not the women have been raped before. Traffickers smell abandonment and vulnerability like sharks smell blood.

The desperate women who accept the scammers' offers would have to travel close to an hour before reaching El Pantanal. Armed men and a Guatemalan woman by the name of Sonia García greet them at the door. Sonia asks them to change out of their conservative clothes (in many cases the women are in evangelist garb) and throw on a miniskirt and gaudy low-cut shirt. She then tells them to report to the main hall of the old, sprawling house and convince the drunk patrons to pay fifty quetzales (about $7) for thirty minutes of action. They, the victims, usually refuse, saying that this wasn't the job they'd signed up for. Then the men surrounding Sonia, most of them Salvadorans, use their fists and maybe a baseball bat to explain that this isn't an offer anymore; it is an order.

In mid-August I went to the Apanteos prison in Santa Ana and spoke with Rigoberto Morán Martínez, one of the six men charged with membership in the Barberena trafficking ring. He told me that in the two years he pimped at El Pantanal, virtually none of his victims would work their first week. Most spent early days with a disfigured, purple face. And the clients at El Pantanal didn't like women with purple faces. Rigoberto, a man who has spent his life using a rifle as a tool, has plenty of lessons for us.

By late 2007, sixteen survivors of El Pantanal testified in a Salvadoran court. Twenty-six women were rescued in an operation led by the Guatemalan Interpol and Salvadoran police investigators. Twenty of the women were Salvadoran. The other six were Nicaraguan or Guatemalan. This demographic breakdown was probably due to the fact that most Barbarena scammers themselves were Salvadoran. Despite coming from vastly different places, most experts and studies agree that trafficking victims have one thing in common: poverty.

One Salvadoran woman rescued from El Pantanal was a minor. She was given the alias "Carmencita" in order to respect her anonymity while testifying in court. In response to the question of why, at fifteen years of age, she accepted an offer to leave behind her family and go work in Barberena, she said: "There were days my *mami* didn't have enough money to buy beans."

In response to the question of what she endured in order to put beans on her family's table, Carmencita said: "There were days I'd serve seven men, but because I didn't like any of that, I would throw tantrums. One day the owner got drunk and he started to hit us with a machete and he hurt my leg. I was crying and I told him I had to go to the hospital. My wound got infected, but he only told me to clean my leg because it was grossing out the clients."

What the clients felt for the fifteen-year-old girl with a deep gash on her leg was not sympathy, but disgust.

The prosecutor asks. Grecia answers.

"Then what happened?"

"That night Mr. Ovidio took me to a stable about four hours away from a river called Las Palmas. It was about eleven at night. I could only see three horses. He told me that his God had spoken, and that I had to be his."

"Did he do something to you?"

"I got really aggressive. I didn't let him touch me. He got violent, he threatened me with a long nail he had, he said it wouldn't be the first time he had killed someone with a nail. I told Mr. Ovidio that I had to go to the bathroom. Then I tried to run away. I ran. I got to a place they call the Battalion. I ran for forty-five minutes. I told them I was running away because Mr. Ovidio wanted to hurt me. One of the soldiers told me not to worry, that I could stay the night there."

According to Grecia's story, on the fifth day after having left El Salvador, now in Tabasco, Mexico, she successfully fled from Ovidio. Grecia remembered Ovidio's words, that he would show her hell on earth. After spending a night at the Mexican military garrison, Grecia made her way along the train tracks to Tenosique, the Mexican city that leads to the Atlantic route of the so-called Train of Death, or the Beast, the cargo trains that Central Americans cling to in search of a better life in the United States. Grecia found a group of migrants from various neighboring countries and asked them if she could join their group. She told them what Ovidio had tried to do to her. They told her she could join them. With them she reached the train tracks, which Grecia described in the following manner: "They're surrounded by shacks and stores, there's an abandoned hotel, and a marsh, there were also more migrants and people who were armed."

Tenosique, a Mexican city close to the border of Petén, Guatemala, is one of those godforsaken cities of migrants. In fact, the hotel Grecia refers to was operating until early 2009, often used by criminal groups to warehouse kidnapped migrants before rerouting them to various northern cities. Ironically, the name of the hotel was California.

The prosecutor asks. Grecia answers.

"What do you mean armed people?"

"They were in charge of bringing people north. They were wearing jeans and T-shirts. They ran the place, they were in charge, they controlled the area surrounding the train tracks. They mentioned they were part of an organization called Los Zetas, and that they ruled the area."

"How many people were there?"

"About twenty."

"What kind of arms did they have?"

"Rifles, big arms, guns, one Honduran said he had an Uzi."

"Who guarded the women in El Pantanal?" I ask Rigoberto. We're seated in a patio known as the green zone in the Apanteos prison of El Salvador. Rigoberto is forty-eight years old and has only had one year of schooling. He's a short man, thick and strong looking, with an angular face punctuated by a wispy mustache. He began working on corn plantations since he was very young. In 1982, at eighteen years old, with the Salvadoran Civil War erupting in the countryside, he was recruited by the Army. When the war ended he found a job that would allow him to continue sporting a rifle: a security guard for a company that outsources men like Rigoberto to watch over pharmacies, shops, supermarkets and hardware stores.

"People he trusted. His family. Armed men," says Rigoberto, referring to the men working for Adán Cerritos, the leader of the Barberena ring.

"Did they carry rifles?"

"Isn't that what we're talking about?"

"Were the women always guarded?"

"Always."

The Barberena ring is typical of Central American trafficking rings. These organizations are made up of closely related people, often relatives, who manage and look after the brothels. Lower on the totem pole are the employees with no power, the scammers, the hit men in charge of attacking the women and keeping them terrified. Barberena was an international network working out of three different countries, and yet it was still a small group. A far cry from the colossal drug cartels, the Barberena ring opted for the comfort of the rural countryside. Being a small organization, however, does not imply being an organization without allies.

"Why didn't you ever report what was going on there?" I ask Rigoberto, taking him, for a moment, for his word when he says he was a simple "barman and a sweeper" for El Pantanal. Rigoberto, after two years on the run, was caught in February 2011 and sentenced to six years behind bars for human trafficking. The maximum sentence for selling someone in El Salvador is ten years, three months and three days, a sentence only applied in extreme cases, such as when the victim is a minor. As Rigoberto tells it, he came to El Pantanal after being deceived by a Salvadoran woman (a professional scammer and cook for the Barberena ring) with whom he had fallen desperately in love.

"Because it wasn't possible, I already told you. The police were all bought out. It wasn't possible. I'd put my life in danger. I could've been killed. I don't know how much they were used to paying [the police]," he answers as the sun starts to dip below the horizon.

"You never saw a woman escape or scream for help?"

"It wasn't possible. Maybe I could've been that person to help them, but it wasn't possible, because that man [Cerritos] had bought out the entire Cuilapa police force. When folks from the capital would come to search for missing women, the police had already warned everyone at El Pantanal to hide the women. Maybe we'd leave a few women around, the ones who were there legally. The rest were hidden somewhere in the same bar, or they'd be taken to that so-called ranch the day before. There were coffee trees, and [Cerritos] had 150 acres of cornfields."

The Barberena ring, small and discreet, with only one brothel under its name, operated at the scale of a criminal network of great proportions. Rigoberto states that the police forces of Barberena and the neighboring town of Cuilapa would come by on a weekly basis to collect their payments from Cerritos, and what's more, the officers themselves were VIP clients at El Pantanal. The same goes for a handful of city government officials.

The strategic alliances of the Barberena ring go even further. Rigoberto explains that even members of the Mara Salvatrucha gang in Ahuachapán, Guatemala, worked as scammers. In fact, one Salvadoran gang member, Marco Antonio Godoy, is now behind bars for trafficking.

The Barberena ring, as small and discreet as it was, operated like a much bigger criminal organization, committing any crime that would bring in the money. During the trial, two women rescued from El Pantanal stated that the owners would often sell the victims' newborn children for US$5,000.

In 2011 El Salvador was able to win eleven trafficking cases against small criminal organizations. And though the cases won may only amount to nothing but an ankle-deep puddle, El Salvador was actually the Central American country that successfully prosecuted the most trafficking cases through that year, which shows progress, though certainly not any breakthroughs.

Though human trafficking is all around us, the victims are often invisible, and the victimizers may not even be on our radar. Often they're first-time entrepreneurs in the world of crime, seeing dollar bills in a cocktail of enticing elements, including weak states and desperate victims. According to the United Nations Office on Drugs and Crime (UNDOC), only one of every thirty cases of trafficking in this region ever goes reported.

The Barbarena ring, in contrast to other trafficking rings, has made sure to diversify its business endeavors. In El Salvador in 2011, for example, Ángel Mauricio Ayala, Kevin Oswaldo Chicas Lobato and Joel Josué Mendoza were sentenced to six years and eight months in prison for having forced two Nicaraguans, who were looking for work in the western state of San Miguel, to either prostitute themselves in a pub or, for the one deemed too old, to work without pay as a domestic servant. The "old one" was twenty-four.

Nelson Orlando Campos and Juan Humberto Ramírez Carranza tricked two teenage Guatemalans who, instead of modeling clothes, ended up working in a bar to get groped by sweaty men. They were sentenced to nine and eight months in jail, respectively. Then there's Juan Alfonso Cuéllar who, similar to the case of Grecia, sold a Salvadoran migrant traveling through Mexico to be sexually exploited. On August 9, 2011, he was sentenced to four years in prison. That means that if he were an exemplary inmate, on August 9, 2013, after serving half his sentence, he could have been released on parole.

"He sold a human being!" complained Violeta Olivares, the coordinator of the Specialized Trafficking Unit of the Public Prosecutor's Office.

The position of the Specialized Trafficking Unit is that the trafficking sentences are absurd. "They're a piece of shit," one prosecutor candidly said to me. In El Salvador, a man who has committed robbery by, for example, holding down a bus by gunpoint and stealing everyone's cell phones, wallets and rings, would be sentenced to more years in prison than Cuéllar, who sold a human being. The thief would get between six and ten years. The trafficker is sentenced to four.

As of 2003, El Salvador began recognizing crimes of trafficking in its penal code. The first conviction was won in 2006. Thirty-nine convictions later and the issue is now beginning to turn more heads with the creation, in 2011, of the National Council Against Human Trafficking. Little by little the National Council is repairing some of the gaping holes in the wall.

Rigoberto Morán Martínez, the trafficker of Barberena, who tells me he was tricked by his lover into going to El Pantanal, slips up in his story, giving away his guilt. His misstep was to tell me that he didn't report what was going on because he was scared, because the police had been bought off, and after all he was just a simple servant always under close watch. But then he accidentally admits that he worked in El Pantanal during two different periods, with a vacation in between, when he left to visit his home in El Salvador.

"When you left El Pantanal the first time, knowing what kind of work they did there, why did you go back?" I ask Rigoberto.

"Why did I come back?" he says, trying to buy himself a little time.

"If you knew these women were locked up and abused, why did you go back?" I press.

"Maybe you don't understand ... There are things ... There are things you might not understand. We know that spells and witchcraft exist! That woman [of Cerritos], that's how she would work. They worshipped this thing called Saint Simón. That's how she operated. When people left and didn't want to come back, she would use these things to make them come back."

The prosecutor asks. Grecia answers.

"The people that you say ran the place, how would they get there?"

"They came in cars, armed. They'd come and go."

"How long would they stay there?"

"Three days, until Mr. Ovidio would come back."

"What would these armed people do?"

"They would tell us to join the organization, tell us that they would give us work and food. They were part of Los Zetas. They told me they'd pay for my trip, that they'd give me food."

"What kind of work did they advertise?"

"Cooking for people who were kidnapped, this was around April 20 or 22 of 2009."

In sum: At this point of her story, Grecia was in Tenosique, Mexico, the first stop in a migrant's journey to the United States. She was in a town ruled by Los Zetas. Grecia had run away from Ovidio after he had tried to rape her in a barren marshland, and she had recently joined a group of undocumented Salvadorans and Guatemalans.

"What happened when Ovidio got there?"

"He looked at me with this mocking smile, and he went to the [Zetas'] house. They were like five yards away from me, he started talking to Chicho, a guy somewhere between twenty-four and twenty-nine years old with a scar on his left cheek. He was from that same organization. They talked for about forty-five minutes. They looked at me, and pointed at me. I was with the group of people I had just joined."

Grecia recounts her train trip with the other kidnapped migrants. They were guarded by armed men who threatened to kill them if anyone dared try to escape. Los Zetas used the train to transport their victims. The train runs from Tenosique to Coatzacoalcos, Veracruz. It makes a series of stops in various small towns and isolated ranches. In one of those remote towns called Chontalpa, a Salvadoran Zeta known as El Pelón tried to sell Grecia to another man. According to Grecia, El Pelón was actually trying to do her a favor. He'd told her that up north, where they were going, she would suffer a lot. But the sale fell through, and Grecia saw firsthand that El Pelón had not been lying to her. At this point in her story, the prosecutor interjects and asks Grecia to clarify.

"When you mention 'selling,' had they already done this to you?"

"Yeah, Mr. Ovidio ... They gave him money for me in front of my face."

"Was Mr. Ovidio on the train with you?"

"No, he went to El Salvador with the money they gave him."

"How much did they give him?"

"They say it was $500 ... That's what Chicho told me."

"Then what happened?"

"They boarded us on buses heading to Reynosa ... It takes about a day and a half to get from Veracruz to Reynosa. It was April 26, 2009, it was a Sunday."

At this point, Grecia describes a classic Zeta kidnapping of undocumented migrants.

Reynosa is a city in the northern Mexican state of Tamaulipas, a state ruled by Los Zetas: It's where seventy-two migrants were exhumed from a mass grave in August 2010, where they caught El Coss, the leader of the Gulf Cartel, the organization that gave birth to Los Zetas, and where forty-nine more bodies were found in May 2012, beheaded, without limbs, under an enormous "Z" painted on a pedestrian bridge over a highway.

The kidnappers divided Grecia's group of about 300 migrants into three safe houses. Locked in rooms that were humid and dark, with no air conditioning, men armed with rifles and baseball bats tortured whoever refused to hand over a family member's phone number. And then, as always, some Central American migrant resisted, didn't want to pay the $300, $500 or $700 Los Zetas always ask for, resisted being tortured, and Grecia and the other migrants had to witness the armed men beat the screams out of a few of them, before leaving and promising to come back. That's how Grecia spent her first three days. On the third day, Omega appeared.

One of the prosecutors asks, and Grecia answers.

"Can you describe him?"

"Tall, fat, with a big double chin, white. They called him Omega, Kike or Apá. They told him there were some Salvadoran women he would like. They pointed at us. He took us out of the room to see if we were pretty. There wasn't much light in the room. He was in charge of the safe house."

"What makes you say that?"

"Because he was one of the people who would call the families and charge the ransom."

"Did you stay in that same house?"

"No, they took me to another house, they took me to a residential neighborhood about ten minutes away. On a bus. A few people came with me. Again they laid us on the floor. That's where I was raped by Omega. He hit me in the face because I told him to wear a condom. He told me I wasn't in a position to ask for anything. They were abusing us nonstop, it wasn't just him."

"Could you recognize these people in person or in photograph?"

"Yes."

"What else happened?"

"The abuse was constant, and it wasn't only him. He raped me about eight or nine times. He said he was enjoying himself, so I had to enjoy myself, too. He would hit me. The same thing happened with the other people, but he was always the first to rape those he liked."

Grecia endured. She remembers three months going by

until, even though her family had already wired ransom money from the United States, she was sold off yet again.

"How long did this go on?"

"All three months, they'd already paid the full amount, but they told me they were going to get more money out of me. They sold me again to a bar called La Quebradita (the Broken One). They sold me as a prostitute. It was like a dance club. I was rejected that first day. The woman who ran the bar told us we needed the mark. Because we were so many, we needed to have a mark. At first I didn't know what it was, but it's a tattoo."

"Where did you get tattooed?"

"On my right calf. They took us to a place where they tattooed us. They fed us and had us smell some chemical that put me to sleep. When I woke up, I had the tattoo. My leg was hurting and was bleeding, not a lot, but dripping a little. It's a butterfly on a branch, together they form a 'Z.' That was the difference, it meant I was theirs, I was merchandise. There were five other women. I saw it on different body parts of four more women, on the arm, the back, the chest, in a bunch of different colors. The one I have is black and green. After marking us we went back to the same place and they started to prostitute us with clients who were part of the same mafia. The clients paid for us, but we never got any of the money. I don't know how much they would pay."

Grecia says that the clients would force her to smoke crack and do cocaine. Grecia says her clients would never use a condom. Grecia says she spent more than a month like this. Grecia says she never left, that her entire life was in the safe house, La Quebradita or at various motels where the clients would take her. Grecia says that if a client took her to a motel, they were always followed closely by a guard. Grecia says they would often hit her, especially if she refused to drink, or if she didn't look enthusiastic before going in with a client. Grecia says that once they hit her so hard they broke her nose.

The broken nose and the tattoo were verified by the Institute of Forensic Medicine of El Salvador, and are documented as evidence in Grecia's case files.

Grecia never tried to escape. Few would have tried if they had seen what Grecia had seen.

"Did something else happen?"

"Yes, to Sonia. They let her go when her family paid the ransom. She reported them to immigration officials. But the immigration officials handed her back over to the traffickers. They burned her alive, they hit her many times with a baseball bat. They told her she wasn't supposed to do that, that no one was allowed to play games with them, that she had lost her chance to be free. They told us the same thing would happen to us if we ever said something."

"What happened to Sonia?"

"Death."

"What did they hit her with?"

"With a bat, but because she wouldn't die, they lit her on fire with gasoline. She screamed with pain, and they hit her more. A half hour, forty-five minutes. Her body was unrecognizable, carbonized, you couldn't see her feet. Burned, hairless meat. They left her in the bar, at an altar they had for Santa Muerte."

The case files attribute the discovery of the Barberena ring to a complainant. Knowing what she lived through, calling her a complainant is as reductive as calling Gandhi an activist. This woman, this survivor, Grecia, is one of the sixteen women who testified in the Salvadoran court as a protected witness.

The owner of El Pantanal, trafficker Adán Cerritos, owned 120 acres of cornfields surrounded by coffee plantations. His ranch was in one of the most rural areas of Barberena, further out than the Boquerón penitentiary, one of the few reasons why anyone talks about Barberena in the first place. The traffickers were beginning to diversify their repertoire and dip into labor trafficking. The same women who worked the fields from Monday to Thursday were abused by dozens of men in El Pantanal from Friday to Sunday.

Cerritos's ranch, according to testimony gathered by the Public Prosecutor's Office as well as the trafficker I spoke with at Apanteos prison, was also the site where the women were punished and hidden away. That's where they would lock up the women when corrupt police officers from Cuilapa and Barberena warned them of missing-person searches. That's where they would warehouse women who, after being beaten, were unfit for clients' tastes. That's also where they would torture their victims.

In court, many of the survivors recounted a night that they were taken to the ranch and made to stand in a circle. In the middle of the circle were two men and a woman. Outside of the circle were armed guards, preventing anyone from running. In the middle of that circle, for many interminable minutes, the two men beat the woman to death. The woman had tried to escape El Pantanal.

She wasn't the only one. Another survivor lived through something similar. Her constant refusals to seduce the clients at El Pantanal cost her a beating so rough that the traffickers thought they had killed her. They left her in a bloody heap at the ranch, planning to get rid of her body the next day. The woman, the survivor, awoke during the night and, little by little, managed to drag herself to the highway. From there, by unknown means, the survivor reached the border and, once on the Salvadoran side, she collapsed before the police and told them her story. In less than a week, the Salvadoran Public Prosecutor's Office orchestrated a rescue mission along with Guatemalan Interpol. Violeta Olivares, the coordinator of the Specialized Trafficking Unit, is very clear when she says why they didn't call the Guatemalan police for help: "We didn't trust them."

In 2006, a judge specialized in organized crime from Santa

Ana, El Salvador, Tomás Salinas, didn't see why the eight Salvadorans accused of forming part of the Barberena ring should remain behind bars during their hearing. He granted them alternative probationary measures and allowed them to leave on the condition that they come to court whenever they were summoned. Some of these eight men, having heard of the operation in El Pantanal, had previously tried to hide themselves. And still the judge thought the eight men wouldn't run this time around. All of them ended up missing. The Public Prosecutor's Office appealed, and the Special Prosecuting Office Against Organized Crime successfully revoked Judge Salinas's decision, ordering all Barberena members recaptured. Of the eight men that Judge Salinas let out, six have been recaptured, the last of whom is Morán Martínez. Two are still on the run.

That wasn't the first time that Salinas had freed a defendant. The most recent example is that of José Antonio Terán, better known as "Chepe Furia." In 2011, Judge Salinas released Chepe so that he could await his trial as a free man. Considering that he wouldn't flee because he was a family man and worked with the city, the judge allowed him parole. His decision was quickly revoked by a superior court, but Terán had already been released and had fled. He was recaptured that same year, and now he's serving a twenty-year sentence.

Murderers murder. Car thieves thieve. And traffickers—they entangle, threaten and kill. Traffickers are like the water cutting through stone: merciless and persistent. They need their victims to be alive and afraid. Alive and terrorized. Alive and submissive. The murders of the Barberena ranch were not a punitive measure intended for those who were killed. The soon-to-be slaughtered victims were, for the traffickers, like living dead. These killings were a warning message for the rest of the women: Look at what could happen to you.

For Central American trafficking rings, the bat, the fist and rape are the primary methods of subjugation. Both the chief of the anti-trafficking unit of Guatemala, Alexander Colop, and his Salvadoran colleague, Smirna de Calles, agree that a pattern among trafficking rings is that the kingpins are the first to rape the victims. "They're the first to bring them down, to use them, to throw themselves on top of them," Colop said. This is exactly what happened to Grecia.

Julio Prado, the assistant prosecutor of Guatemala's Specialized Unit Against Impunity, says that even though most trafficking gangs of northern Guatemala, like that of El Pantanal, come from broken worlds and primarily use hand-guns and simple techniques, that doesn't mean that there aren't more sophisticated gangs out there.

Prado says that in the worst places where he's participated in search-and-rescue operations, victims were forced to sell themselves for 50 quetzales ($6) for fifteen minutes of service, but that he's also seen cases in which Colombians or Russians were sold for $500 an hour. "The question," Prado says, "is what type of client can pay that amount of money to have a good time for an hour?"

In 2006 the Guatemalan government investigated a trafficking ring with a slant toward the wealthy client. Prado helped uncover a dance club called Caprichos, owned by businessman Herman Smith—he forced his victims to call him "Papito"—a man known to rub elbows with Guatemalan politicians and high-society members. In the bar, government agents found minors from El Salvador, Honduras and Russia. They also found a system of trick doors and tunnels connected to neighboring houses where there were books of self help and economic theory that, according to one survivor, Smith used to explain to the victims how they could use their captivity as an opportunity to become businesswomen: mastering the art of turning their bodies into merchandise. Smith, a persuasive trafficker, would convince his victims that he was not their victimizer, but their benefactor. He was never brought to trial;

on May 6, 2008, Smith was shot in the head inside of his own dance club. The hit man fled.

Guatemala has sentenced a handful of Colombian traffickers who work for what's known as the ring of Pereira, a gang that was dedicated to bringing Colombian women overseas by telling them that they would be hired as models. These rings, Colop says, would even mold their victims, giving them breast and butt implants, telling them surgery was necessary to enter into the world of runway fashion. "They'd bring them to Honduras and when they were no longer a hot commodity over there, they'd bring them here," Colop explains. The women would be told that they had to use sex to pay for their implants, their trip, their food and their clothes. One survivor says it was impossible to pay off her debts. Prado explains that the logic behind bringing Colombians to Guatemala speaks to the traffickers' business savvy, as Colombian narcos living in Guatemala would pay a lot of money to sleep with beautiful compatriots.

In El Salvador, the vice minister of justice and safety, Douglas Moreno (ex-warden of Apanteos prison), is charged with developing strategies to combat trafficking. "There's a network," Moreno told me, "of well-organized people with a lot of economic power who are greatly benefiting from this situation and of whom, until now, we were unaware. These are people we would never have imagined to be associated with this business and yet, unfortunately, we lack sufficient evidence to incriminate them."

The Herman Smith ring or the ring of Pereira represent another face of trafficking that, like modern-day slavery, uses capitalist reasoning to keep people in bondage: You need to pay back your debt because I'm helping you get ahead, because you have no papers and you need to give me something in exchange for my protection. The more common forms of trafficking in Central America function like the Barberena ring and rely on local corruption, having only a small arsenal at its disposal and preferring cheaper methods of subjugating their victims: fists, sticks, fire and fear.

Silvia Saravia has seen dozens of cases of women falling prey to these types of run-of-the-mill trafficking organizations. "Those who have been locked up suffer from extreme fear, a tremendous fear for the safety of the other women and for their own families, fear that they will suffer the consequences of their escape. Emotionally blocked, they are completely locked inward. Many require psychiatric attention. Suicidal ideation, fear of disappearing, fear of persecution. They don't believe they can trust anyone. They know that there are people out there who are not playing around, that the victimizer will do what he says ... Anxiety, insomnia, loss of appetite ... Grecia, for example, she'll have to receive ..." Saravia thinks a few seconds, "a whole process of holistic attention."

After almost three months of being forced to see clients in La Quebradita, a week after witnessing Sonia in flames, after her aunt wired $3,500 in ransom, Grecia was freed by Omega. They gave her 300 pesos (some $25), left her at a bus station in Reynosa and told her to go somewhere far away. One of the prosecutors who interviewed Grecia during the trial says Grecia thought something strange was going on at the time, that Los Zetas seemed to be shutting down their safe houses and fleeing. With 300 pesos, Grecia could only go as far as Monterrey, some 100 miles south. There, Grecia met a taxi driver who asked her if she was undocumented and took her to a state-run immigrant assistance center where someone easily identified Grecia's symptoms. According to medical tests, Grecia arrived at the center with a vaginal infection and pelvic inflammatory disease.

The prosecutors asks. Grecia answers.
"What happened in the center for migrants?"
"When they saw my behavior, when the shift supervisor

saw me crying and screaming, they saw I wasn't acting normal, they started asking me questions. Little by little I started to explain ... They found me a religious shelter for people who have suffered crimes of trafficking ... They scheduled me an appointment with a psychologist ... They took me to Mexico City ... For five months I was given psychological and legal help."

"Did you participate in an investigation?"

"Yes. The whole time I was there."

"Were people detained?"

"Yes, for kidnapping and human trafficking. They showed me some pictures, approximately ten to twelve Honduran and Mexican people [were detained]."

On November 23, 2009, Grecia was in Mexico City with the Special Prosecutor's Office for Violence Against Women and Human Trafficking (FEVIMTRA). According to the case files, in her first psychological assessment Grecia was found to be "depressed, mistrustful and unable to cry." Officials had to meet with her a total of eleven times before they were able to record her entire declaration. Thanks to Grecia's report to the Mexican government, a series of raids were conducted in 2009 that led to the arrest of twelve alleged Zetas who ran kidnapping gangs. Their trial is pending.

When Grecia went back to El Salvador in December 2009, her situation got worse. Grecia explained that Ovidio, just as she feared, had threatened both her mother-in-law and her mother. The psychological assessment done by the Institute of Forensic Medicine in El Salvador states that Grecia "cannot sleep at night, she registers any sound as gunshots, she goes two or three days without eating, whenever she lights a fire she remembers Sonia, her libido is nonexistent, she pushes her partner away when they have relations." The assessment ends with various conclusions.

Emotional state: depressive, anxious.

General orientation: She states that there are gaps in her

declaration because there are events she can't remember. Mental craters.

Psychological state: neurotic.

On Wednesday May 26, 2010, a twenty-nine-year-old Salvadoran woman caught sight of a newspaper snapshot of someone who looked familiar. The man in the photograph was getting out of a pickup truck and was handcuffed to two other men. The police had detained a Mexican man, four Salvadoran men, one Salvadoran woman and one other fat man in a black four-wheel-drive truck with Guatemalan plates in the parking lot of a dance club called Kairo's. The club is on Boulevard Los Heroes, one of San Salvador's biggest streets. Inside the truck, in a secret compartment that was opened by an electric switch, the police found a Galil rifle, two M16s, a .30-30 carbine, two shotguns, a revolver, a military LED light and eleven cell phones. The twenty-nine-year-old woman thought she recognized the fat man in the picture, but she tried not to think about it. That night, the fat man's face was again blasted on every news site. When he spoke she had to endure hearing his shrill, familiar voice. The woman finally had to admit to herself that she knew him. She knew him well. The woman was Grecia. The man was Omega.

Omega's real name is Enrique Jaramillo Aguilar. He's thirty-five years old, was born in Apatzingán, Michoacán, Mexico, and in December 2011 he was sentenced to serve nine years in a Salvadoran prison for illegal possession of fire-arms and false documentation. He's currently serving time at Apanteos prison. Jaramillo identified himself to Salvadoran authorities as a Guatemalan and flashed them false documents to prove it. His arrest that Wednesday, May 26, was the result of a police operation that tied him to Los Zetas. He was on the police radar thanks to an informant who discovered that the false Guatemalan was involved in the 2008 massacre of Agua Zarca in Huehuetenango. The massacre was an hours-long shoot-out between Guatemalan members of the Sinaloa Cartel and Los Zetas, which resulted in nineteen bodies hitting the streets. The massacre shed light on the infiltration of Mexican cartels in Guatemala. Jaramillo was arrested on suspicion of being one of the participating Zetas, but the Guatemalan Public Ministry was unable to prove it in court.

When Grecia recognized the man who raped her in Reynosa, sold her to La Quebradita and robbed her aunt of $3,500, she decided to testify before the Salvadoran Public Prosecutor's Office. That's when Grecia began her job in court, testifying before a judge, two prosecutors, two defense lawyers contracted by Jaramillo, and Jaramillo himself. Grecia requested that she be allowed to send in her declaration beforehand, not wanting to go through the entire judicial process in person. She was deathly afraid that Omega would send people to hurt her. Later, with the support of the International Organization for Migration and the United Nations Refugee Agency, Grecia left the country for an undisclosed location, created a new identity for herself and began to remake her life.

Wednesday, July 4, 2012. 8:30 a.m. Specialized Sentencing Court of San Salvador. Final allegations against the accused, Enrique Jaramillo Aguilar and Jesús Ovidio Guardado.

Jaramillo waits with Ovidio outside the courtroom. Jaramillo's loose skin hangs off his chin. He's lost a lot of weight since his arrest at Kairo's dance club. He's lost hair as well. He wears it closely cropped on the sides and longer on top, where it looks as if someone ripped it out instead of cut it. Ovidio looks even more miserable, more wasted away. It's been a year since his arrest. His white button-down shirt and his khaki pants hardly suit him.

Inside, Jaramillo's two private attorneys try to bring a little cheer into the room. They joke about a suicide attempt that Grecia supposedly survived during her teenage years.

"They say she took 200 pills, she was a narcotic," one of them says.

"No, I can't help but ask myself how she could've packed so many in," the other says. They crack up.

Then the first one plays reggaeton on his cell phone and turns the volume up as high as it will go. The court registrar asks them to please leave the room.

The two prosecutors make their final allegations: Ovidio sold her on the train ... La Quebradita ... She's treated like merchandise ... Jaramillo raped her continuously ... Tattoo on her left leg ... The expert says the victim's current suffering is due to what happened in Mexico ... For Ovidio, attempted rape and aggravated forms of trafficking ... For Jaramillo, continual rape and aggravated trafficking ... Maximum sentences in both cases.

Jaramillo's lawyers offer their rebuttal: What about Los Zetas? Where does it say that? Lies ... The assessment speaks of mental craters ... The victim says one thing and then another ... She's an unstable person ... Her seven-year-old son dresses like a girl ... Her son doesn't have these abnormalities because of what she says happened ... A victim without credibility.

Ovidio's court-appointed lawyers follow: Tentative crimes don't exist. Was there penetration or wasn't there? There's no middle ground.

Then, surprisingly, Jaramillo asks to speak. With his shrill voice he calls the judge "your honor" and lays down his arguments. The first is that Ovidio is too old to be working in the world of migration. The second is a little confusing. He says that Grecia had said that Ovidio only had five teeth, but that when they asked her how many teeth a human being should have she answered thirty-six. "But as far as I know, people only have thirty-two teeth." His third argument is that he doesn't live in Reynosa, nor does he know anyone from there. He says he's from another state, from Michoacán (his criminal record states that he's been a fugitive since 2006 in Reynosa,

Tamaulipas, running from charges of property damage). His fourth argument is that he has never been a member of the military and that Los Zetas are made up of soldiers. He says he's heard songs that state that Los Zetas are thirty members large, and that he certainly isn't one of those thirty members.

Friday, July 6. The verdict.

Absolved.

Judge Roger Rufino Paz Díaz states that Grecia contradicted herself. Grecia gave a different version of the facts to the Salvadoran Public Prosecutor's Office and the Mexican Public Prosecutor's Office. In Mexico, she omitted Ovidio's name and said she had been sold to Los Zetas by people linked to a shelter in Veracruz. The prosecutors argue that Grecia did this because she knew Ovidio to be in the country, that he knew her family well and lived close to her mother. The prosecutors argue that Grecia was afraid to report Ovidio in Mexico, that he would find out and ultimately harm her family. That's why she erased him from her story and only included him when she was in El Salvador and could warn her family of potential danger. The prosecutors argue that Grecia's psychological evaluation lends credibility to this theory. Grecia, as the psychologists wrote, was afraid. She was very afraid.

El Salvador's Public Prosecutor's Office, under the chief of the anti-trafficking unit, Smirna de Calles, held a press conference that same day. She explained that they were disappointed in the verdict, that the victims of these crimes have to recon-front their traumas as they are testifying. She promised to appeal and take it to the Supreme Court. Justice had not been issued.

Grecia will not testify again. Not even the Public Prosecutor's Office knows where she is. She's surviving somewhere else.

13

The Prayers of El Salvador's Anti-Gang Police Unit

January 2015

More than a dozen families abandon their homes after Barrio 18 threatens a massacre. A man cries angrily because tonight he and his wife and three children will sleep on a family member's floor. The subdirector of the Anti-Gang Unit arrives and tells the families to start praying.

This is the story of the families fleeing the San Valentín condos in the Mejicanos suburb of San Salvador.

Breaking news this Tuesday, January 20, 2015. There is a live audience, watching as if it were a soccer game: people peeking out from their kitchen windows as they eat lunch. Live and direct: more than a dozen families fleeing their San Valentín condos in the city of Mejicanos. There are also film crews, cops directing traffic, and other idling spectators. The police are offering protection for families who have been threatened by the Barrio 18 gang. Gang members threatened to kill by tonight. The residents of San Valentín, taking the threat seriously, are now fleeing on live national television.

The midday heat is suffocating. The families started emptying out their homes around ten in the morning — the gang had warned them the night before, at seven o'clock, that they had twenty-four hours. And then: They would get massacred. The families look exhausted as they drag out mattresses, refrigerators, televisions, chairs ... And yet, sweating in the raging heat, they keep on. They believe the threat: that if they don't leave by seven tonight, they'll all be killed.

The San Valentín condos are in the Delicias del Norte neighborhood of Mejicanos, on the outskirts of San Salvador. On the way to Argentina Park along the 2-C bus route. The condos are four blocks from where, on March 6, 2013, assassins murdered Giovanni Morales, otherwise known as El Destino (Destiny), a veteran member of the Guanacos Criminal Salvatruchos clique of the Mara Salvatrucha, which controls the nearby neighborhood of Montreal. The murder of Morales made big news because he was the assistant to Father Antonio Rodriguez, the famous Passionist (a Catholic sect) accused of being an accomplice to the gangs and was thus forced out of the country to his native Spain a year previously. If you don't remember Father Toño (as Antonio Rodriguez was known) or El Destino, you might at least remember this reference: The San Valentín condos are seven blocks from where, on Sunday June 20, 2010, members of the Colombia Locos Sureños clique of Barrio 18, from the Jardín neighborhood, set fire to a Route 47 bus while the passengers were still inside. Seventeen people died. They were either burned or shot while they were trying to escape through the windows. The bus was headed toward the Buenos Aires neighborhood of Mejicanos, which was controlled by the Maras, though to arrive it would have to take a number of turns through a zone controlled by Barrio 18. The territorial dispute leading to the savage act of violence turned heads around the world, even appearing on the front pages of dozens of international newspapers that rarely remember this fierce corner of the world.

In the middle of all this death lie the San Valentín condos. There are forty-six families living in these architecturally drab boxes: From a cement-lined axis opening up to streets on either side, rows of small box houses branch off in both directions. Three rows on each side, plus a vertebral strip down the middle. Tiny little houses with a one-room dining/kitchen/living room. In total: just a single room and a bathroom. The inhabitants have become experts in converting these spaces to serve their needs. At night the mattresses hit the floor and the chairs go on the tables. By day the mattresses are stuffed into the small patios in the back and the chairs ring the table again, or are propped in front of the televisions.

This is life in the San Valentín condos, where reporters cluster around looking for quotes, and cops stand guard.

One of the families is lingering outside their small home, sweating and crying. Since ten this morning they have been hauling out chairs, appliances and mattresses. They're piling everything they can into a pickup truck. The pickup takes off but soon returns, now emptied, to haul off a little more. There are only adults packing up in this family: two twenty-something men and three women, one in her fifties, one in her forties and pregnant, and a twenty-year-old. Two of the other women in the family, wives of the two men, as well as their four children, have already left for a cousin's house. They put the kids (the eldest is six, the others are still infants) out of the way for the move. This extended family rented three of the one-room San Valentín condos. Each little home costs them a hundred dollars a month. They pay their rent by washing windshields at intersections in San Salvador.

Fully loaded, the pickup heads out again for the cousin's house in another similarly small condo unit. Some of the family will crash there until they find a new home. Others will find space at one of the young men's parents' apartments, hoping that their landlord doesn't realize how many people are sleeping in the apartment and kick them out.

Despite the fact that the condos being packed up are surrounded by daily violence, residents point out that San Valentín wasn't always run by the gangs. You need some context: For the working class in El Salvador, the gangs are always just around the corner. Sometimes, if you're lucky, they never knock directly on your door. A few months ago, however, in the second house from the main gate, "four young female gang members" moved in. The house had been for sale, but the gang members moved in without making a purchase. They just took over. Soon, at night, tattooed youngsters from the Jardín neighborhood, members of Barrio 18, started coming by. They made a racket, but none of the other residents said anything.

The two men from the family packing up tell me how it all started. Meanwhile, the women are crying as their homes are emptied.

Last Saturday, January 17, the police came and raided the house of the "young female gang members." None of the gangsters, however, were home, so the police took everything that was inside.

The police were doing their job. They were responding to a call. They broke into the house, took everything they could and then left. But this is the problem. Gangs don't leave. They are part of the social fabric. They live here. They are the sons and daughters of women who live in the neighborhood. They are brothers and sisters of young men and women who live here. They are fathers, uncles and friends of the locals. Gangs are part of El Salvador. They are as rooted to the block, and to the neighborhood, as the corner store.

The female gangsters came back. On Sunday, the day after the raid—seven different neighbors, all in the process of moving out, confirmed it for me—the four women came back at night, accompanied by two men, both armed with pistols. The group went to a neighbor's house and told them to let the other residents know that they would all have to help refurnish the emptied house, that "the rat," as they put it, who snitched to the cops was living in those condos, and so those same residents were responsible for putting a new door on the house, installing a new refrigerator, television, kitchen appliances, dining table, chairs and couch. On top of the demand to refurnish, they told the neighbor that the residents would have to sign a letter saying that the women were honorable residents of San Valentín. Or, Plan B: They would move into a different condo unit, which would be paid for by the residents. And if none of this happened, the gang would start killing off the families who live in San Valentín. The neighbor who first heard this message was the first to start packing. He believed the threat. The next day, after he had already told some of his neighbors about the women's demand, he received a text message. It was the same story, but with another ingredient tacked on: "You all have 24 hours to meet our demands or there will be a massacre." The man showed some of his neighbors the text, including one of the men of the first family I started talking to. That same night is when the panic started spreading throughout San Valentín.

Somebody told the police about the threat, and, that night, a few officers came to try to calm the people who were already talking about leaving. By the next morning, Tuesday, at least five families had already made a decision: They were leaving. These first five families sparked another five, and by noon there were seventeen households packing their furniture into trucks, pickups and old cars, or hauling their stuff away however they could, on their way to another gang's turf.

"This is what it comes down to," one of the young, dark-skinned windshield-washers tells me. "Where do we go if there are gangs every place we can afford to live? If there are gangs every place with rent below $300, where do we go? What do we say if the new gangsters ask us where we're coming from? If they're from the 18s they're not going to like what went down here. If they're from the other gang, they're not going to want us either. Right now we're just leaving, later on we'll see how to live." The young man looks tough, hardened by a life washing windshields. He finishes his phrase, pauses for a moment, and then he begins to cry. He doesn't weep openly like his aunt who was crying earlier, or break into sobs, or need to wipe his eyes with a handkerchief. Skin crisped by a life working under the sun, the man doesn't want to cry. Or at least doesn't want to be seen crying. He tries to stop, but he can't and, screwing up his face, I can see that he is crying from somewhere deep. His stomach spasms. He is humiliated, and he says it: "I'm humiliated."

This man, who squeegees windshields all damn day long on the corner of a street in this baking hot country, has had to empty his house that he furnished and rented with his own sweat because a few lipsticked women threatened a whole condo complex. This man, after standing out on that corner day in and day out under the scrutinizing glare of thousands of drivers, after living under the motto that "there's no reason to mix with them," this man who always went straight "from work to the safety of his home" now has to leave because these women have the gangs standing behind them.

Seeing him crying, the man's brother-in-law starts up himself. He hangs his head down, humiliated, and begins shaking and crying.

Tonight, these men and their families will sleep squeezed into somebody else's apartment. They'll pack themselves in as well as they can, try to get some sleep. And then, tomorrow, they'll get back to washing windshields, trying to start over. Or maybe they'll throw in the towel and try to head to the United States.

It's one in the afternoon and seven policemen are watching over the fleeing families. Suddenly, fifteen more cops, all wearing balaclavas, arrive. The subdirector of the Anti-Gang Unit, Pedro González, is riding with them. Everything so far has been on live television, and now the police want viewers to see that something is being done.

The newly arrived anti-gang agents escort all the media off the grounds of San Valentín. As I'm standing at the far corner of one of the alleyways, they overlook me, and I'm able to stay. Subdirector González calls out to the residents:

"Gather together, please. All of you, come here, there are no more cameras. We got rid of the media because we want to give you a message."

About twelve residents gather in front of the subdirector. The rest either continue their hurried packing or stay locked in their homes.

A woman walks out of her apartment and calls out, "I'm coming by myself because my husband has heart trouble."

Subdirector González tells people to go home, wash their clothes, prepare their lunches and watch TV. Go about your daily lives. He tells them that his agents will capture "all the gangsters." He says, "We're going to lock up all the gangsters in the neighborhood." He then turns and shouts at his agents: "Comb the area!" He lifts his pointer finger and sort of sweeps it around in the air.

None of the agents move. He turns back to the cluster of residents before him and tells them to pray. "It doesn't matter if you're Catholic or evangelical, let's pray. This is what's most important. Let's pray to the Lord." He asks for a volunteer to lead the prayer. Nobody moves. The subdirector insists, asking again for someone to pray. Nobody moves. He then tells the woman standing in front of him, who seems to be in her seventies, that she "looks devout." He asks her if she will pray. She doesn't pray. Finally, another woman starts the oration. I have a hard time hearing but make out the words, which I scribble into my notebook: "Lord, put an angel in front of every door."

The family of windshield washers continues their hurried exodus.

Another ten families, within view of the head of the nation's Anti-Gang Unit—who is asking families not to leave, who is promising to protect them—continue packing up their homes.

At least fifty people don't believe that the police can keep them safe.

A few minutes later Subdirector González will tell me

something that his boss the national chief of police and even his boss the minister of security and justice have both said to me before. He will say: "It's also a question of how you perceive this reality."

Yes, it's possible to think the threat is nothing but those young women making a point in front of their gang. In fact, some families aren't leaving. They think that the threat was more chest thumping than a real danger. But even if some families are staying, who is to say that those who are leaving don't have legitimate fears? The same gang who threatened them last night was responsible for a multiple homicide just a few blocks away. The same gang burned, shot and massacred a busload of people just seven blocks in the other direction. The same gang, just ten days earlier, killed the son of the *pupusa* maker from one of these very condos. They kidnapped him just outside the front gates as he was hauling home a tank of gas; they dumped his body a day later on the outskirts of the nearby Panamá neighborhood.

It is about how you perceive reality, but the reality is of a very real death threat. It's not the reality of the weatherman, whom you decide to believe and take a raincoat with you as you walk out the door or not believe and just head out in your T-shirt. It's not the reality that someone might steal your car and so you better lock the doors. It's about perceiving the reality that tonight, in just a few hours, your family may or may not be massacred.

Would you pack up? Or would you chance it and stay in your home?

The prayer Subdirector González asked for is over. In the next few hours his unit will capture six people accused of illicit association—gang membership.

In San Valentín, a woman asks: "So are the police going to stay?" González responds: "We will stay until you feel safe."

"And then?" the woman asks. "And when you leave? When we have to get on the bus to drop our kids off at school? And when we need to go to work?" The woman waits a moment for an answer, and then turns to resume her packing.

Another woman asks: "Could you leave a policeman to guard every one of our doors forever?"

The prayer circle has disbanded. Nobody responds to the question.

14

The Unfortunate History of an Undocumented Man Who Was Sold, Extorted and Deported

April 2014

According to one of the oldest coyotes in Chalatenango, in northern El Salvador, there are rules that every good coyote should follow and there are questions that every good migrant will ask. This is the story of a coyote who didn't follow any rules and a man who didn't ask any questions.

Señor Coyote, sprawled out on his rubber-stringed chair in the midday heat, looks just like what he is: the patriarch of a long lineage of men in the Salvadoran state of Chalatenango. Men who work as migrant guides to the United States. Men who work to smuggle people into countries that try to stop them from coming.

Señor Coyote is—according to the cigarette and cheese trafficker who introduced me to him—the most experienced coyote in the state. He began working in 1979 when most Salvadorans who wanted to go north had to hire a Guatemalan. Which is what Señor Coyote did the first time he went north. Then, after his first trip, he started working for the Guatemalan, helping him find Salvadoran clients. Soon he was accompanying him on the trips. And then, after deciphering the rules of the road, he struck out on his own.

Now, as a veteran, Señor Coyote focuses on, as he says, "coordination." The time of traveling coyotes, he tells me, is over. Now the labor is separated. The first coyote finds his

Salvadoran clients, sends them with an employee to Guatemala City, or maybe to the Mexican border, where the clients are turned over to another coyote, usually a Mexican, who takes them to Mexico City and delivers them to a colleague who ferries them up to the US border, where he hands them off to another coyote, usually known as a "passer" or "shooter," who is in charge of crossing them and dropping them off at a safe house in the United States where the migrants will be locked up until the families hand over the second half of the payment. The first half is paid at the beginning of the trip.

Nobody—"nobody, nobody," Señor Coyote repeats—will charge less than $7,000 for a trip starting in El Salvador. At least not a "serious coyote."

A serious coyote, according to this large man, this Señor Coyote, who still wears work boots from his harvesting days, is a coyote who doesn't get on the train. Many Central Americans—approximately 250,000 a year are detained by Mexican immigration authorities—take the cargo trains, the Beast, to travel north. They hook themselves onto the roof as best they can and munch away the kilometers along desolate, unprotected strips of Mexico. A serious coyote, according to this cowboy-hatted man, uses the money his migrants deliver to send payments ahead to the chain of coyotes working to guide the migrant to the United States. For this service of coordination, a coyote like Señor Coyote comes away with $1,500 per migrant. There are ways, of course, of cutting costs: The classic is putting your migrants on the train, or nearly suffocating them under a false-bottom in a truck, or, if you're scared or stupid, not giving them $200 in cash to pay Los Zetas the quota they charge migrants to cross into their territory. Los Zetas control scattered swaths of the country, pieces of the puzzle that make up the cartel map of Mexico.

To paint a clearer picture: If the puzzle pieces controlled by Los Zetas were red, the map would be bloody in the states of Tabasco, Veracruz and Tamaulipas. Those are three states where the trains run and where the banana trucks rumble.

If anybody is still unfamiliar with them, Los Zetas are a Mexican-based criminal organization that got its start toward the end of the last century. The cartel was basically a private army run by one of the capos of the Gulf Cartel, Osiel Cárdenas Guillén—imprisoned in the United States since 2007—which then broke off from the Gulf Cartel and formed its own independent wing, using, among many criminal tactics, migrants as a source of money and power: robbing them, selling them, raping them, trafficking them and kidnapping them for ransom. A serious coyote, Señor Coyote says in a very serious tone, doesn't cut costs, no matter how brutal the business partner. A serious coyote pays Los Zetas their quota.

If you were to take the information above and convert it into questions that you ask your coyote, then you would be, according to the rubric of Señor Coyote, a good migrant. If he were a migrant, he would ask his coyote how many coyotes he would be transferred to throughout the trip. He would ask how he was going to cross Mexico. He would ask how his money was going to be used. He would ask—just to be sure— if he was going to get stuffed into a banana truck, and if he wasn't going to get on the train and was going to take buses and collective taxis instead, he would ask if his coyote knew the right Mexican authorities to be able to pass through the checkpoints without problems. He would ask, over and over, if the payment included the quota to Los Zetas. And then, he would ask it all again.

If you don't ask, you lose. So says Señor Coyote.

"These days, $7,000 is the minimum. The biggest threat is getting swindled. The law should punish the coyotes who swindle. But those who do a good job should get subsidized."

There are, according to Señor Coyote, some low forms of swindling: Form 1, the coyote asks the migrant for the money up front, telling him that he'll be leaving on Day A, but he still needs the money right away, and then they don't end up leaving until Day Z; Form 2, the coyote asks for the money up front, telling the migrant he'll be leaving on Day A, and then never leaves; Form 3, the coyote knows that the migrant can't pay anything up front, so asks for some collateral, an object of value, a favor, a land title. The coyote says that it's only temporary, that he'll give the object or title back after he gets paid, but he never gives it back; Form 4, the coyote says he's only going to charge $3,000 for the trip, or maybe $4,000, or anything at all under $7,000.

It may seem hard-hearted that a coyote won't drop below that price, but Señor Coyote says that any coyote who charges less than that should make you think twice.

If a coyote quotes you a low price—here Señor Coyote doesn't mince his words—he won't be able to answer a migrant's questions. He will lie.

Sifting through some judicial records, I come across the case of a young man named Adán, whose story seems to back up everything Señor Coyote tells me.

Adán is, according to the rubric of Señor Coyote, a bad migrant. José Ricardo Urías is—again, according to the rubric of Señor Coyote—a swindling coyote, a coyote who perfectly fits into Señor Coyote's Fourth Form of bad coyotes.

Adán, a twenty-five-year-old man from Chalatenango, began his trip to the United States on September 14, 2011. José, a thirty-four-year-old coyote (and currently serving a four-year prison sentence for human smuggling) took charge of Adán and a friend that same day.

September 14, at eight in the morning: After sleeping in hammocks in José's aluminum-roof home, Adán and his friend began their trip toward the United States.

Adán had previously lived in the United States, for eight years. He entered without papers for the first time in 2003. He was later deported on a flight back to El Salvador on July 27, 2011, at 4:39 in the afternoon.

Adán and his friend thought that they were guaranteed passage to the United States. They were so convinced they were going to make it that they gave José $1,500 the night before the trip. The total price, according to the prosecutor's file on José, was going to be $4,500.

Let's recall one of Señor Coyote's sayings: "These days, $7,000 is the minimum."

Adán told the prosecutor that his coyote, José, promised him "he wasn't going to suffer, that he was going to be eating beef and chicken" on the journey.

Coyote José is not a rich man; he's not a white-collar criminal. He is poor. His house is made of scrapped-together material, it has an aluminum roof, and is set on a numberless plot in the El Zamorano neighborhood of the city of Jiquilisco, in Usulután state.

Coyote José wouldn't figure into the category of "serious coyote," according to Señor Coyote, because, first of all, he doesn't charge what he should be charging, and second, because he himself travels with his migrants. According to Señor Coyote, the time of traveling coyotes has passed. The work of a "serious coyote," according to that large man lounging on the rubber-stringed chair, is to coordinate the migrant's journey.

Without asking if Coyote José was going to pay off Los Zetas, without asking if they were going to travel by train, or what his money was going toward, Adán and his friend left the El Zamorano neighborhood for the bus station, Puerto Bus, in San Salvador, then rode to Guatemala City where they transferred to another bus heading toward La Mesilla, a border town across the river from Ciudad Cuauhtémoc, Chiapas, Mexico.

From there they hoofed it on dirt trails into Mexico, riding shared taxis to Estación Chontalpa, a small city in Tabasco, on the border with the state of Chiapas. There they went into the woods and waited for the train that was coming north from the city of Tenosique. For a week, Adán recalled, they never got off the train, riding north into Veracruz, straight into the chamber of the heart of Zetas territory.

By train they reached the state of Mexico, on the outskirts of Mexico City, and then pushed north to Celaya in Guanajuato state. They'd made 700 kilometers so far, clinging to the steel backside of the Beast.

"A serious coyote," Señor Coyote says, "doesn't take the train."

Adán testified that Coyote José made a call in Celaya: "They're here," he said to someone. "Come and get them."

Adán and his friend thought he was talking to another coyote, someone who would come and guide them north.

The men who came, however, didn't seem like coyotes. A Chevy Silverado pulled up and a man known as El Trenzas (the Braids) hopped out. Then another truck pulled up, a Dodge Ram, and three men (El Trenzas's bodyguards) jumped out.

El Trenzas handed $800 to Coyote José, who said to Adán, "I'll be right back." That was when Adán realized that he and his friend had just been sold.

El Trenzas, who claimed to be a member of Los Zetas, told them, "If you don't pay up, I'm gonna fuck you up."

They took them to a ranch, where there was also a Honduran man locked up, where they would spend the next few days. They were forced to call family members and ask them to wire $1,500. Adán's ex-wife wired the money from the United States. His friend's mother did the same.

At this point, everything was normal. It was a normal Los Zetas kidnapping.

Normal as in it happens to almost 10,000 people a year. Normal as in something so common it can profit kidnappers about $50 million a year.

In 2009, the National Commission of Human Rights in Mexico (CNDH) interviewed 9,758 migrants crossing through Mexico who had been kidnapped by criminal groups—mostly by Los Zetas. The CNDH concluded from this report that the groups profited about $25 million in just six months.

That type of normal.

El Trenzas repeatedly threatened Adán and the other two kidnapped men locked up on the ranch, telling them that he had eyes everywhere on that part of the migrant trail. Finally, he put them on a bus that took them 1,000 kilometers north, to the eastern Mexican state of Coahuila, bordering Texas. They got off the bus at the station in Piedras Negras.

Piedras Negras is a Mexican border town. Across the wall, on the US side, is the small highway town of Eagle Pass. Between the two cities flows what is known in Mexico as the Río Bravo, or, in the United States, the Rio Grande. At this point the river has already been fed by its two biggest sources, the Pecos River on the US side and the Conchos River on the Mexican side.

El Trenzas told Adán and the other two migrants to get off the bus in Piedras Negras, that somebody would be waiting for them.

Outside the bus station a Mexican man was sitting in a red truck.

From your armchair, from the desk in your furnished home, from the bed in which you are reading the story of Adán, it's easy to say he was an idiot for following, like an automaton, El Trenzas's orders.

Why didn't he get off the bus and look for help, or go back to El Salvador? It's easy to wonder from your armchair.

For over three years I traveled on the migrant trails of Mexico. I discovered that what you would think of as stupid while sitting in your armchair is a different story on the actual trails. What you think is stupid sitting at home can be the most logical thing in the world on the trails.

Once, I interviewed a Salvadoran man who wanted to get out of the Mexican border town of Altar. His brother had been kidnapped about a hundred kilometers away, and he just wanted to get out. He knew there was nothing he could do, no authorities to help him. And he was right.

Another time I heard about a couple of policemen in Veracruz who returned an escaped migrant back to a Los Zetas safe house. The migrant had fled his kidnappers, but once he was free, instead of continuing to run, he reported the crime. The municipal police of Coatzacoalcos took him right back to his kidnappers. The man was turned into a bloody mass of flesh that could barely breathe. Two young Guatemalan migrants, who shared a room with the man in the safe house, told me his story. The Guatemalans didn't escape: They were set free after each of their families wired the Zetas $500.

Another time I spent a few days in Ixtepec, Oaxaca, talking to a Mexican coyote, El Chilango, who was on the run. He was guiding three Honduran migrants, but he hadn't reported his work to his coyote boss, a man known as Don Fito. Based in the northern Mexican city of Reynosa, Don Fito paid Los Zetas $10,000 a month to let him work in their territory. His coyotes were only supposed to guide migrants who were his clients. El Chilango, however, thought that he could sneak a few migrants under his boss's radar, pocketing all of their money for himself. Don Fito found out and then started hunting El Chilango up and down the whole 5,000 kilometers of migrant trails running from Guatemala to the United States.

Los Zetas have eyes everywhere. They think they are omnipotent, all-seeing—that they know everything—and though it may be an exaggeration, one thing is true: On the migrant trails, Los Zetas have eyes almost everywhere.

A few days after I'd been talking to El Chilango, I received a call from him. I could barely make out voices and scratching on the other end of the line.

"Heeeey ... Help. Sssssss. They got me. They're ... Help ..."

The line cut.

He never answered his phone again. For a year afterward, I asked around on the migrant trails for El Chilango. Nobody ever saw him again.

The Mexican man led Adán and the other two migrants to a house in Piedras Negras. There, Adán remembers, a "fat woman" told them that they'd have to pay "$300 a head or you die." The fat woman was also tending to another kidnapped migrant, a Mexican, who was locked up in the house.

They called their families again. The $300 came through in money wires, but they were still locked up thirteen days later. They were fed once a day.

Adán and his friend, the other Salvadoran, decided to escape. The Honduran and the Mexican, who were also locked up, decided to stay. "They were scared," Adán said, according to the judicial report. They escaped but only made it a few blocks away. A couple gangsters who worked for the fat woman saw them and dragged them back to the safe house.

On October 11, 2011, a couple of the fat woman's thugs took Adán, his friend, the Honduran, and the Mexican out of the house, along a series of dirt roads, to an isolated bank of the Rio Grande. The stretch of river before them was shallow. On the bank, Adán recalls, there were eight sacks of marijuana. Each sack, he figured, weighed about thirty-five pounds.

"Take them across," one of the thugs ordered, pointing to the other side of the river.

"I'm not taking them," Adán responded. "They'd give me twenty years for that in the United States."

One of the other thugs took out a machete and held it up to Adán's neck, convincing him to heft up one of the sacks of marijuana.

The four men, plus one guide, waded across the river. In the United States they walked for three hours until they were met by a car driven by two men, who took the sacks and left. The guide, seeing that the marijuana had crossed safely, turned and started heading back to Mexico. The migrants were left alone in the desert. They waited, not sure what to do. Two hours later, the two men in the car returned and drove them to a hotel in Eagle Pass.

One of the thugs told Adán that they would give him a ride the next day to San Antonio, where he would be able to call his family. His terrible journey finally looked like it was going to turn out OK.

The next day, however, things took another bad turn. US officers, from more than one federal agency, surrounded the hotel and detained the two thugs, two women they were traveling with, and four migrants who were waiting to be taken to San Antonio.

Adán told Salvadoran authorities that he declared to the US agents what had happened to him, that the two thugs, as far as he understood, were members of Los Zetas and had been on the run in the United States for a few months. Adán spent two months in an immigrant detention center in Texas. The US government, after making use of Adán's testimony in their case against the two Zetas members, deported him.

On January 12, 2012, at 4:37 in the afternoon, on federal flight N593AN, Adán was flown back to his country.

He contacted Coyote José, the same man from Usulután who had sold him to El Trenzas for $800. All he wanted was his $1,500 back. Coyote José told him, as if it were a loan he was being asked for, that he didn't have it.

Like it was no big thing.

Adán filed a police report. In 2013, Coyote José was

sentenced to four years in prison for human trafficking. That's to say, for selling a human being, José received a four-year term. A pickpocket who steals a cell phone can be sentenced to between six and ten years. A man who sells another man to Los Zetas, only four. That's the law.

Señor Coyote from Chalatenango says that the government should give a subsidy to the good coyotes. He says that a good coyote doesn't pay attention to the swindlers swirling around, trying to scare migrants. He says that a good coyote lives by his word, which is passed person to person. Señor Coyote says that he himself is a good coyote. He says that to a good coyote there is nothing better than a happy migrant. Señor Coyote says it like a moral: A good migrant is a migrant who asks questions. He repeats, if he were a migrant, he would ask his coyote how many coyotes he was going to meet on the trails. He would ask how he was going to cross through Mexico and what his money was going toward. He would definitely ask if he was going to get smushed into a banana truck, or if he was going to ride the Beast, or if the coyote knew Mexican officials so they could pass the checkpoints with ease. And he would ask, more than once, if the payment included the quota for Los Zetas. And then he would ask it all again.

On the Typeface

This book is set in Sabon, a narrow Garamond-style book face designed in 1968 by the German typographer Jan Tschichold. Tschichold had been a leading voice of sans-serif modernist typography, particularly after the publication of his *Die neue Typographie* in 1928. As a result, the Nazis charged him with "cultural Bolshevism" and forced him to flee Germany for Switzerland.

Tschichold soon renounced modernism—comparing its stringent tenets to the "teachings of National Socialism and fascism"—and extolled the qualities of classical typography, exemplified in his design for Sabon, which he based on the Romain S. Augustin de Garamond in the 1592 Egenolff-Berner specimen sheet.

Sabon is named after the sixteenth-century French type-founder Jacques Sabon, a pupil of Claude Garamond and proprietor of the Egenolff foundry.